I0816798

The Pioneer Woman Cooks

THE ESSENTIAL RECIPES

THE ESSENTIAL RECIPES

120 Greatest Hits, New Twists, and Perfected Classics

REE DRUMMOND

WILLIAM MORROW
An Imprint of HarperCollinsPublishers

ALSO BY REE DRUMMOND

The Pioneer Woman Cooks: Dinner's Ready!

The Pioneer Woman Cooks: Super Easy!

The Pioneer Woman Cooks: The New Frontier

The Pioneer Woman Cooks: Come and Get It!

The Pioneer Woman Cooks: Dinnertime

The Pioneer Woman Cooks: A Year of Holidays

The Pioneer Woman Cooks: Food from My Frontier

The Pioneer Woman Cooks: Recipes from an Accidental Country Girl

Frontier Follies

The Pioneer Woman: Black Heels to Tractor Wheels

CHILDREN'S SERIES

Charlie the Ranch Dog

Little Ree

Without limiting the exclusive rights of any author, contributor or the publisher of this publication, any unauthorized use of this publication to train generative artificial intelligence (AI) technologies is expressly prohibited. HarperCollins also exercise their rights under Article 4(3) of the Digital Single Market Directive 2019/790 and expressly reserve this publication from the text and data mining exception.

THE PIONEER WOMAN COOKS: THE ESSENTIAL RECIPES. Copyright © 2025 by Ree Drummond. All rights reserved. Printed in the United States of America. No part of this book may be used or reproduced in any manner whatsoever without written permission except in the case of brief quotations embodied in critical articles and reviews. For information, address HarperCollins Publishers, 195 Broadway, New York, NY 10007. In Europe, HarperCollins Publishers, Macken House, 39/40 Mayor Street Upper, Dublin 1, D01 C9W8, Ireland.

HarperCollins books may be purchased for educational, business, or sales promotional use. For information, please email the Special Markets Department at SPsales@harpercollins.com.

hc.com

FIRST EDITION

Designed by Kris Tobiassen
Food photography by Ed Anderson
Lifestyle photography courtesy of Ree Drummond and family except the following:
Ashley Alexander: opposite title page
Betsy Dutcher: 205
Buff Strickland: 20, 74, 122, 206, 220
Caroline Lima: 196, 258, 312, 314, 336, 340, 359, 382, 385
Ed Anderson: 378
Sara Slover Brown: viii bottom right, 154

Library of Congress Cataloging-in-Publication Data has been applied for.

ISBN 978-0-06-327663-5

25 26 27 28 29 WOR 10 9 8 7 6 5 4 3 2 1

For Sofia

Contents

Cowboys
OKLAHOMA STATE
FOOTBALL
OSU
COWBOYS

Introduction

I just have to get this out of the way, friends: I am *so darn excited* to share this cookbook with you. It has been in the works for two full years, but the truth is that it's actually been a lot longer than that. It is jam-packed with all (yes, all!) of the recipes that I consider absolutely essential, dishes that have been a huge part of my family's life for as long as I can remember.

In 2006, on a dark and stormy night—just kidding, it was a bright and sunny morning—I started blogging about life on the ranch with my husband and four kids. After many months of covering such topics as cow manure in my yard and getting four little kids dressed to go work cattle at 4 a.m., I shared a recipe on a whim. That led to another recipe, and another . . . and before long I was regularly sharing recipes on the internet, alongside goofy tales of cows and kids. The food section of my website took off and would lead to my very first cookbook, published in 2009—something I never would have predicted when I first started blogging. At the time, I thought writing my own cookbook would be a fun project and a nice memory. Both of those things were true! I filled the cookbook with everything I cooked back in those days, and I told stories and posted photos of my four little country kids. Little did I know that more cookbooks would be in the cards for me—and this is officially my ninth.

I mention my very first cookbook because it is relevant here. When I set out to develop the idea for this book, I pondered and jotted down various themes that I'd noticed with my cooking in recent months and years. I considered focusing on recipes for two people, since it's just Ladd and me at home now. I thought about taking a Tex-Mex angle, since I make so much of that category of food. I deliberated protein-rich recipes and a pasta angle, and even started down the road of a dessert-only cookbook. But finally, when I really looked at the food I was continuing to cook day in and day out, the lightbulb went on.

What I was cooking day in and day out were the recipes I've always cooked, the tried-and-true absolute favorites that my crew keeps requesting and coming back for. And I mean that literally: my kids are all grown now (I repeat from earlier: They were tiny when I started blogging! Life flies by!), and when they come home to visit, the meals they look the most forward to are the ones that were part of their childhood, their teenage years, birthdays, holidays, and every day. My pot roast, which I have refined to juicy perfection through the years. My mom's

cinnamon rolls, which I still make every Christmas. (They're more luscious than ever.) The legendary mashed potatoes I've always served. My pancakes, which I've worked on through the years and are dangerously delicious.

When I thought about these recipes, I also realized how much these classics have evolved in the past almost twenty years. All home cooks make adjustments to their standby recipes, and my tweaks have always sought to turn these already fantastic dishes into more magnificent versions of themselves.

So that's where I decided to head with this cookbook! I'm sharing with you all of the most important recipes in my repertoire, and the most popular on any platform I've shared them . . . but with an important twist: Each one has been put through the paces and tested—and not in a test kitchen somewhere, but right here in my kitchen, on my stove, in my oven, and on my table. If I never cooked another recipe outside of the ones in this cookbook, I would be a happy woman.

Life has changed so much in our family! The kids are now adults. Alex and her husband have a new baby, Sofia. (I'm in love! My gosh!) Paige just married the love of her life, David, and moved from the ranch to Dallas. Bryce graduated from both college and football and swooped into the spot on the ranch Paige's move opened up. And Todd, still in college, is doing great and, by the way, is the tallest Drummond sibling. (I would say he got the last word, but Paige's husband, David, has him beat by three inches. Ha!) And Ladd and I find ourselves empty nesters, almost thirty years after we got hitched.

My point is, everything is in constant change, and I think in a way this makes us cling to the things that anchor us to home. And right or wrong, in our family, food is the primary anchor. (I'd say football runs a close second!) So while variety is the spice of life and it's fun to throw in surprises every now and again, I don't discount the emotional importance of embracing the dishes that will forever be associated with the good ol' days. I hope you fall in love with every single recipe in this cookbook. I hope that if you've made some of these through the years, you find yourself delighted by the tweaks and refinements. And most of all, I hope they turn into dishes that your family wants to keep coming back to. That's what it's all about.

Love,

Breakfasty Food

Breakfast is my crew's favorite meal of the day, hands down. Whether it's seven in the morning or pushing noon—or, let's face it, the middle of the afternoon or even midnight (true story!) —there is no breakfast food that Ladd and the kids have ever turned down. This is my most beloved collection of Drummond family breakfast faves through the years. They've seen me through busy summers, holiday mornings, lazy brunch days, and just the everyday grind of the ranch. These recipes are made for mornings, but most all of them can cross over into different categories, from dinners to desserts. I was hard-pressed to narrow down my choices for this chapter, and I hope when you try them you'll understand why!

Light and crisp!

WONDERFUL WAFFLES

MAKES ABOUT 8 WAFFLES

In the category of breakfast breads that are topped with butter and doused with syrup before being served to hangry family members on a weekend morning, and by family members I mean me, waffles are far and away my very favorite. (Don't tell pancakes and French toast. I like them both as friends.) There's something about those lightly crisp waffle wells, man. I am powerless in their presence! This wonderful waffle recipe has been slowly perfected through the years, and the secret lies in using egg yolks and whites separately. Don't worry—they'll eventually wind up reuniting in the same waffle! It's much like marriage in middle age: Sometimes it can be healthy when the two spouses pursue their own interests, then come together in harmony . . . in their matching comfortable chairs . . . to watch their favorite TV show together . . . before retiring to bed at 8:47 p.m. (Hypothetically speaking, of course.)

2 cups all-purpose flour

2 tablespoons granulated sugar

2 tablespoons packed brown sugar

1 tablespoon baking powder

½ teaspoon kosher salt

1½ cups buttermilk, homemade (see page 5) or store-bought

2 egg yolks

1 tablespoon plus 1 teaspoon vanilla extract

½ cup (1 stick) salted butter, melted, plus more for the waffle iron and softened butter, for serving

4 egg whites

Maple syrup or pancake syrup, warmed, for serving

1. Preheat a waffle iron to medium heat.

2. In a medium bowl, sift together the flour, granulated sugar, brown sugar, baking powder, and salt

3. In a small bowl, whisk together the buttermilk, egg yolks, and vanilla, then slowly whisk in the melted butter.

4. Pour the wet ingredients over the dry ingredients . . .

5. And gently fold the mixture with a rubber spatula until halfway combined.

6. In a small bowl, beat the egg whites with a hand mixer (or you can use a stand mixer!) until they're stiff.

7. Slowly fold them into the batter . . .

8. Stopping just short of mixing them all the way through. You should see little pockets of egg whites here and there!

9. Generously brush melted butter all over the surface of the waffle iron plates.

10. Scoop ⅓ to ½ cup of the batter into each well (depending on the size of the wells), then close the waffle iron and cook the waffles according to the manufacturer's instructions . . .

11. To achieve a deep golden color and crisp texture.

12. Serve immediately with a scoop of softened butter and warm syrup. The cure to hangriness! (Hanger?)

Variations

- *Make a batch of berry butter from French Toast with Berry Butter (page 9) and add a slice on top of each waffle.*
- *Sprinkle the waffles with sifted powdered sugar before serving.*

WAFFLE IRONS FOR THE WIN!

If you've been avoiding buying a waffle iron because you don't think you'll eat waffles very often, I want to encourage you by sharing a handful of other things I use mine for. Waffle irons are fun!

Wafflewiches: Use the waffle maker as a makeshift panini press by building a sandwich with deli meats, cheeses, and any other fillings you like. Butter both sides of the sandwich and close it in the waffle iron. Cook till golden, then remove and slice.

Waffle Iron Hashbrowns: Grate a baked potato (or use thawed frozen hash browns), toss with salt, pepper, and a little grated cheddar, then spoon the mixture into the waffle wells and grill until golden and crisp. Addictive!

Wafflet: A cross between a waffle and an omelet! Whisk some eggs and add salt, pepper, finely diced ham, cheese, and a little grated onion. Pour into the waffle wells and cook on low until set.

Waffle Iron Cinnamon Rolls: Cook store-bought or homemade cinnamon roll dough in waffle iron wells until golden brown and cooked through. Remove and drizzle on icing or glaze. So quick and yummy!

HOMEMADE BUTTERMILK

MAKES A LITTLE OVER 1½ CUPS

I breastfed my babies. I didn't do this for any particularly admirable reasons; I just never wanted to wash bottles. In that same vein, I make my own buttermilk. I don't do this because I am an all-natural homesteading goddess; I just never have store-bought buttermilk in my fridge. Historically, anytime I've ever bought buttermilk at the store, I use a half a cup or so (of the half-gallon container!) and forget about the rest of it until it eventually goes bad. Who needs these burdens?!? Friends, make your own buttermilk! It takes about ninety seconds. It's super cheap. You won't have any waste. And best of all? You'll feel like a natural homesteading goddess. (Even if you have Totino's pizza rolls in your freezer.)

1½ cups whole milk
2 tablespoons distilled white vinegar (or you can use lemon juice)

1. Pour the milk into a jar or other glass container. Add the vinegar and stir it in.

2. Let sit for a few minutes to thicken; it will happen quickly!

3. Use it immediately or seal the jar and store it in the fridge for up to 2 weeks.

Perfect in salad dressings, pancakes, or cakes!

My number one homemade hack!

EVEN MORE PERFECT PANCAKES

MAKES ABOUT TWELVE 5-INCH PANCAKES

Sometimes it's the simplest recipes that challenge us home cooks the most. I made a pancake recipe for years that I loosely called "perfect pancakes," both on my website and in my heart, and in my defense, I did think those pancakes were pretty darn good. However, because I'm a restless redhead (or is it a restless middle child today? I get confused about my life excuses), I decided a year or so ago that I wanted to tinker with it and explore whether "perfect" could be taken a step further. And by golly . . . I reckon I cracked the code!

There were two main adjustments I made from the original: First, I tried a combination of both milk and buttermilk, since I never could decide which was better. Second, I tried resting the batter for 1 hour before cooking the pancakes, which was painful and difficult considering I have very little pancake patience. Both improvements resulted in the texture I've always sought! Fluffy and tender, with a beautiful flavor to boot. Will you believe me if I tell you that these are, in fact, at long last, finally, the most perfect pancakes? I mean it this time!

2 cups all-purpose flour

¼ cup sugar

1 heaping tablespoon baking powder

½ teaspoon baking soda

½ teaspoon kosher salt

1¼ cups whole milk, plus more as needed for thinning the batter

¾ cup buttermilk, homemade (see page 5) or store-bought

1 large egg

1 generous tablespoon vanilla extract

4 tablespoons (½ stick) salted butter, melted, plus more for greasing the griddle and serving

Maple syrup (or pancake syrup), warmed, for serving

1. In a large bowl, stir together the flour, sugar, baking powder, baking soda, and salt.

2. In a separate bowl, combine the milk, buttermilk, egg, and vanilla. (Notice I'm being generous with that vanilla! My tablespoon runneth over.)

3. Whisk the wet ingredients with a fork until well combined.

4. While continuing to whisk, drizzle in the melted butter until it's mixed in. You should see little bits of butter throughout!

5. Pour the wet ingredients into the dry ingredients, gently stirring as you go.

6. When all the wet ingredients have been added, very gently fold the batter until just barely combined.

Time-tested and absolutely perfected!

7. Stop when you can no longer see pockets of flour, but the batter should still look lumpy! Don't try to stir out the lumps.

8. Cover the bowl with plastic wrap and allow the batter to rest on the counter for 1 long, agonizing hour. (If you don't have the time or patience to wait, don't worry. The pancakes will still be good.)

9. After that time, the batter will be bubbly and very thick. If you want thick pancakes, don't stir the bubbles away!

10. If you decide you want slightly thinner pancakes, add a tablespoon or two of milk and very gently stir it into the batter.

11. Heat a griddle or skillet over medium heat and smear the surface with butter.

12. Use a ⅓-cup measure to drop helpings of batter onto the griddle. You'll need to use the measuring cup to coax the thick batter into rounds.

13. Let the pancakes cook until bubbles form on the surface (2½ to 3 minutes), then flip them and cook for another 1½ minutes or so.

14. Remove a stack to a plate . . .

15. Put a little butter between the pancakes (and on top of the stack) . . .

16. Then grab that warm syrup and go for it!

Variations

- *Instead of butter, spread a thin layer of peanut butter between the pancakes.*
- *Sprinkle mini chocolate chips between the pancakes and sprinkle more over the top. (Whipped cream would be great, too!)*

FRENCH TOAST WITH BERRY BUTTER

MAKES 4 SERVINGS

French toast, when it ticks all the boxes, is truly sublime. This recipe is the result of years and years of mediocre-to-disappointing French toast experiences, which were marked by soggy bread and eggy flavor that overpowered everything. I've finally landed forever on this version, which nails the yummy balanced flavor and the various textures of the bread (thicker crust, softer middle, crisp surface—yum!). Make this on Saturday mornings for the rest of your life.

BERRY BUTTER

½ cup fresh blackberries

1 teaspoon granulated sugar, if needed

½ cup (2 sticks) salted butter, softened

2 tablespoons sifted powdered sugar, or more if desired

FRENCH TOAST

4 egg yolks

1½ cups half-and-half

1 tablespoon plus 1 teaspoon vanilla bean paste (or vanilla extract)

Grated zest of 1 lemon

2 tablespoons granulated sugar

Eight 1-inch-thick slices crusty French bread

2 tablespoons salted butter, for the griddle

Sifted powdered sugar, for serving

Maple syrup or pancake syrup, warmed, for serving

1. Make the berry butter: Place the blackberries in a small bowl and mash them with a fork until they're mostly broken up. If they're too firm, add a teaspoon of granulated sugar and let them sit for 10 minutes before mashing.

2. In a medium bowl, use a beater to whip the butter until fluffy.

3. Add the mashed berries and powdered sugar . . .

4. And stir until everything is evenly mixed.

5. Place the berry butter on the center of a long piece of plastic wrap . . .

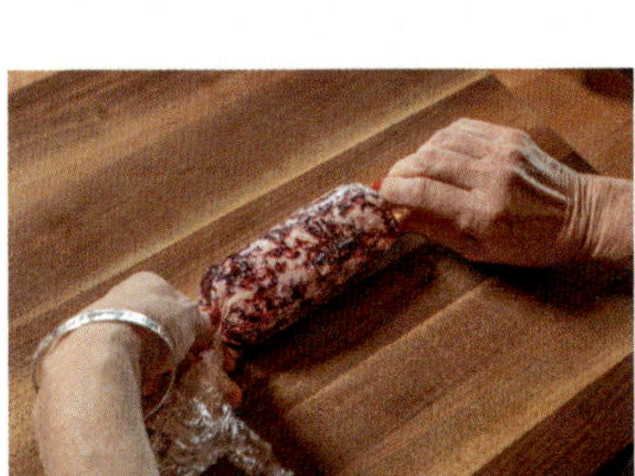

6. And form the butter into a compact roll, wrapping it in the plastic wrap and twisting the ends to tighten. Place the butter in the fridge so it will be firm enough to slice (or in the freezer if you need to use it soon!).

7. Make the French toast: In a large shallow dish, combine the egg yolks, half-and-half, and vanilla bean paste.

8. Add the lemon zest and granulated sugar . . .

9. And whisk until totally combined. Meanwhile, heat a griddle over medium heat.

10. Place the bread slices in the dish and allow them to soak up the custard for about 30 seconds. Turn the pieces over to absorb for another 30 seconds.

11. Smear the griddle with the butter and place the French toast on the pan.

12. Cook the French toast for about 3 minutes on the first side, watching carefully so it doesn't burn, then flip it and cook the other side for 1½ to 2 minutes. Lower the heat if you need to prevent the French toast from getting too brown; you want to give the inside of the bread a chance to heat up and cook.

13. Remove the slices to a platter and sprinkle with a little powdered sugar.

14. Slice the berry butter into thick rounds. Wrap any extra butter in the plastic and store it in the fridge for up to 4 days, or in the freezer for up to 3 months.

15. Place the butter on the French toast, then pour on the warm syrup!

Don't skip the
berry butter!

COWBOY BREAKFAST BURRITOS

MAKES 18 TO 20 BURRITOS

I was hesitant to include breakfast burritos in this cookbook. By now everyone knows how to make them, right? But one morning in recent months, I was making a batch to take to Ladd and the cowboys, and out of curiosity I glanced at my very first cookbook to compare my present to my past. I was surprised by how much I have evolved in the past fifteen years! (In a breakfast burrito sense, anyway.) In a nutshell, my current burritos are meatier, messier, and dirtier (more delicious bits!), and it appears I've also become a tortilla snob in my old age. I have Alex or Paige grab me a hundred at a time at a market in Dallas, then I freeze them in batches and thaw them whenever I make tacos, burritos, or quesadillas. Totally worth it, and even if you loved my O.G. breakfast burritos, I think these are going to excite you a lot.

1 pound bacon

1 pound breakfast sausage

18 eggs

¼ cup half-and-half

2 teaspoons ground black pepper

½ teaspoon kosher salt

½ teaspoon seasoned salt

Several dashes of hot sauce

18 to 22 very good quality 6-inch flour tortillas

LOADED BURRITOS

1 cup grated cheddar cheese, plus more as needed

½ cup jarred jalapeño slices, plus more as needed

Hot sauce

Special equipment: 18 to 20 precut aluminum foil sheets

1. Begin by cooking the bacon in a large cast-iron skillet over medium-high heat, then remove it to a plate lined with paper towels.

2. Pour off all but ¼ cup of the bacon grease, then brown the sausage in the same pan, crumbling it as it cooks.

3. Remove the sausage to a plate and set it aside with the bacon. Turn the heat under the skillet to low.

4. In a large bowl or pitcher, combine the eggs, half-and-half, pepper, kosher salt, seasoned salt, and hot sauce . . .

Plain
Loaded

5. And whisk the mixture until it's all combined.

6. Pour the eggs into the skillet . . .

7. And cook slowly, scraping the bottom of the skillet to get all the little bits mixed in with the eggs. Let it continue to cook, stirring and scraping frequently.

8. While the eggs are cooking (or you can do this before you start the whole process!), char the tortillas by holding them with metal tongs over the stovetop flame for about 20 seconds per side. (Or you can place them in a very hot cast-iron skillet for about 40 seconds per side.)

9. Chop the bacon into small pieces.

10. When the eggs are scrambled and set, turn off the heat and add the sausage . . .

11. And bacon . . .

12. And stir it until it's all mixed. It should be as much meat as eggs!

13. I often make two types of burritos: a basic one and a loaded version. For the basic, place a tortilla on the front half of a precut foil sheet. Add a couple of heaping spoons of the egg/meat mixture . . .

14. Then fold up the bottom end and tuck it under the top end.

15. Fold the top end over, keeping things as tightly enclosed as possible . . .

19. In this case, "L" is for "Loaded!" Either way, just be sure to label all your burritos!

20. Serve/hand them out immediately, or put them in a foil baking pan, cover it with foil, and keep them warm in a 200°F oven for up to 1 hour.

16. And roll it up in the foil sheet and fold in the ends.

17. Once rolled, I label the burrito with a marker. This is "P" for "plain"! (Though there's nothing plain about it.) I should probably just label it "L" for "Ladd."

18. The loaded version is the more popular: After you add the egg/meat mixture, sprinkle on a little cheese, a few jalapeño slices, and a few dashes of hot sauce!

We're both still early birds!

THE MOST PERFECT BISCUITS

MAKES 12 WONDERFUL, BUTTERY BISCUITS

Ladd and I opened a restaurant, The Mercantile, in our town back in 2016, and if you were to poll visitors over the years about the one food item that made the biggest impression on them, I would guess 85 percent would say these biscuits. And that's saying a lot, considering we have quite a few memorable menu items! But these biscuits, friends . . . they are absolutely delectable, and more buttery than any biscuit you've probably ever tasted. They've long since replaced my go-to biscuit recipe I shared in my very first cookbook, and I will make them for the rest of my life knowing they're absolutely, officially, the best. (A close second are Drop Biscuits, page 19. There's room in the world for both beauties!)

1 pound (4 sticks) frozen salted butter (place sticks in the freezer at least 2 hours in advance), plus more for greasing the pan

4 cups self-rising flour, plus more for scoring the biscuits

3 mounded tablespoons sugar

1 mounded tablespoon baking powder

1 mounded teaspoon kosher salt

2¼ cups heavy cream, plus a bit more if needed

½ cup buttermilk, homemade (see page 5) or store-bought

1. Preheat the oven to 350°F. Rub butter all over the inside of a 9 × 13-inch metal baking pan.

2. In a large bowl, whisk together the self-rising flour, sugar, baking powder, and salt.

3. On the large holes of a cheese grater, grate the frozen butter. (Be sure to grate it straight out of the freezer, and just before you need it for the next step.)

4. Add the butter to the dry ingredients . . .

5. Then use a pastry blender or two knives to totally mix everything together. The frozen butter will ensure even, very fine crumbs.

6. Pour in the heavy cream . . .

7. And the buttermilk . . .

Strawberry
Freezer Jam
(page 25)
Legendary
for a reason!

8. And gently fold it together until everything is combined. It will be a slightly sticky dough.

9. Dump the dough into the buttered pan . . .

10. And gently press it into an even layer, making sure to leave the top very craggy and natural-looking. (Don't press it flat!) Dab a little extra heavy cream on your hands if the dough is sticking too much.

11. Use a floured bench scraper or dinner knife to score 12 squares . . .

12. Then bake the biscuits until light golden brown, about 50 minutes. Check on them after 30 minutes; if they look like they're browning too fast, lay a sheet of foil loosely on top of the pan for the rest of the baking time.

These biscuits are best reheated individually in the microwave! Place one biscuit on a plate and cook it for 25 seconds. Let it sit a minute before eating. Buttery wonderfulness!

Serve with

- *Sausage gravy (see page 22)*
- *Strawberry Freezer Jam (page 25)*
- *Any dinner, as a side*
- *Any salad, as a side*
- *Any soup, as a side*
- *(Are you getting the drift here?)*

NEXT-LEVEL BREAKFAST

Everyone loves a breakfast sandwich on a biscuit, but they become next level on one of these perfect biscuits! I like to make them in a batch and freeze them for reheating later: Pile the biscuits with scrambled eggs, bacon or ham, and your favorite cheese. Wrap them in parchment, then transfer them to a plastic freezer bag to store for up to 6 months. To reheat, microwave individual sandwiches with the parchment on for 2½ minutes. Let sit for 2 minutes before eating.

DROP BISCUITS

MAKES 6 LARGE BISCUITS

There are biscuits . . . and then there are drop biscuits. To me, the two are as different as night and day, and I would honestly be hard-pressed to pick which one I prefer. So I'll just say this: I make drop biscuits whenever I want to remember my Grandma Helen and cry a little. Sleepovers at her house always included drop biscuits and sand plum jelly for breakfast the next day, and there is no biscuit memory in my heart, mind, or soul that is stronger than that one. (Excuse me . . . I need to go cry a little!)

Whether you make drop biscuits or a more traditional version (see page 16) is entirely up to you, and I'll make it easy for ya: There is no wrong answer.

1½ cups all-purpose flour

1 heaping tablespoon baking powder

¼ teaspoon kosher salt

½ cup (1 stick) cold salted butter, cut into small pieces, plus 2 tablespoons, melted, for brushing

¾ cup buttermilk, homemade (see page 5) or store-bought

Flaky sea salt

1. Preheat the oven to 400°F. Line a sheet pan with parchment paper.

2. In a large bowl, stir together the flour, baking powder, and salt.

3. Add the pieces of cold butter to the bowl . . .

4. And use a pastry blender or two knives to cut the butter into the flour mixture until the mixture resembles coarse crumbs.

5. Add the buttermilk while stirring gently with a wooden spoon . . .

6. And stop right when the mixture comes together. Not overmixing is key!

7. Using two large spoons, *drop* (hence the name) six mounds onto the parchment-lined sheet pan. Leave them craggy on top!

8. Bake the biscuits until just the craggy edges turn golden, about 20 minutes.

9. Generously brush the remaining 2 tablespoons melted butter on top of each biscuit.

10. Sprinkle the tops with a little flaky sea salt. Serve with absolutely everything!

Store in an airtight container overnight, then reheat them in the microwave (20 seconds per biscuit) or on a sheet pan in a 300°F oven for 10 minutes.

It helps to be flexible in ranching.

Craggy, crisp,
and crazy good.

BISCUITS AND SAUSAGE GRAVY

MAKES 12 TO 24 SERVINGS, DEPENDING ON APPETITES!

You'll see chicken-fried steak later in this cookbook, and between that recipe and this one, you've pretty much got the cowboys in your life covered. I'll tell you a little secret about biscuits and gravy, though: It's not just for cowboys. It's also not just for boys. It's also not required that you even know what biscuits and gravy is. You may even assume it's not for you. But just trust the process and go to town! You won't regret it!

I love this chunky gravy approach, which I've been making more and more in recent years as store-bought sausage has become less and less greasy. (A pound of sausage used to yield a good ¼ cup of grease; now it seems to be a tablespoon at most?) Before, when I cooked the sausage patties and removed them from the pan before making the gravy (which was my method for twenty-five years), I sent a lot of the grease to the plate with the sausage and barely had any for the gravy stage. Crumbling the sausage and using it as the courier for the flour solved my issues!

This is wonderful, hearty, comforting . . . and there's absolutely no excuse for it. My favorite kind of dish!

2 pounds pork breakfast sausage (such as Jimmy Dean or J.C. Potter)

⅔ cup all-purpose flour

7 to 8 cups whole milk

1 tablespoon ground black pepper, plus more to taste

½ teaspoon kosher salt, plus more to taste

½ teaspoon seasoned salt

12 warm The Most Perfect Biscuits (page 16) for serving, or you may use Drop Biscuits (page 19)

1. In a large skillet over medium-high heat, crumble and cook the sausage until it's browned and slightly crisp. The finer the bits of sausage, the better!

2. Reduce the heat to medium-low and sprinkle the flour all over the sausage.

3. Stir until the flour disappears into the sausage and cook the mixture, stirring constantly, for 2 minutes.

4. Add 7 cups of the milk while stirring constantly, scraping the bottom of the skillet the whole time to loosen the delicious bits from the bottom.

5. Add the pepper, kosher salt, and seasoned salt . . .

6. Then stir or whisk gently for 10 to 12 minutes. As the gravy cooks and bubbles, it will get thicker and thicker. Turn up the heat slightly if needed. Cook until the gravy is thick but still pourable. If it gets too thick, thin with a little milk, up to 1 additional cup.

#1 cowboy breakfast
of all time!

7. Grab a piping-hot biscuit . . .

8. Split it through the middle and lay both halves on a plate, cut side up.

9. Spoon gravy all over the biscuit (don't be shy!) and serve immediately with a generous grind of pepper.

Serving gravy to a crowd

During the course of serving this to a roomful of biscuits-and-gravy lovers, the gravy will naturally start to thicken. Sometimes I'll pause and stir in a little milk over medium heat to get the consistency right again. Just takes a minute!

The most important quality of biscuits and gravy is that the plate of food be steaming hot. It's best to have folks waiting in the wings with their appetites and their forks, ready to grab the plate and go dig in. Make sure the gravy is steaming hot in the skillet before spooning it over the biscuits!

Post-biscuits-and-gravy smiles!

STRAWBERRY FREEZER JAM

MAKES ABOUT 6 CUPS

Any kind of strawberry jelly or preserves has always been my jam. For all the peach, berry, plum, and grape versions in the world, to me it doesn't get more homey or family friendly than strawberry! I have made (and canned) strawberry jam through the years—including sterilizing jars, hot water baths, and waiting for that mason jar lid to "pop" when it seals—and it's a fun, rewarding process. It's also a pain in the butt! So I want to share this slightly less complicated option with you—one that's made in a bowl and stored in the freezer. Less fuss, tons of strawberry sweetness—this has definitely become an essential staple for me.

2 cups (1 pound) fresh strawberries (or use frozen, just let them fully thaw)

4 cups sugar

One 1.75-ounce envelope powdered fruit pectin (such as Sure-Jell)

¼ cup fresh lemon juice

1. With a small knife or spoon, hull the strawberries. Place them in a large bowl.

2. Using a chopper or potato masher, smash the berries . . .

3. Until they are juicy and mashed, with lots of larger bits throughout.

4. Add the sugar (it's a lot—jam is sweet!) . . .

5. And stir, then let the strawberries sit for about 10 minutes to release their juices.

6. Meanwhile, sprinkle the pectin into a skillet with ¾ cup water.

7. Cover the pan and bring the mixture to a gentle boil over medium heat. Continue to boil for 1 minute. Remove from the heat.

8. Stir the lemon juice into the macerated strawberries . . .

9. Then slowly pour in the warm pectin, stirring gently as you add it.

10. Stir the mixture a couple more times to make sure everything is evenly mixed.

11. Ladle into clean jars* or plastic containers and let it cool completely with the lids off.

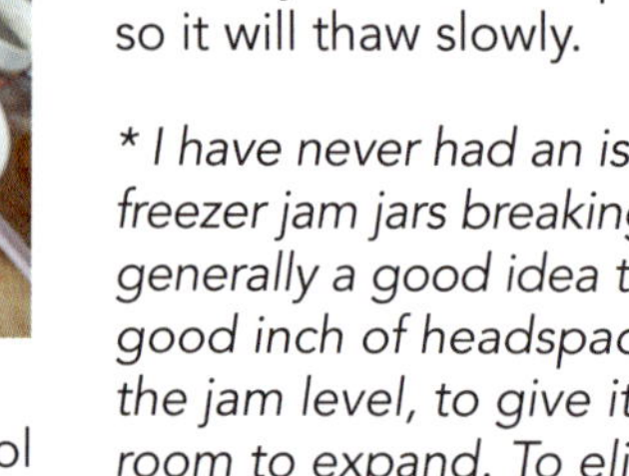

12. Once cool, put on the lids and put the jars in the fridge (the jam will keep for up to 3 weeks!) or the freezer (for up to 1 year). I routinely move a jar from the freezer to the fridge when the current jar is about a quarter full, so it will thaw slowly.

** I have never had an issue with freezer jam jars breaking, but it's generally a good idea to leave a good inch of headspace above the jam level, to give it more room to expand. To eliminate concern, you can use plastic freezer containers!*

Three (four!) generations of biscuit makers.

The easiest
homemade jam!
The Most Perfect
Biscuits (page 16)

CINNAMON ROLLS

MAKES APPROXIMATELY 45 ROLLS

On one hand, these cinnamon rolls deserve not just an introductory headnote but an entire book. That's how essential this recipe is to me, my life, my family, and the globe. On the other hand, I could leave this section entirely blank and just let the rolls speak for themselves and it would make absolute sense. I'm torn between the two approaches, so I'll just keep this brief: These are the best cinnamon rolls of all time. Many make that claim, but they haven't tried mine. Well, technically my mom's! She and I made them through my childhood, and they solidified my love of both bread and butter. (Essential indeed!) Make these soon, friends. Follow the steps and I promise you will succeed. These rolls are as forgiving as they are perfect.

DOUGH

1 quart whole milk

1 cup vegetable oil

1 cup granulated sugar

Two 0.25-ounce packets active dry yeast (4½ teaspoons)

9 cups all-purpose flour, plus more for rolling out the dough

1 heaping teaspoon baking powder

1 scant teaspoon baking soda

1 tablespoon table salt

FILLING

1 cup (2 sticks) salted butter, melted, plus more for the baking pans

2 cups granulated sugar

2 generous tablespoons ground cinnamon

MAPLE ICING

2 pounds powdered sugar, sifted

1 tablespoon maple flavoring, plus more as needed

½ cup whole milk, plus more as needed

⅓ cup (⅔ stick) salted butter, melted

¼ cup strongly brewed coffee, plus more as needed

Pinch of table salt

Special equipment: Six 9-inch round aluminum cake pans or metal pie plates or three 9 × 13-inch pans

1. First, make the dough: In a large pot, whisk together the milk, vegetable oil, and sugar.

2. Heat it to a strong simmer over medium heat, then remove it from the heat and let it cool to between 105 and 110°F. (An instant-read thermometer takes away the guesswork!)

3. Sprinkle the yeast over the surface and let it sit undisturbed for 1 minute.

4. Add 8 cups of the flour . . .

5. And whisk or stir together until it's just combined. It will be very thick and sticky at this point!

6. Cover the pot with a dish towel and set it in a relatively warm (at least draft-free!) spot for 1 hour.

The best
cinnamon rolls
you will ever eat.

7. During that time, the mixture will get bubbly and rise quite a bit.

8. Add the remaining 1 cup flour, along with the baking powder, baking soda, and salt . . .

9. And stir/fold until you can't see any more of the dry ingredients. The dough will be thick, so this might take a couple of minutes.

10. Dump the dough onto the countertop (you can add a little flour first!) and form it into a long log. Begin to roll it out . . .

11. And keep going, rolling the dough very thin, until you have a very large rectangle around 30 × 10 inches. (Note: If your countertop space won't allow this size, you can divide the dough in half and work in two batches!)

12. For the filling: Pour the cup of melted butter over the dough and use your fingers to smear it evenly, going all the way to the edges.

13. Sprinkle the 2 cups of sugar over the dough, getting it all the way to the edges. The butter should soak up a lot of it.

14. Sprinkle the cinnamon over the sugar, making sure it's well covered.

15. Starting at the top long edge, begin rolling the dough toward you, keeping it as tight as possible.

16. Keep going back and forth across the length of the dough, rolling as you go. (I have always jokingly referred to this as my typewriter technique!) If gooey butter doesn't ooze out as you go, you're doing it wrong!

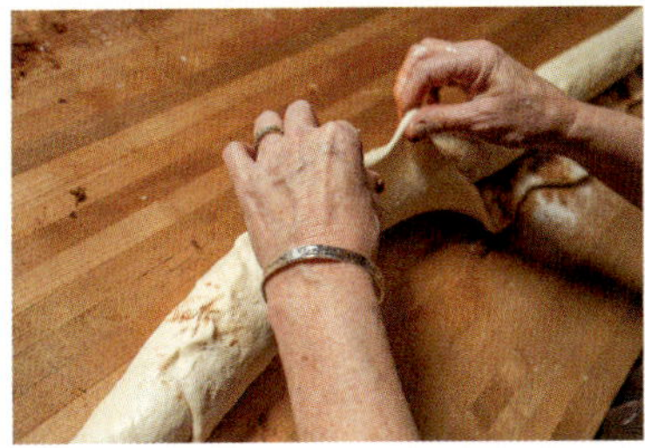

17. When the rolling is almost finished, pull the edge up to the top of the roll, pinching to seal.

18. Turn the log over so that the seam side is down and use a sharp knife to slice it into rolls about ½ inch thick.

19. Whether you're using round disposable pans (my standard!) or larger baking dishes, drizzle in a little melted butter and smear it around to coat. For a round pan, I use about a tablespoon of butter; for 9 × 13-inch pans, I'd use about 2 tablespoons in each pan.

20. Lay the rolls in the pans so that they're touching one another but not stuffed or cramped. You want to give them room to rise.

21. Keep going until all the rolls are in pans, then cover them with dish towels and let them rise on the countertop for 30 to 40 minutes. Preheat the oven to 375°F.

22. See how nice and plump they look? Bake the cinnamon rolls until they are golden (but not too dark/crisp on top!), 17 to 20 minutes. (You can bake them in stages if oven space dictates; they are fine to continue to rise on the counter for a while.)

23. While the rolls are baking, make the maple icing so that you can pour it on when the rolls are warm! In a large bowl, whisk the powdered sugar, maple flavoring, milk, melted butter, coffee, and salt.

24. Mix until the icing is thick but still pourable, adding more coffee or milk as needed to get to the right consistency. I usually add a little more maple flavoring, too!

25. Remove the pans from the oven and the second they go on the countertop, pour or ladle on the icing.

26. Keep adding icing evenly over the surface and around the edges, and be sure to use it all! The rolls should look like they're swimming in icing.

27. Let the rolls sit for 10 to 15 minutes to drink up the icing. Serve them warm and give the extras to your neighbors!

Sofia's birthday! The best day of our lives—so far!

Cinnamon roll tips

- *After the dough rises in the pot, I sometimes put it in the fridge for a few hours. It can be easier to roll, fill, and cut the rolls when the dough is chilled. (Note that this means it will take longer for the rolls to rise in the pan before baking.)*
- *You can make the dough the day before you plan on making the rolls. Store it in the fridge; just be prepared to punch the dough every once in a while to keep it from overflowing!*
- *Be sure to ice the rolls when they're piping hot! It is essential for the texture, and it's fun to watch those rolls drink it up.*
- *Deliver these the same day you make them so they're super fresh. To store the baked and iced rolls, wrap the pan after they've cooled, first in a layer of plastic wrap and then a layer of aluminum foil, and freeze them for up to 4 months. To reheat them from frozen, allow them to thaw, then remove the foil and plastic wrap and reheat them in a 275°F oven for 15 minutes.*
- *Individual rolls can be reheated in the microwave for 12 to 15 seconds.*

EGGS BENEDICT

MAKES 3 TO 6 SERVINGS

If you were to watch a reel of my life from the date I was born (back in 1822) to today, you would see a recurring character pop in during all the ages and stages. I'm talking about the beautiful, elegant, sublime Eggs Benedict type of character. My mom made it on Christmas morning during my teenage years. I made it for college friends on lazy Sunday mornings in Los Angeles. It was the birthday breakfast I made my father-in-law, Chuck, more times than I can count. And it's the one thing I still look for first on any brunch buffet or hotel room service menu, whether I'm traveling alone for work or cavorting in the mountains with Ladd. Yes, the buttery, toasted English muffin is delicious. Yes, the Canadian bacon is juicy and salty-good. Yes, Ladd does occasionally cavort. But it's the egg-on-egg mischief (eggy hollandaise on poached egg . . . who said this was legal?) that keeps me coming back again and again. I have tried to change and tweak this basic recipe from time to time, but the plain truth is that there's no possible way to improve on the original. So please don't even try!!

4 tablespoons (½ stick) salted butter, softened

3 English muffins, halved

12 slices Canadian bacon

2 tablespoons distilled white vinegar

6 large eggs

Blender Hollandaise Sauce (page 36), freshly made and warm

Paprika, for sprinkling

1. Preheat the oven broiler and arrange a rack in the lower half of the oven.

2. Spread the butter evenly on the English muffin halves and place them on a sheet pan with the slices of Canadian bacon. Place the pan in the oven on the lower rack to warm the Canadian bacon and lightly toast the English muffins, 7 to 8 minutes, watching to take care not to burn them.

3. Meanwhile, bring a gallon of water to a gentle boil in a large pot and add the vinegar.

4. Crack an egg into a small ramekin or bowl.

5. Using a wooden or metal spoon, gently stir the water in a circular motion to create a whirlpool.

6. Quickly drop the egg into the center of the whirlpool. The whites will immediately move around and start folding in.

My all-time favorite breakfast.
Long live Benedict!

7. While the water is moving, feel free to add a second egg. (You can do one at a time or in batches of two.)

8. Cook the eggs until the whites are set and the yolks are partly set but still soft and oozy, 2½ to 3 minutes.

9. Remove them to a paper towel to absorb the excess water, then keep going with the rest of the eggs.

10. Remove the English muffins and Canadian bacon from the oven.

11. Lay two English muffin halves on a plate, then overlap 2 slices of Canadian bacon on each muffin half.

12. Lay a poached egg on each one . . .

13. And top with a generous amount of hollandaise.

14. End with a sprinkle of paprika!

Note: To ensure that everything is hot when it's ready to serve, you can plunge the poached eggs back into the hot water just before serving. You can also warm the hollandaise by stirring in a tablespoon of very hot water or stirring the sauce over a double boiler.

BLENDER HOLLANDAISE SAUCE

MAKES 1½ CUPS

Hollandaise is one of the five mother sauces of French cuisine . . . but that isn't why I started making it. To me, it's always been that utterly luscious sauce my mom made during my upbringing in ol' Bartlesville, Oklahoma (say that with a twang), which is about 4,500 miles from France, by the way. Also, she made it in a blender, which is about 100,000 miles away from the French way, figuratively speaking. But by Bartlesville (and I dare say, most!) standards, her version is perfectly perfect—not just for Eggs Benedict, but for veggies, beef, even fries!

1 cup (2 sticks) salted butter

3 large egg yolks

Juice of 1 lemon, plus more to taste

Pinch of kosher salt and ground black pepper, plus more to taste

Pinch of cayenne pepper

1. In a small saucepan, melt the butter over low heat. Keep it warm, as you will need it to be sizzling for the next step; be careful not to brown or burn it.

2. Add the egg yolks to a blender.

3. Squeeze in the lemon juice and pulse the mixture three times to start to mix.

4. Place the lid on the blender and remove the pour cap. Get the butter to the sizzling stage (it has to be very hot for the sauce to form), then—with the blender on low speed—slowly drizzle in the butter in a thin stream. You will hear the sauce start to thicken as you pour.

5. Add the salt, black pepper, and cayenne and pulse a couple more times to blend.

6. The sauce should be silky and thick! Taste it and blend in a little more seasoning if needed. If it is overly thick, blend in a little more lemon juice or 1 teaspoon very hot water.

What to do with hollandaise

- *Serve it over Eggs Benedict (page 33).*
- *Drizzle it over Roasted Asparagus (page 316).*
- *Spoon it over medium-rare steak. (Heaven!)*

Best blender sauce ever!

LEMON POPPY SEED MUFFINS

MAKES 1 DOZEN MUFFINS

If you came to this cookbook to find out once and for all what the differences is between a muffin and a cupcake, I can tell you plainly that you are barking up the wrong tree. I say that with love! I also say that because I have no idea what that difference is, and I'm pretty sure all muffins are really just cupcakes that happen to be early risers. When deciding which of my cupcake, I mean muffin, recipes is indeed essential to my life and happiness, I really didn't even have to think about it. These lovely lemon numbers are positively puckery!

STREUSEL

2 tablespoons granulated sugar

1½ tablespoons turbinado sugar

1 teaspoon grated lemon zest

¼ cup plus 2 tablespoons all-purpose flour

¼ teaspoon kosher salt

3 tablespoons cold salted butter, cut into small cubes

MUFFINS

1 cup granulated sugar

¼ cup freshly grated lemon zest (from about 4 lemons)

2 cups all-purpose flour

2 teaspoons baking powder

½ teaspoon baking soda

½ teaspoon kosher salt

2 tablespoons poppy seeds

¾ cup buttermilk, homemade (see page 5) or store-bought, at room temperature

¼ cup fresh lemon juice (from about 2 lemons)

2 large eggs, at room temperature

1½ teaspoons vanilla extract

Yellow gel paste food coloring (optional)

½ cup (1 stick) salted butter, melted

1 tablespoon turbinado sugar, for sprinkling

GLAZE

1 cup powdered sugar

2 tablespoons fresh lemon juice, plus more to taste

1 teaspoon grated lemon zest

½ teaspoon vanilla extract

Yellow gel paste food coloring (optional)

1. Preheat the oven to 375°F. Line 12 cups of a muffin tin with paper liners.

2. First, make the streusel: In a medium bowl, combine the granulated sugar, turbinado sugar, and lemon zest.

3. Rub the mixture together with your fingers until the mixture is fragrant and the sugars are damp.

4. Add the flour and salt and whisk until combined.

5. Add the butter and use a pastry blender or two knives to cut it in until the mixture resembles coarse crumbs. Stick it in the fridge while you make the muffin batter.

Perfectly puckery!

6. Make the muffin batter: Starting in a similar way to the streusel, in a large bowl, rub together the granulated sugar and lemon zest with your fingertips until fragrant and damp. If you have a few minutes, let it sit to make the flavor more intense.

7. Add the flour, baking powder, baking soda, salt, and poppy seeds . . .

8. And stir until well combined.

9. In a small bowl, combine the buttermilk, lemon juice, eggs, vanilla, and a little yellow food coloring if you're using it.

10. Whisk until combined, then drizzle in the melted butter, whisking constantly.

11. Add the wet ingredients to the dry ingredients . . .

12. And stir gently until the mixture just comes together; it's very important not to overmix the dough, lest you wind up with "tuff" muffins!

13. Divide the batter evenly among the cups of the muffin tin. I use an ice cream scoop to make it easy!

14. Top each one generously with the streusel and sprinkle the turbinado sugar evenly over the 12 muffins.

My little muffin!

15. Bake the muffins until they are just turning golden, 16 to 18 minutes. Allow them to cool in the pan for 5 minutes, then remove them to a wire rack.

16. When the muffins have cooled, make the glaze: In a small bowl, whisk together the powdered sugar, lemon juice, lemon zest, and vanilla, along with a few drops of yellow food coloring, if you're using it. Taste it and make sure it's nice and tart! Feel free to add a little more lemon juice if you think it needs it.

17. Drizzle the muffins with the glaze and allow it to set before serving. These are great to make ahead of time, too! Just allow the glaze to set, then store the muffins in an airtight container for up to 24 hours.

Famous for a reason!

THE MOST BEAUTIFUL BLUEBERRY SCONES

MAKES 6 LARGE SCONES

These are the famous blueberry scones we have served in our Mercantile bakery since we opened almost ten years ago, and they are right at the top of our Do Not Discontinue list. They are absolutely legendary and will spoil you forever on scones of any kind. The difference is the laminating, or layering, process we've always used. It traps the vanilla and blueberry flavors inside the most glorious layers and makes for the best texture you could imagine. And you don't have to imagine it: These scones may be rich and special, but they're very easy to make at home. I can't wait for you to experience them!

SCONES

10 tablespoons cold salted butter

½ cup heavy cream, plus more for brushing

½ cup sour cream

1½ cups cake flour

1 cup all-purpose flour, plus more as needed

⅓ cup granulated sugar

1 tablespoon baking powder

¼ teaspoon baking soda

1 teaspoon kosher salt

1¼ cups blueberries (about 6 ounces)

GLAZE

2 cups powdered sugar

1 tablespoon salted butter, softened

1 to 2 tablespoons heavy cream

1 teaspoon vanilla bean paste

Pinch of kosher salt

Pearl sugar

1. Preheat the oven to 400°F.

2. Make the scones: Grate the butter onto a plate using the large holes of a cheese grater. Place the plate in the freezer until the butter is frozen, 15 to 20 minutes.

3. In a small pitcher, mix together the heavy cream and sour cream. Set aside.

4. In a stand mixer, mix the cake flour and all-purpose flour together, then add the granulated sugar, baking powder, baking soda, and salt.

5. Turn the mixer on low to combine the dry ingredients, then increase the speed to medium-low and add the frozen grated butter.

6. Continue mixing for 1 minute, until the mixture resembles coarse crumbs.

7. Add the cream mixture and mix until everything just comes together, 30 to 45 more seconds. You don't want to overmix!

8. Turn the crumbly dough out onto a sheet of parchment paper. Bring the crumbs into a pile and pat gently until it all comes together.

9. Gently pat the dough to a 12 × 10-inch rectangle.

10. Use the parchment to fold the left one-third of the dough over the middle one-third of the dough . . .

11. Then fold the right one-third of the dough over the middle.

12. Use the bottom of the parchment sheet to fold the tri-fold in half. Press in the center of the rectangle to help with folding.

13. So here's where we are so far! We folded the rectangle into thirds, then folded that in half. Rotate the piece of dough 90 degrees (a quarter-turn), sprinkle with a little flour . . .

14. And press it again into a 12 × 10-inch rectangle, as shown in step 9.

15. Fold it in thirds again . . .

16. Then fold it in half . . .

17. And again rotate it 90 degrees, sprinkle it with flour, and use a rolling pin to roll it out . . .

18. Into a 12 × 10-inch rectangle.

19. Sprinkle the blueberries over the surface of the dough and lightly press them in.

20. Grab the bottom of the parchment and use it to help roll the dough tightly . . .

21. And keep going until it is fully rolled.

22. Place the roll seam side down in the middle of the parchment, sprinkle on a little flour, and roll it into a 12 × 4-inch rectangle.

23. Cut the rectangle into thirds, then cut each third in half diagonally to make 6 scones.

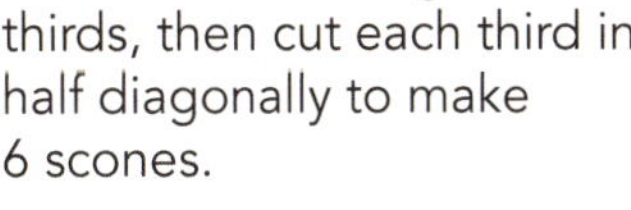

24. Place the scones on a parchment-lined sheet pan and brush the tops with heavy cream. Transfer to the oven . . .

25. And bake until the scones are just turning golden on the edges, about 20 minutes. Let them cool completely on the pan.

26. When the scones are cooled, make the glaze: In a medium bowl, whisk the powdered sugar, butter, 1 tablespoon of the heavy cream, the salt, and vanilla bean paste. Add small splashes of more heavy cream as needed to get the icing to a thick consistency, but not so thick that you have to spread it.

27. Spoon icing over each scone, letting it naturally drip over the sides. Be generous, the thick icing is part of the joy!

28. Sprinkle pearl sugar on each scone, then let the icing set. Scones can be stored in an airtight container at room temperature for up to 3 days, but they never last that long!

Variation

- *Use this exact method and substitute any of the following for the blueberries: raspberries, chocolate chips, chopped strawberries, chopped pecans, dried cranberries, chopped white chocolate . . . or just leave plain!*

Lunchy Food

It was a little tricky for me to fill a specific chapter with recipes devoted to lunch, because in our neck of the woods, lunch is often dinner . . . and a lot of cowboys even call it dinner! On a ranch, the work starts early and by the time the guys are finished (anywhere from 11 a.m. to 2 p.m.) they are ready for a huge plate of food, whether it's called dinner, lunch, or supper. Yet, I am a girl still solidly stuck in her non-agriculture past, where no one rose before 8 a.m. and where "lunch" meant salad, soups, and sandwiches. I put my very favorite and most classic of those recipes in this chapter. I always want to eat them with my sister, Betsy—forever the lady I most want to lunch with.

SHERRIED TOMATO SOUP

MAKES 8 TO 10 SERVINGS

I've made (and tasted) so many different bowls of tomato soup through the years, and I've never found a recipe I love more than my friend Cathy's, which she shared with me when my kids were babies. It's simple, slightly sweet, and made special by both cream and sherry, which add such yummy flavor. In the original, the sweetness is due to the addition of sugar, but through the years I switched it out for carrots, which accomplishes the same task while also adding a little more veggie flavor and more saturated color to the tomatoes. This soup is a star on its own, but add a grilled cheese (see page 51) and we're talking pure unadulterated happiness. *Mmm, mmm, good.* (Sorry, Campbell's. Couldn't help myself.)

1 heaping tablespoon chicken base, such as Better Than Bouillon (or 6 bouillon cubes)

½ cup (1 stick) salted butter

1 medium yellow onion, finely diced

3 large carrots, peeled, ends trimmed, and cut into thirds

1 teaspoon kosher salt, plus more if needed

½ teaspoon ground black pepper, plus more for serving

3 garlic cloves

1¼ cups dry sherry or dry white wine, such as Sauvignon Blanc (or more chicken broth)

Three 28-ounce cans crushed tomatoes

1 cup heavy cream

Extra virgin olive oil, for serving

Grated Parmesan cheese, for serving

1. In a microwave-safe pitcher or bowl, bring 1 cup water to a boil in the microwave. Add the chicken base or bouillon cubes . . .

2. And stir to combine until it's all dissolved.

3. In a 5-quart pot, melt the butter over medium heat and add the onion and carrots.

4. Sprinkle in the salt and pepper . . .

5. And stir and cook until the onions are translucent and the carrots have started to soften, 5 to 7 minutes.

6. Grate in the garlic and stir it in . . .

The Grilled Cheese
Sandwich of Your Dreams
(page 51)

7. Then pour in 1 cup of the sherry . . .

8. The tomatoes . . .

9. And the bouillon.

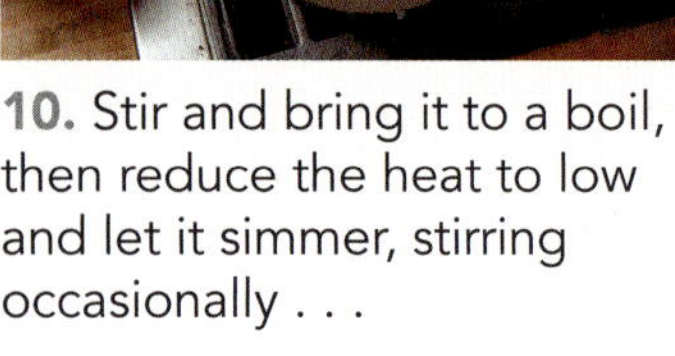

10. Stir and bring it to a boil, then reduce the heat to low and let it simmer, stirring occasionally . . .

11. Until the soup has thickened and the carrots are very tender, about 30 minutes. Turn off the heat.

12. Using an immersion blender, blend the soup until everything is totally pureed—including the carrots! (You can also use a regular blender; you will just need to puree in very small batches, since it's hot. Use caution when blending hot soup!)

13. Add the remaining ¼ cup sherry . . .

14. And the heavy cream. Stir until everything is mixed. Taste the soup and add more salt as needed. (Carrots on the sweeter side might need up to an additional teaspoon of salt for balance.)

15. Ladle up a big bowl . . .

16. Drizzle on a little olive oil . . .

17. And add some grated Parmesan and a little sprinkle of pepper.

THE GRILLED CHEESE SANDWICH OF YOUR DREAMS

MAKES 1 SERVING

A grilled cheese is absolutely required to accompany any bowl of tomato soup (see page 48), but that isn't the full story here. The real news about this particular version of, let's face it, one of the most common sandwiches in America (second only, I'd say, to PB&J) is that there is *nothing* common about it. Friends, after eighteen years of sharing recipes with you, and after fifty-plus years of eating grilled cheeses, I'm thrilled to present to you the very best grilled cheese sandwich I have ever made. I won't go into descriptive detail about the whys of the cheeses or the science of what I spread on the bread because I'd rather just show you here. All I will say is this: If you've never listened to me before, and I'm a middle child so I would totally understand if you haven't, this recipe is the place to start.

Two ½-inch-thick slices Soft White Sandwich Bread (page 55) or any good sandwich bread*

2 tablespoons salted butter, softened

2 tablespoons mayonnaise, homemade (see page 67) or store-bought

4 slices good-quality American cheese (I use Dietz and Watson brand from the supermarket deli counter)

2 generous tablespoons freshly grated sharp cheddar cheese

2 generous tablespoons freshly grated Monterey Jack cheese

**** For best results, make or buy a whole loaf of bread and slice it when you are about to make the sandwich. Pre-sliced bread is often cut a little too thin or is too soft to hold up to the cheese and butter/mayo mixture. Sourdough bread would work great, too, though take care not to slice it too thick since it has more structure than plain white bread. The most important thing is to keep the heat low enough to melt the cheese before the bread burns.***

1. Heat a cast-iron skillet over low heat.

2. On one slice of bread, spread 1 tablespoon of the butter . . .

3. Then (again, trust me!) cover the butter with a tablespoon of the mayo.

4. Place the slice in the skillet, butter/mayo side down.

5. Overlap 2 slices of American cheese so that they cover the bread but don't hang too far over the edges.

6. Sprinkle on the grated cheddar and Monterey Jack . . .

7. And top with the other 2 slices of cheese, again overlapping.

8. Spread the remaining 1 tablespoon each of the butter and mayo on the second slice of bread . . .

9. And pop it on the top, butter and mayo side up.

10. To hasten the cheese melting, put a lid (or inverted metal sheet pan!) on top of the pan to trap the heat.

11. After about 4 minutes, check the underside of the bread to make sure it isn't too brown. Flip it when it's deep golden and crisp, and let it cook on the other side until the bread is golden and all the cheese is wonderfully melted.

12. Remove the sandwich from the skillet . . .

13. And let it sit on a board for 1 minute before slicing.

Sherried Tomato Soup
(page 48)
You have to try
this crust!

My favorite
everyday bread!

SOFT WHITE SANDWICH BREAD

MAKES 1 LOAF

I have long proclaimed that baking bread is not my calling. I love homemade bread, I'll eat it willingly and enthusiastically, but I have never had the passion (or even an itch) to perfect the art of baking it. The sourdough craze of the past few years served only to solidify my obstinance. I love to watch it made, I love to eat it, but again . . . I don't wanna make it. So I hope you'll take all of this pontificating as an indicator of just how fantastic this simple sandwich bread recipe—which I have made again and again and again in recent years—truly is. It's neither artisan nor complicated, and it doesn't ferment. It is meant to be a substitute for regular ol' sliced sandwich bread, and I'm talking about the soft Wonder bread variety. Except you slice it only when you need it. It truly is a wonder, and making a loaf a couple of times a week may just become a habit!

2 cups all-purpose flour, plus more for rolling out the dough

1½ cups bread flour

⅓ cup whole milk

One 0.25-ounce packet instant yeast (2¼ teaspoons)

2 tablespoons sugar

4 tablespoons (½ stick) salted butter, softened, plus more for greasing the pan and serving

1 teaspoon kosher salt

Vegetable oil, for the bowl

1. In a medium bowl, combine the all-purpose flour and bread flour and whisk it together.

2. Combine the milk with 1 cup water in a measuring pitcher and warm it in the microwave for about 1½ minutes.

3. Remove it from the microwave and let it cool to between 110 and 115°F.

4. Pour the liquid into the bowl of a stand mixture fitted with a dough hook.

5. Sprinkle in the yeast . . .

6. And the sugar.

7. Turn the mixer on low and stir the mixture for 30 seconds . . .

8. Then add the butter . . .

9. And the salt. Turn the mixer on medium and let it mix for 30 seconds . . .

10. Then add the dry ingredients in three additions, letting each one incorporate before adding the next.

11. Let the mixer run for 2 minutes, then turn the speed to medium low . . .

12. And let it mix for 6 more minutes, until the dough is smooth and almost fully pulls away from the sides of the bowl. If it doesn't quite look smooth, mix for another minute or two.

13. Transfer the dough to a lightly oiled bowl, then cover the bowl with plastic wrap and let it rise in a relatively warm place . . .

14. Until doubled in size, 1½ to 2 hours. (If it hasn't risen much, keep it covered and give it another 45 minutes. Make sure it's sitting in a draft-free spot.) Grease 9 × 5-inch metal loaf pan with butter.

15. Sprinkle a light coating of all-purpose flour on the work surface. Dump out the dough . . .

16. And shape/stretch it into a rectangle about 8½ × 15 inches. (The short side of the dough will fit neatly into the loaf pan.)

17. Roll the dough away from you . . .

USE SANDWICH BREAD FOR

- *French Toast with Berry Butter (page 9): Substitute for the French bread.*
- *A perfectly simple BLT: Use Homemade Mayonnaise (page 67) to make it extra good.*
- *Egg Salad Sandwiches (page 64): Sublime.*
- *Good ol' toast with softened butter and honey! It will rock your world.*
- *Crispy-Chewy Croutons (page 81): Substitute for the French bread.*

18. Until you have a nice, tight roll.

19. Place the roll seam side down in the greased pan, cover it lightly with plastic wrap, and set it in a draft-free place for an hour (or more if needed) . . .

20. Until it has risen over the rim of the pan by a good inch (but isn't spilling over the sides). Meanwhile, preheat the oven to 350°F with a rack in the center position.

21. Bake the loaf on the center rack until it's lovely and golden, 30 to 40 minutes. It shouldn't look perfect on top; rustic and real is fine!

22. Let the loaf cool in the pan for 10 minutes to settle before tipping it onto a board. Slice with a serrated knife to your heart's content!

The bread is perfect to eat right away, with softened butter. Or allow it to cool completely to room temperature, then wrap it in plastic wrap, a plastic storage bag, or even a thin kitchen towel to keep it fresh. Trust me, it won't last longer than 24 to 36 hours . . . at the most!

SPINACH SALAD WITH WARM BACON DRESSING

MAKES 4 TO 6 SERVINGS

My favorite kind of salad is one that has so many toppings you can barely see the greens. That pretty much sums up this beauty, which I've loved since I was a teenager. Bacon is one of the overarching themes, as it forms the foundation for not only the toppings, but the dressing as well. And lest you think the spinach is merely a vessel, it actually becomes an even more sublime version of itself once the warm bacon dressing goes on. This is the salad of my dreams, and I'm very happy to share my dreams with you.

6 slices thick-cut peppered bacon

1 medium red onion, thinly sliced

8 ounces white button mushrooms, sliced

Kosher salt and ground black pepper

3 tablespoons red wine vinegar

1 teaspoon Dijon mustard

2 tablespoons honey

8 ounces baby spinach, washed and dried

6 Hard-Boiled Eggs (page 63), sliced

1. In a large skillet, cook the bacon over medium-high heat until it's crisp around the edges but still chewy.

2. Drain it on a paper towel.

3. Remove 3 tablespoons of the bacon grease from the skillet and set it aside.

4. Pour out most of the rest of the grease (but don't clean the pan!) and add the onion. Cook, stirring often . . .

5. Until deep golden and caramelized, about 15 minutes.

6. Remove the luscious onion to a plate and set it aside.

My favorite since 1988.

7. Add the mushrooms to the skillet . . .

8. And cook, stirring occasionally, until they are deep golden, about 12 minutes. Season with salt and pepper, then stir . . .

9. And remove the mushrooms to a plate. Turn the heat to low . . .

10. Then pour in the reserved bacon grease . . .

11. The red wine vinegar . . .

12. The mustard . . .

13. And the honey.

14. Stir this dressing mixture, scraping the bottom of the skillet and loosening all the flavor, until slightly thickened, about 2 minutes. If it needs a little more volume, add a tablespoon or two of hot water.

15. Place the spinach in a large bowl and drizzle the dressing all over . . .

16. Then toss it to coat all the leaves.

17. Pour the spinach into a wide, shallow bowl . . .

18. And arrange the ingredients in piles: The onions . . .

19. And then the mushrooms.

20. Chop the bacon and slice the eggs . . .

21. And arrange those, too. Serve it immediately! What a salad.

Definitely in my dahlia era!

Easy to peel,
perfectly cooked!

HARD-BOILED EGGS (ONCE AND FOR ALL!)

MAKES 6 EGGS

I am actually scared to post this method for making hard-boiled eggs, and here's why: Even though I've personally had a 99-percent success rate using it, I recognize that things can always go wrong and there are exceptions to most rules, and if you follow this method and it doesn't work, you might get mad at me—or even if you don't get mad at me, you might not love me quite as much as you did before I shared the method . . . and then, I ask myself, why take that risk? I would like to say this is tongue in cheek, and it probably is to some degree, but again . . . middle child of fifty-six years over here. But I'm going to step out on a limb and share it despite my fears because the truth is, it works! Gone are the days of crying over hard-to-peel eggs and chipped, nicked eggs. I promise you, it works!

6 large eggs

1. Fill a medium saucepan with enough water to completely submerge the eggs. Cover the pan and bring the water to a boil over high heat. Uncover and gently lower the eggs into the water using a slotted spoon or metal spider—don't drop them into the pan or they may crack!

2. Lower the heat as necessary to maintain a low, steady boil and cook the eggs to your desired doneness: 7 minutes for a jammy egg, 8 minutes for a jammy center with set edges, or 12 minutes for a drier, sturdier hard-boiled egg that's perfect for egg salad or deviled eggs!

3. While the eggs are cooking, prepare a bowl of very icy water. When their time is up, transfer them to the ice water to shock them. Watch the clock and wait 2 minutes . . .

4. Then remove the eggs to a dry kitchen towel. Peel them by tapping both ends of an egg on the countertop and gently rolling it on the countertop to loosen the peel. It should come right off!

5. Keep going until you have the number of peeled eggs you need; there should be very few (if any!) nicks in the egg.

Peeled eggs can be refrigerated in an airtight container for 1 day; unpeeled eggs can stay uncovered in the fridge for up to 1 week!

THE PERFECT PACKAGE!

Hard-boiled eggs have less than a hundred calories each, and about 6 grams of protein, which is a nice bang for your nutritional buck. Egg yolks contain protein, vitamins, and amino acids, while the whites are all protein, all the time.

EGG SALAD SANDWICHES

MAKES ABOUT 3 CUPS EGG SALAD, FOR ABOUT 4 SANDWICHES

It's entirely possible that one would have to be born before 1983 in order to consider egg salad an essential recipe in their life. That said, I would encourage you post-'83 youngsters to consider delving into the sublime beauty that is a good egg salad. And good egg salad, to me, is kept very simple; while I'll spike tuna or chicken salad with crunchy celery and other add-ins (including hard-boiled eggs! How meta!), my egg salad keeps the eggs front and center, without a lot of distraction. This version is insanely wonderful, thanks to the homemade mayo and from-scratch sandwich bread . . . but even if you use the store-bought version of both of those ingredients, this sandwich is still absolute heaven.

12 Hard-Boiled Eggs (page 63)

½ cup mayonnaise, homemade (see page 67) or store-bought, plus more as needed

2 tablespoons Dijon mustard, plus more as needed

3 dashes Worcestershire sauce

½ teaspoon smoked paprika

1 teaspoon kosher salt, plus more as needed

1 teaspoon ground black pepper, plus more as needed

Soft White Sandwich Bread (page 55) or store-bought bread, sliced thin

1. Peel the eggs and place a wire rack over a large bowl.

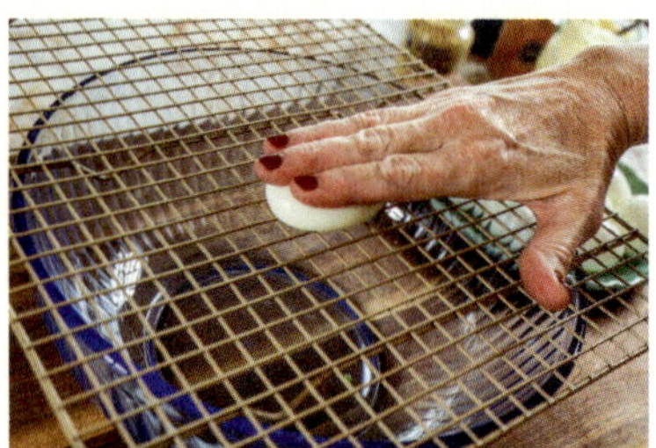

2. One by one, place the eggs on the rack . . .

3. And press the egg through the grates.

4. Keep going until all the eggs are "chopped"!

5. Add the mayonnaise, mustard, Worcestershire, paprika, salt, and pepper . . .

6. And stir very gently to mix all the ingredients evenly.

Homemade bread and
mayo make this heavenly!

7. Taste the egg salad and add more salt and pepper as needed. If you like, you can even add more mayo or mustard, depending on your preferences. Cover the egg salad and refrigerate it for at least 2 hours to allow the flavors and textures to meld.

8. For each sandwich, pile about ¾ cup of the egg salad onto a slice of bread . . .

9. And lightly press a second piece of bread on top.

Variations

- *Stir 3 tablespoons minced chives into the egg salad for a punchy onion flavor throughout.*
- *Add ¼ to ½ teaspoon cayenne pepper to the egg salad before mixing for a bit of heat.*
- *Serve the egg salad on top of pretty lettuce leaves instead of building sandwiches.*
- *Stir 1 mashed avocado into the egg salad for a yummy green option! (Serve immediately after mixing.)*
- *Place a few slivers of Pickled Red Onions (page 76) on the sandwich!*

"A clover and one bee" . . . and me!

HOMEMADE MAYONNAISE

(with Roasted Garlic Mayo as a bonus!)

MAKES ABOUT 1 PINT

I use store-bought mayo all the time, and I have no idea why. Every time I make a little jar of the homemade stuff, I find myself scratching my head as to why store-bought mayonnaise is even legal! It takes approximately ninety seconds to make a batch yourself, after all, and the difference in texture and flavor is huge. Here are both a basic version and a yummy roasted garlic version—and they're both *a-ma-zing*! Use them to your heart's content! The regular mayo is more straightforward, and is good for mixing into Chicken Salad (page 70) and for making salad dressings like ranch (see page 238). The roasted garlic version packs a punch when you want more flavor on your turkey sandwich or need a glorious dip for Roasted Asparagus (page 316).

1 large egg*

1 cup neutral oil, such as canola, sunflower, or avocado (I used canola)

1 tablespoon fresh lemon juice

¼ teaspoon kosher salt

Pinch of ground black pepper

**** I am generally not concerned about the raw egg in mayonnaise, but if you prefer to avoid it, you can use pasteurized eggs; they work just great!***

1. In a 16-ounce wide-mouth jar, combine the egg with the oil.

2. Add the lemon juice . . .

3. And the salt and pepper.

4. This is the fun part! Place the immersion blender all the way into the jar so that the head is resting on the bottom. Turn the blender on . . .

5. And slowly pull it up. You'll see the mixture immediately turning into mayo!

6. Continue pulling the blender up . . .

7. And stop when you get to the top! The oil should all be mixed in. (Don't move the blender up and down and continue to blend; it's perfect as is!)

8. Use the mayo immediately or store it in the fridge to chill. It will keep in the fridge for up to 1 week.

MAYO VS. AIOLI

Many think mayonnaise and aioli are the same thing, but there is a distinct difference: Mayo typically includes egg and a neutral oil, while aioli has to start with garlic and olive oil. Aioli uses egg yolks, or no egg at all. (I'll take them both, BTW!)

VARIATION: ROASTED GARLIC MAYO

Make an absolutely phenomenal roasted garlic version, which is wonderful as a sandwich spread or dip for fries!

1. Add 6 roasted garlic cloves (roast your own, or use store-bought) to a 16-ounce jar with an egg . . .

2. Along with a teaspoon of Dijon mustard . . .

3. And a dash of Worcestershire.

4. Add the same ingredients as the regular mayo: 1 cup oil, 1 tablespoon lemon juice, and ¼ teaspoon kosher salt, and a pinch of black pepper.

5. Blend as above until very creamy! You'll see delicious little bits of roasted garlic and flecks from the Dijon. Marvelous mayo.

4 cups shredded cooked chicken (see page 216) or rotisserie chicken

2 celery stalks, diced small

3 green onions, sliced

2 cups red or green grapes, halved, more if desired

½ cup mayonnaise, homemade (see page 67) or store-bought

½ cup sour cream

1 to 2 tablespoons brown sugar, to taste

Juice of 1 lemon

1 teaspoon kosher salt, plus more to taste

¾ teaspoon ground black pepper, plus more to taste

¼ teaspoon cayenne, plus more to taste

3 tablespoons minced fresh dill

1. In a large bowl, combine the chicken, celery, and green onions . . .

2. Along with the grapes.

3. Make the dressing by combining the mayonnaise, sour cream, and brown sugar in a medium bowl . . .

4. Along with the lemon juice, the salt, pepper, and cayenne.

5. Stir until combined, then taste and add more salt and/or pepper (or cayenne!) if you like.

6. Pour all but ¼ cup of the dressing on top of the salad . . .

7. Sprinkle on the dill . . .

8. And stir until all the ingredients are coated in the dressing. Take a look and see if you think it has enough dressing for you; feel free to add more or the rest of it if you like. (Any leftover dressing can be stored in the fridge for 1 week and used for any regular green salad.) Cover the salad bowl with plastic wrap and chill the salad for at least 4 hours or up to 24 hours before serving, to let the flavors meld.

How to serve

- *On a flaky croissant. Perfection!*
- *On toasted white bread with iceberg lettuce.*
- *On a bed of green leaf lettuce, as a salad.*
- *Inside a rolled whole wheat tortilla, as a wrap.*

WEDGE SALAD

MAKES 6 SERVINGS

I'm going to just come right out with it: This salad takes about 2½ hours to make. Wait, don't turn the page!! Please hear me out. I realize an iceberg wedge salad should be simple and fast to make (hunk of iceberg, big spoonful of dressing, right?), but after a few decades of ordering them in restaurants and making them at home, I found myself getting bored with the wedge salad portion of my life. Well . . . this version is the opposite of boring, and if you make it just once, it will likely become the go-to salad you serve to company going forward. Between sizzled cubes of pork belly and sweet oven-roasted tomatoes, not to mention the tastiest ranch in the West, this is going to alter the course of your wedge-salad-eating life! It sure altered mine, and I would consider this an essential salad in my world.

OVEN-ROASTED TOMATOES*

16 ounces grape or cherry tomatoes, halved

2 tablespoons olive oil

Kosher salt and ground black pepper

** As a simpler alternative, just add halved fresh grape tomatoes to the finished salad.*

PORK BELLY CROUTONS**

2 pounds pork belly, cut into 1½-inch cubes

½ cup packed brown sugar

1 generous tablespoon kosher salt

1 tablespoon coarsely ground tricolor peppercorns

1 teaspoon garlic powder

1 teaspoon onion powder

*** As a simpler alternative, just add chopped cooked bacon to the finished salad.*

ASSEMBLY

1 head iceberg lettuce

2 cups Ree's Favorite Ranch (page 238)

6 tablespoons store-bought balsamic glaze, for serving

½ cup Pickled Red Onions (page 76)

1½ cups grated sharp cheddar cheese

6 Hard-Boiled Eggs (page 63), sliced

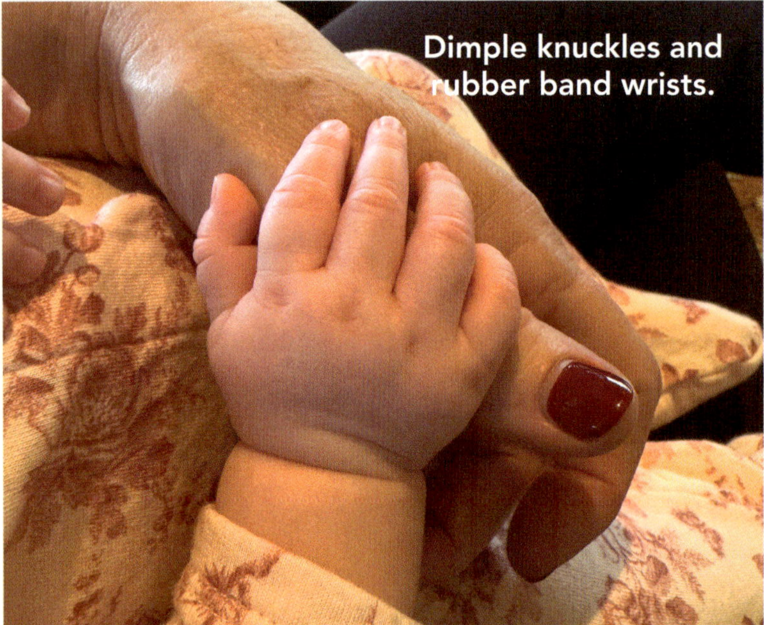

1. Preheat the oven to 300°F with racks in the top third and lower third of the oven. Line a sheet pan with parchment paper.

2. First, roast the tomatoes: In a medium bowl, drizzle the tomatoes with the olive oil.

3. Sprinkle them with salt and pepper and stir to evenly coat.

4. Arrange the tomatoes on the prepared sheet pan, cut side up, taking care not to crowd them. Bake them on the top rack for 2 hours!

5. Meanwhile, make the pork belly croutons: Line a baking dish with foil. Heat a heavy skillet over medium-high heat and sear the cubes of pork . . .

6. Until golden and crisp on all sides.

7. Remove them to the prepared baking dish.

8. In a small bowl, mix together the brown sugar, salt, tricolor pepper, garlic powder, and onion powder.

9. Sprinkle the mixture over the pork belly . . .

10. And toss until the pork is totally coated and there isn't much of the mix left in the bottom of the pan (though a little is fine!).

11. When the tomatoes have been roasting for 1 hour, set the pan with the pork on the lower rack of the oven. Roast until the pork is both crisp and tender, about 1½ hours. Set them aside to cool slightly.

12. After 2 hours, the tomatoes should be nice and shriveled. Set them aside to cool while you assemble the salad.

13. Cut around the core of the iceberg head and remove the core.

14. Slice it into 6 wedges.

15. To build each salad, place a wedge on a dinner plate, cut sides up. Spoon a generous amount of the ranch dressing on top. (Dribbling on the plate is fine! Recommended, even.)

16. Drizzle the balsamic glaze in a zigzag motion over the dressing . . .

17. Then arrange the pickled red onions and roasted tomatoes on the salad and around the plate.

18. Sprinkle on some cheddar . . .

19. And arrange a sliced egg on the side of the plate.

20. Add 4 to 5 pieces of pork belly evenly around the outside of the plate. Wild times we're in! (I love this salad!)

Paige with her aunt Missy, taking a break.

I promise there's lettuce under there!

PICKLED RED ONIONS

MAKES ABOUT 1 CUP

I didn't go back and count the number of appearances these onions have made in my cookbooks through the years. I'd like to say only once before, but it's possible that it's more than that. This would be fitting, however, considering how perfectly versatile this bright, happy condiment/adornment/garnish/finishing touch is! I gave it multiple definitions in that sentence because it really defies categorization; I put slivers of these onions on salads, in quesadillas, on burgers, stirred into potato salad, in grilled cheeses . . . I could write a long list! And while these are now offered in jars in many supermarkets, they're best (and certainly cheapest!) made at home. Make a batch and discover the magic!

⅔ cup distilled white vinegar

2 teaspoons sugar

½ teaspoon kosher salt

½ medium red onion, sliced very thin

1. In a medium saucepan, combine the vinegar with ⅔ cup water.

2. Add the sugar and salt . . .

3. And bring it to a gentle boil over medium-high heat.

4. Pack a pint jar tightly with the sliced red onion . . .

5. And slowly pour the hot liquid to within ¼ inch of the top of the jar. Let sit to cool completely, then place the lid on the jar.

6. Within an hour, you've got pickled red onions! Place the jar in the fridge and they'll continue to get more purple-pink within hours. The onions will keep in the fridge for 2 weeks!

They go with everything!

BROCCOLI CHEESE SOUP

MAKES 8 TO 10 SERVINGS

In a cookbook of Drummond family recipes, I couldn't leave out my third child's favorite soup. Bryce has loved broccoli cheese soup since he was a towheaded sweetie-pie whose cherished blankie was actually a worn-out yellow towel from J.C. Penney. I still love seeing the twinkle in his eyes when this soup is on the stove. It's the key to his heart (and Bryce is one of the keys to mine!). I haven't adjusted this much through the years, but have upped the seasonings and added garlic as my tastebuds are requiring more excitement in my old age. However, the addition of Havarti cheese is probably my favorite update. Try it!

5 tablespoons salted butter

1 yellow onion, finely diced

2 garlic cloves, finely minced

⅓ cup all-purpose flour

1 teaspoon kosher salt, plus more to taste

½ teaspoon seasoned salt

1 teaspoon ground black pepper, plus more to taste

2 cups Homemade Chicken Stock (page 136) or store-bought stock or broth

1 quart whole milk

2 cups half-and-half

¼ teaspoon ground nutmeg

4 heads broccoli, broken into florets (about 8 to 9 cups)

2½ cups grated sharp cheddar cheese, plus more for serving

2½ cups grated Havarti cheese (or Monterey Jack), plus more for serving

Crispy-Chewy Croutons (page 81), for serving

1. In a 5-quart pot, melt the butter over medium heat. Add the onion and garlic . . .

2. And cook, stirring continually, until the onion is very tender, 4 to 5 minutes.

3. Sprinkle the flour, kosher salt, seasoned salt, and pepper on top.

4. Stir to cook the flour for about a minute . . .

5. Then pour in the chicken stock . . .

6. The milk . . .

Big broccoli flavor—
and so much cheese!

7. And the half-and-half.

8. Stir, then sprinkle in the nutmeg.

9. Throw in the broccoli and stir to combine.

10. Put the lid on the pot, reduce the heat to low, and simmer the soup until the broccoli is tender, about 30 minutes.

11. Use an immersion blender to carefully blend the soup to your heart's content!

12. I like to blend until the soup is mostly pureed and the broccoli is broken into tiny bits, with a few remaining chunks here and there.

13. When the soup is the consistency you want, add the cheeses . . .

14. And stir until they are totally melted. Taste at this point and add more salt and pepper if needed.

15. Serve with a little extra cheddar and Havarti and dot croutons on the surface.

Variations

- *Use dill or herbed Havarti if you can find it. Yum!*
- *Add 4 ounces goat cheese (chèvre) to the finished soup and stir to melt. Delicious sharpness.*
- *Serve in bread bowls if you can find them!*

CRISPY-CHEWY CROUTONS

MAKES ABOUT 4 CUPS

Sometimes it's the simplest recipes that trip me up. I have been on what feels like a lifelong quest to make the perfect crouton for salads and soups (and snacking). I've always tried croutons in the oven, with endless combinations of olive oil, butter, herbs . . . even the shape and size of the bread pieces. Ten times out of ten, they've come up short: either too crisp or too dry or too bland, or (this was a dark crouton day) all of the above. I thought perfect croutons weren't in the cards for me! Fortunately, these beauties fell out of Heaven and into my lap (well, onto my plate) in the past year. They are perfect and chewy and oh so delicious. They have brought crouton hope back into my life, and I think they'll do the same for you. (Thank you, Jess!)

½ loaf crusty bread (French, Italian, or sourdough)

1½ cups extra-virgin olive oil

8 garlic cloves, smashed and peeled

Kosher salt and ground black pepper

1. Tear the bread into bite-size chunks.

2. In a large pot or skillet, heat the olive oil over medium-high heat and add the smashed garlic.

3. Carefully stir them in the oil for 2 minutes to infuse the flavor.

4. Add the bread to the pan in a single layer, making sure not to overcrowd it. (I fry them in batches!)

5. Cook the croutons for about 1 minute, then flip them to the other side . . .

6. And let them cook for another minute or so. You want the edges to be crisp and golden.

For salads, soups,
and snacking!

Bryce is back on the ranch! His washing machine is getting a workout.

7. Remove the croutons from the oil and let them drain on a sheet pan lined with paper towels. Keep the garlic sizzling in the oil . . .

8. And add the second batch of bread.

9. Cook them the same way (if there's still any oil left in the pan, you can always tear more bread and make another mini-batch!).

10. Season the croutons (and the fried garlic!) with salt and pepper—you want them to be well-seasoned—and shake the pan to toss. Enjoy them warm, or let them cool to room temperature to achieve their best slightly chewy texture.

Enjoy with salad, soup, or as a dipper for hummus or other dip.

Store leftover croutons in a plastic storage bag at room temperature for up to 3 days. They won't last that long!

Ticks all the Caesar salad boxes!

CLASSIC CAESAR SALAD

MAKES 6 TO 8 SERVINGS

Caesar salad can be a very personal thing, right on down to the lettuce. I remember the moment my old college roommate and I discovered that one of us (she) liked the crunchy, lighter green parts of the romaine and the other of us (me) preferred the darker green parts of the leaf. From that day forward, we loved splitting/sharing Caesar salads in restaurants and delighting in our differences!

This recipe is everything I want in a Caesar: Deep, rich dressing with tons of flavor and even more Parmesan. I don't add egg to my dressing, but that's an option if you like things creamier. Don't skip the croutons on this one! They are an essential part of this very essential recipe.

4 anchovy fillets

Kosher salt

2 tablespoons Dijon mustard

1 tablespoon balsamic vinegar

1 teaspoon Worcestershire sauce

2 garlic cloves

Grated zest and juice of 1 lemon

½ cup olive oil

¼ cup freshly grated Parmesan cheese, plus more for garnish

Ground black pepper

3 romaine lettuce hearts, sliced into 1-inch pieces

Crispy-Chewy Croutons (page 81)

1. First, make the dressing: Place the anchovies in a medium bowl.

2. Sprinkle a pinch of salt on top . . .

3. And use a fork to mash them into a paste.

4. Squeeze in the mustard . . .

5. And add the balsamic and Worcestershire.

6. Grate in the garlic . . .

7. Add the lemon zest and juice . . .

8. And whisk the mixture together. Slowly add the olive oil, whisking constantly . . .

9. Until the dressing is smooth and emulsified.

10. Whisk in the Parmesan . . .

11. And plenty of pepper. After mixing, taste and add more salt if it needs it! If you have time, cover and refrigerate the dressing for a couple of hours to let the flavors marry.

12. Place the lettuce in a large bowl and pour the dressing on top.

13. Toss until the lettuce is evenly coated.

14. Grate in more Parmesan and give it one more toss.

15. Transfer the salad to a serving bowl and top with plenty of croutons . . .

16. As well as more Parmesan and pepper!

Variations

- *For a creamier Caesar dressing, add a raw egg yolk to the bowl after the anchovies are mashed and incorporate it into the dressing.*
- *Use a blender for either version of the dressing to make it very homogenized and smooth.*
- *Top the salad with any cooked protein (chicken, shrimp, salmon).*

FRENCH ONION SOUP

MAKES ABOUT 8 SERVINGS

French onion soup is one of those things I make once or twice a year, tops. And that's because it is my favorite soup on the planet, and if I have it at home, I have a hard time limiting myself to just one portion, as I would do in a restaurant (and by the way, if a restaurant has it on the menu, I'm ordering it). This version is the same one I've made since forever, and I learned the onions-in-the-oven trick from my mom's old book of service league recipes. It results in the most deep, delicious onions, which results in the most deep, delicious soup, which is only one component of the finished dish! There's also the bread, there's also the cheese, and if you'll excuse me, I'm going to go make it right now. And have more than one portion.

½ cup (1 stick) salted butter

6 large yellow onions, thinly sliced

2 garlic cloves, chopped, plus 1 peeled clove for the bread

⅔ cup bourbon or dry sherry (or you can substitute more beef stock for the alcohol)

2 quarts Homemade Beef Stock (page 160) or store-bought stock or broth

1½ teaspoons Worcestershire sauce

1 teaspoon kosher salt, plus more for the bread

½ teaspoon ground black pepper, plus more for the bread

1 small baguette, cut into ½-inch-thick slices

Olive oil, for drizzling

16 ounces Gruyère cheese, grated

2 tablespoons chopped parsley, for garnish

1. Preheat the oven to 400°F.

2. In a large heavy ovenproof soup pot or Dutch oven, melt the butter over medium-low heat. Add the onions and chopped garlic and cook, stirring frequently, and placing the lid on the pot when you're not stirring . . .

3. Until the onions are very soft, about 20 minutes.

4. Set the lid slightly ajar on the pot, place the pot in the oven, and continue cooking the onions in the oven for 1½ hours, stirring twice during that time to ensure the onions don't stick to the pot and burn.

5. After their time in the oven, the onions should be very deep golden brown! Return the pot to the stovetop, but leave the oven on.

6. Before turning on the heat under the Dutch oven, pour in the bourbon.

7. Stir for 1 minute, scraping the bottom of the pot (be careful—the pot will be very hot after being in the oven!), then turn the heat to medium and allow the bourbon to reduce for another 5 minutes, stirring occasionally.

8. Add the beef stock . . .

9. And the Worcestershire, salt, and pepper. Let the soup simmer for 30 minutes. Meanwhile, decrease the oven temperature to 375°F.

10. Place the baguette slices on a sheet pan. Drizzle both sizes generously with olive oil.

11. Sprinkle on salt and pepper.

12. Transfer to the oven and bake until golden and crisp, 12 to 14 minutes. Switch the oven to broil and place a rack just above the center of the oven.

13. Rub each slice of toast with the peeled garlic clove to give them a nice flavor punch.

14. Dish up portions of soup in ovenproof bowls or crocks, making sure to get a balance of broth and onions in each bowl.

15. Arrange 2 to 3 pieces of bread on top of each portion, depending on the circumference of the bowl. You want the bread to cover most of the surface of the soup!

16. Place the crocks on a sheet pan and sprinkle ⅓ cup cheese on top of each bowl.

17. Broil the soup until the cheese is melted and bubbling and starting to blacken in a couple of spots, 3 to 4 minutes (watch carefully in case it starts to burn too quickly). Remove the pan and let the soup sit and settle for 3 minutes. (The cheese is hot hot hot!) Garnish with parsley and serve.

Come to Mama!

Pizza

You'll find lots of pasta recipes in this cookbook, scattered throughout a number of different chapters depending on their ingredients. But I knew even before I got started that I wanted a dedicated chapter for pizza that stood on its own. First of all, my name is Ree Drummond and I never met a pizza I didn't like. Second, I have made more pizzas in my life than I think I could even count. Third, I own a pizza restaurant! Fourth, I happen to think pizza is the most universally loved, crowd-pleasing, no-brainer, everyone-will-love-it food you can possibly serve, whether it's to your sweet family or a kitchen full of friends. Oh, and another thing: It's a veritable blank canvas, and there is no end to the combinations and permutations a pizza maker can come up with. Still, I wanted to narrow it down to the pizza varieties I don't think I could live without, and those are the ones you'll find in the pages to follow. There are a couple of fancy ones, a couple of super-basic ones, and a few in between. But don't overlook my no-fail pizza crust and no-cook pizza sauce, both of which can turn an average pie into an absolute marvel. Go forth and make pizza, my friends!

The dough that's never
let me down!
Best-Ever Pesto
(page 107)

THE BEST PIZZA DOUGH IN THE WORLD!

MAKES ENOUGH FOR TWO 15-INCH PIZZAS

If you have any kind of pizza game at home, a good pizza crust makes all the difference in the finished product. This is my BFF in terms of pizza crusts (I've used it since the turn of the century, around the time my girls were babies) and it has never let me down. The only difference now is that I call for a little more salt, which I found makes the pizza crust so delicious that there's never a piece left on anybody's plate. Get into the habit of making a batch of this weekly and parking it in the fridge. It's better if it sits in there for at least a couple of days!

1 teaspoon active dry yeast

4 cups all-purpose flour

2½ teaspoons kosher salt

⅓ cup extra virgin olive oil, plus more as needed

1. Sprinkle the yeast over 1½ cups warm water—between 105 and 110°F is best, if you have an instant-read thermometer to check! Let this mixture sit undisturbed for 5 minutes, then stir it gently.

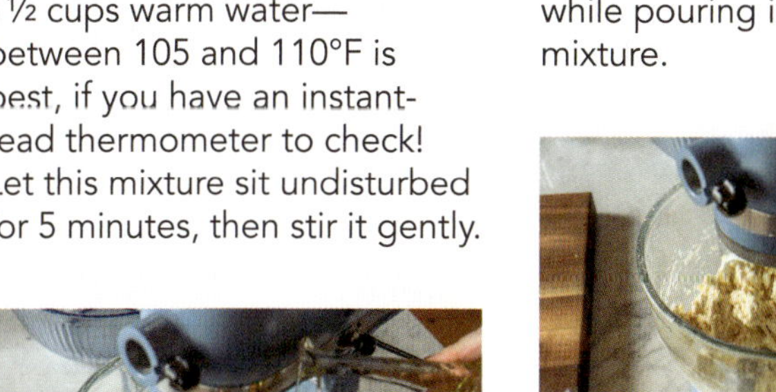

2. In the bowl of an electric mixer fitted with the paddle attachment, combine the flour and salt. On low speed, drizzle in the olive oil until it's been fully incorporated.

3. Continue mixing on low while pouring in the yeast mixture.

4. Continue mixing for 1 minute, increasing the speed if needed, until the dough just barely comes together. You don't want to overwork the dough, so a minute is enough.

5. Coat a large bowl with olive oil, then dump in the dough. Turn the dough over to coat it in the oil, then cover the bowl with plastic wrap and store it in the fridge. Give it at least 24 hours to rise and develop, but 3 days is best! (If you're in a hurry, you can let it rise on the counter for 2 hours to make pizza the same day.)

6. Either way, the dough should rise until at least doubled! When you're ready to make the pizza, divide the dough in half. If you just make one pizza, you can cover the bowl and refrigerate the other ball of dough for up to 3 days, or freeze it (with a bit of extra room in the freezer bag) for up to 6 months.

P-TOWN'S PIZZA SAUCE

MAKES 7 CUPS

For most of my pizza cooking life, I used jarred marinara as the sauce. There is absolutely nothing wrong with this approach, whether you use Homemade Marinara Sauce (page 148) or the store-bought stuff, but I want to show you another way. At P-Town Pizza, my place in Pawhuska, we have a no-cook sauce that focuses entirely on the ingredients without much fuss at all. It's just mixed up in a blender and does all its "cooking" on the pizza in the oven. Let me tell ya, if pizza sauce has always been a bit of an afterthought for you, this is going to turn that upside down.

One 28-ounce can peeled whole San Marzano tomatoes

One 28-ounce can crushed San Marzano tomatoes

1 generous tablespoon crushed Calabrian chili paste (sold in a jar), plus more to taste

3 garlic cloves, peeled

1 cup packed basil leaves

2 tablespoons olive oil

1 teaspoon sugar

½ teaspoon kosher salt, plus more to taste

½ teaspoon ground black pepper, plus more to taste

1. In a blender or food processor, combine the whole tomatoes and crushed tomatoes.

2. Add the Calabrian chili paste . . .

3. The garlic . . .

4. The basil . . .

5. And the olive oil, sugar, salt, and pepper.

6. Blend the mixture for 2 minutes to ensure it is totally pureed and thick. Give it a taste and blend in more salt, pepper, or chilies, depending on what you like.

7. Transfer the sauce to jars and store it in the fridge for up to 2 weeks. Makes incredible pizzas!

Le Parfait
Super
This'll make your pizza more magical.

TRIPLE THREAT PEPPERONI PIZZA

MAKES ONE 15-INCH-LONG OVAL PIZZA

Of all the pizza variations we have on the P-Town Pizza menu—and I think we have ten to twelve—our best seller has been pepperoni since the day we opened. I attribute this to two things: First, pepperoni is America's favorite pizza. Second, our pepperoni pizza, which inspired this one, is utterly fantastic! We use three different sizes of pepperoni, all of which serve different purposes. Large deli-sliced pieces cover a lot of ground and sink into the cheese underneath; classic pepperoni fills in a lot of the gaps; and the smaller pepperoni cups while the pizza bakes and gives the pizza a nice little crunch here and there. Forget the floppy pepperoni pizzas you ordered to your dorm room in 1987—those served their own unique purpose, I guess—this one is a keeper for life!

½ recipe The Best PIzza Dough in the World! (page 93)

½ cup P-Town's Pizza Sauce (page 94) or jarred marinara

¾ cup grated low-moisture mozzarella cheese

¾ cup grated provolone cheese

6 large pepperoni slices (from the deli counter)

⅓ cup classic pepperoni slices

⅓ cup 1½-inch-wide pepperoni slices (such as Hormel Cup N' Crisp)

Garlic Butter (page 106)

¼ teaspoon red pepper flakes, plus more to taste

1. Preheat the oven to 475°F.

2. On an ungreased sheet pan (18 × 13-inch), stretch and press the dough into a rustic oval about 15 inches long. Form the edges so they are a bit thicker.

3. Spread the pizza sauce all over the crust, leaving a 1-inch border around the edge.

4. Sprinkle on the mozzarella and provolone . . .

5. Then arrange pepperoni on top of the cheese. Start with the large deli pepperoni, covering as much surface as you can.

6. Next comes the classic pepperoni: Use it to fill in some of the larger gaps.

7. Fill in the rest of the gaps with the smallest 1½-inch pepperoni.

Three different
kinds of
pepperoni!

8. Brush the outer crust generously with garlic butter . . .

9. Then sprinkle red pepper flakes over the pepperoni.

10. Bake until the crust is golden and the cheese and pepperoni are sizzling, about 18 minutes. Brush the crust with a little more garlic butter if you like!

With my sister, Betsy, and our dad at P-Town Pizza.

SCRUMPTIOUS SAUSAGE PIZZA

MAKES ONE 15-INCH-LONG OVAL PIZZA

It would be impossible for me to pick my favorite pizza in this cookbook, because I truly consider every pizza in this cookbook essential. All of them are in my rotation of pizza favorites, but *if* I had to choose one pizza to eat for the rest of my life, it would be this one. I've always loved a sausage pizza—and I'm talkin' good ol' country sausage, not Italian sausage—and this one is topped with sweet, spicy little jalapeños, which seals the deal for me. I cannot wait for you to try it.

¾ pound pork breakfast sausage, such as Jimmy Dean or J.C. Potter

½ recipe The Best Pizza Dough in the World! (page 93)

½ cup P-Town's Pizza Sauce (page 94) or jarred marinara

¾ cup grated low-moisture mozzarella cheese

¾ cup grated provolone cheese

2 tablespoons grated Parmesan cheese

Garlic Butter (page 106)

¼ cup Candied Jalapeños (page 103)

1. Preheat the oven to 475°F.

2. In a large skillet, cook the sausage over medium-high heat until fully cooked, crumbling as you go. Remove from the heat and set aside.

3. On an ungreased sheet pan (18 × 13-inch), stretch and press the dough into a rustic oval about 15 inches long. Form the edges so they are a bit thicker.

4. Spread the pizza sauce all over the surface, leaving a 1-inch border around the edge.

5. Sprinkle on the mozzarella and provolone . . .

6. Then spoon the sausage on the cheese.

7. Sprinkle the Parmesan over the sausage . . .

8. And brush the crust around the edge with garlic butter.

9. Bake the pizza until the crust is golden and the cheese is melted, bubbling, and golden, 16 to 18 minutes (watch to make sure it doesn't brown too much!).

10. Slide the pizza onto a cutting board and top with the jalapeños.

**David and Mauricio—
best sons-in-law ever!**

I love this pizza!
Candied Jalapeños
(page 103)

Scrumptious
Sausage Pizza
(page 99)
Absolutely
irresistible!

CANDIED JALAPEÑOS

MAKES ABOUT 1 CUP

These sweet, sticky little peppers are sometimes known as cowboy candy because they truly are a delicacy for anyone who loves a little spice. They're delicious dotted on pizza, but I like to spoon them over a block of cream cheese and serve them with crackers, sprinkle them on tacos, or pile them on burgers. To. Die. For!

1 cup honey

1 tablespoon distilled white vinegar

2 garlic cloves, grated

Pinch of kosher salt

3 jalapeños, stemmed and thinly sliced into rings

1. In a small saucepan, combine the honey and vinegar.

2. Add the garlic and salt . . .

3. And the jalapeños.

4. Stir and bring it to a gentle boil over medium-high heat. Reduce the heat to low and simmer the jalapeños . . .

5. Until they are cooked down and very sticky, about 10 minutes.

6. Spoon the jalapeños into a small jar . . .

7. And pour in enough of the liquid to submerge the peppers. (If there is any liquid left, you can pickle a few more jalapeño slices in any small container you can find, or you can discard the liquid.)

8. Use immediately or put the lid on the jar and store them in the fridge for up to 2 weeks. (Hint: They won't last that long!)

Note: Cooking jalapeños can cause fumes that are irritating to some. Turn on your stove ventilation and/or open a window to help lessen the effect.

A very
"ree-licious" pizza!

PIZZA REE-A

MAKES ONE 15-INCH-LONG OVAL PIZZA

This pizza is my namesake. It has a loyal following with P-Town customers, and it's a marvelous, magnificent meatless wonder. It celebrates all that is right about tomato and basil, and it most certainly celebrates cheese—you'll find four of them melted on top of this gorgeous pizza (plus a sprinkle of Parmesan—that's five!). It's hard to beat a pepperoni or sausage pizza in terms of pleasing a crowd, but this pizza will satisfy the foodies in your life. It's bursting with bountiful beauty, and it'll be an essential recipe for the rest of my days.

½ recipe The Best Pizza Dough in the World! (page 93)

3 tablespoons olive oil

Kosher salt

⅓ cup Best-Ever Pesto (page 107)

¾ cup grated low-moisture mozzarella cheese

¾ cup grated provolone cheese

4 ounces fresh mozzarella cheese

4 ounces goat cheese (chèvre), cold and firm

Ground black pepper

Garlic Butter (page 106)

1 cup cherry tomatoes (I used a mix of orange and red), halved

Grated Parmesan cheese, for sprinkling

Balsamic glaze

8 to 10 basil leaves

1. Preheat the oven to 475°F.

2. On an ungreased sheet pan (18 × 13-inch), stretch and press the dough into a rustic oval about 15 inches long. Form the edges so they are a bit thicker. Drizzle on the olive oil and sprinkle on a little salt.

3. The pesto is the pizza sauce in this case! Spread it all over the crust, leaving a 1-inch border around the edge.

4. Sprinkle on the low-moisture mozzarella and the provolone . . .

5. Then tear the fresh mozzarella into chunks and dot them all over the pizza.

6. Do the same with the goat cheese. (If it's a little too soft, place it in the freezer for 10 minutes to make it easier to pinch.)

7. Sprinkle on a pinch of salt and a few grinds of pepper.

8. Brush the crust with garlic butter . . .

9. Then bake the pizza until the crust is golden and the cheese is melted and starting to brown around the edges, 16 to 18 minutes.

10. Dot the top of the pizza with the tomatoes . . .

11. Sprinkle on the Parmesan . . .

12. Then drizzle on the balsamic glaze in a crisscross pattern. (The glaze is heavenly on this pizza!)

13. Finally, sprinkle torn basil all over the top. Love, love, love this pizza!

GARLIC BUTTER

I started routinely brushing the edges of my pizza crust with freshly made garlic butter years ago, and there was seriously no going back after that. I'm a fan of the crusty edge of pizza slices anyway (I always clean up Ladd's after he eats pizza!), and the little brush of garlicky butter makes this irresistible. A bonus: This butter makes your house smell like an Italian restaurant!

½ cup (1 stick) salted butter

¼ teaspoon kosher salt

5 garlic cloves, grated

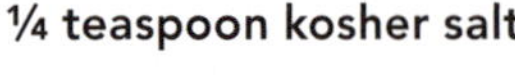

1. In a small skillet or saucepan over low heat, combine the butter, salt, and garlic.

2. Let the butter melt and slowly simmer for about 5 minutes to deepen the garlic flavor. Turn off the heat and set aside.

Leftover garlic butter?

- *Cook scrambled eggs in it.*
- *Toss it in cooked pasta.*
- *Use it on bread for panini.*
- *Drizzle it over a baked potato.*

BEST-EVER PESTO

MAKES ABOUT 2 CUPS

Pesto. It's the stuff that dreams are made of. I used to use it a teaspoon at a time, every once in a while. Now, in the summertime anyway, I can go through a jar of it weekly! Add it to pasta sauces and salad dressing, mix it with mayonnaise as a sandwich spread, mix it with sour cream for a delightful veggie dip. It goes with every protein, every cheese, and every green and vegetable. And it's a perfect pizza sauce! Yes, you can buy it in the supermarket . . . but once you've made your own batch, it'll be hard for you ever to go back.

⅓ cup pine nuts

5 cups basil leaves

¼ cup fresh oregano leaves

Grated zest and juice of 1 lemon

¾ cup grated Pecorino Romano cheese (or Parmesan)

2 garlic cloves, peeled but whole

½ teaspoon kosher salt

Pinch of ground black pepper

¾ cup olive oil, plus more as needed

1. In a small skillet, toast the pine nuts over medium heat, shaking the pan until they just start to become golden, 3 to 4 minutes. Take care to ensure they don't burn. Set them aside to cool for 20 minutes.

2. Pack a food processor with the basil leaves . . .

3. Then add the oregano.

4. Add the lemon zest and juice . . .

5. The pine nuts . . .

6. The cheese and the garlic.

7. Sprinkle in the salt and pepper . . .

8. Then put the lid on the food processor and slowly pour in the olive oil while pulsing constantly.

9. Keep going until the mixture is well mixed. You want the pesto to be evenly combined but still with great texture. Blend in a little more olive oil if the pesto looks too dry or leafy.

10. Transfer the pesto to a pint jar and store in the fridge for up to 10 days.

My garden is the source of boatloads of basil!

Incredibly intense basil flavor!

If you love mushrooms,
you are home.

"I'M A FUN-GI" MUSHROOM PIZZA

MAKES ONE 15-INCH-LONG OVAL PIZZA

One of the things I'm most grateful for in my life (my eating life, anyway!) is that I've loved mushrooms since I was a child. A pretty picky eater as a kid, I certainly did not willfully or intentionally set out to try a mushroom. Instead, my gateway drug was a mushroom pizza—which I didn't know had mushrooms on it, but which wound up being the tastiest pizza I thought I'd ever eaten in all my nine years. Well, I've been a mushroom pizza–eating *fungi* ever since! (Get it?) The only caveat I'll offer is that the addictive umami nature of this pizza can take over and result in more pieces being eaten in one sitting than is acceptable in polite society. But if you're okay with that, I sure am, too!

2 tablespoons salted butter

2 tablespoons olive oil, plus more for drizzling on the dough

16 ounces mushrooms (I used cremini, white button, and shiitake), quartered

2 garlic cloves, finely grated

2 teaspoons fresh thyme leaves

⅓ cup dry white wine (or veggie stock or chicken stock)

½ teaspoon kosher salt, plus more as needed

Ground black pepper

½ recipe The Best Pizza Dough in the World! (page 93)

¾ cup grated low-moisture mozzarella cheese

¾ cup grated provolone cheese

Garlic Butter (page 106)

1. Preheat the oven to 475°F.

2. In a large skillet, melt the butter in the olive oil over medium-high heat. Add the mushrooms . . .

3. And cook, stirring occasionally, for about 10 minutes. The mushrooms will give off moisture, which will cook down during that time.

4. Add the garlic and the thyme . . .

5. And continue cooking for 3 more minutes.

6. Pour in the wine . . .

7. Add the salt and a few twists of pepper . . .

8. And cook until the wine has cooked down and the mushrooms are very dark in color, another 5 minutes.

9. On an ungreased sheet pan (18 × 13-inch), stretch and press the dough into a rustic oval about 15 inches long. Form the edges so they are a bit thicker.

10. Drizzle the crust with a little olive oil, then sprinkle on a little salt and pepper.

11. Scatter most of the mushrooms over the crust, leaving a 1-inch border around the edge.

12. Sprinkle the mozzarella and provolone over the mushrooms, allowing some to show through.

13. Arrange the rest of the mushrooms on top of the cheese.

14. Brush the garlic butter on the crust . . .

15. And sprinkle the top with salt and pepper.

16. Bake the pizza until the crust is golden and the cheese is bubbling, 16 to 18 minutes.

Variation

- *Make the pizza using leftover Burgundy Mushrooms (page 311) for a crazy-good mushroom pizza experience. Just skip the sautéing step, quarter the Burgundy mushrooms, and add them to the pizza crust as shown above.*

POTATO LEEK PIZZA

MAKES ONE 15-INCH-LONG OVAL PIZZA

I went through a leek stage in my thirties. I guess there are worse stages to go through in one's thirties! Leeks kept me out of trouble, I guess you could say. Anyway, during this leek era of my life I started making this pizza, which has stood the test of time and still shows up on my table with great regularity. The flavor of the leeks is second-to-none (they're cooked in bacon grease, after all), and a layer of thin potatoes bakes into the crust and brings a great texture to the whole thing. I love everything about this pizza, and if you haven't yet gone through a leek stage, I hope this kicks one off for you!

3 medium leeks

6 slices thick-cut bacon

Kosher salt and ground black pepper

3 small Yukon Gold potatoes, unpeeled

½ recipe The Best Pizza Dough in the World! (page 93)

3 tablespoons olive oil

6 ounces fresh mozzarella cheese, sliced

¼ cup grated Parmesan cheese

Garlic Butter (page 106)

4 ounces goat cheese (chèvre), crumbled

1. Preheat the oven to 475°F.

2. First, trim the leeks: Cut off the root ends, then slice the leeks in half lengthwise.

3. Cut off the tough dark green ends . . .

4. Then slice the leeks thinly.

5. Rinse the leeks by submerging in them in a medium bowl of cold water, stirring them around with your hands to loosen any sand or dirt. Drain them and let them dry on a paper towel.

6. In a large skillet, fry the bacon over medium heat until chewy (it will crisp further in the oven). Remove it to a plate lined with paper towels.

7. Add the leeks to the bacon grease in the skillet and stir them around.

8. Season with salt and pepper and cook the leeks, stirring constantly, until they're starting to soften, about 3 minutes. Remove them from the heat.

9. Use a mandoline slicer or sharp knife to very thinly slice the potatoes. They should be as paper thin as possible—use caution with the sharp blade!

10. On an ungreased sheet pan (18 × 13-inch), stretch and press the dough into a rustic oval about 15 inches long. Form the edges so they are a bit thicker. Drizzle on the olive oil and sprinkle with salt and pepper, leaving a 1-inch border around the edge.

11. Lay the potato slices all over the crust, overlapping as you go.

12. Sprinkle more salt and pepper on top of the potatoes.

13. Cut the mozzarella slices in half and lay them evenly over the potatoes.

14. Sprinkle the leeks on top . . .

15. Then slice the bacon into bite-size pieces . . .

16. And arrange them over the top as well.

17. Sprinkle on the Parmesan . . .

18. Brush the crust with the garlic butter . . .

19. And bake the pizza until the crust is golden and the cheese is melted and bubbling, 16 to 18 minutes. As soon as it's out of the oven, dot the top with chunks of goat cheese. What a pizza!

The Pioneer Woman
Thin potatoes are
part of the crust!

OSU
Oklahoma State

Casseroles

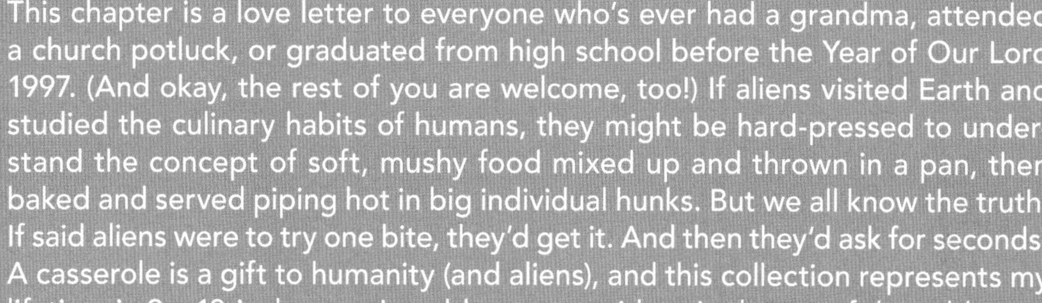

This chapter is a love letter to everyone who's ever had a grandma, attended a church potluck, or graduated from high school before the Year of Our Lord 1997. (And okay, the rest of you are welcome, too!) If aliens visited Earth and studied the culinary habits of humans, they might be hard-pressed to understand the concept of soft, mushy food mixed up and thrown in a pan, then baked and served piping hot in big individual hunks. But we all know the truth: If said aliens were to try one bite, they'd get it. And then they'd ask for seconds. A casserole is a gift to humanity (and aliens), and this collection represents my lifetime in 9 x 13-inch pans. I could not part with a single one of these blessed recipes. They're as much a part of my makeup as red hair and freckles. And whether you serve them to your family on a Tuesday night or deliver them to friends who need a hug, I hope they grace your oven (and your 9 x 13-inch pans) for years to come.

I've cracked the
mac-and-cheese code!

THE CREAMIEST MAC AND CHEESE

MAKES 8 TO 12 SERVINGS

If I had to estimate how many batches of mac and cheese I've made in my life, I'd never be able to guess. I cooked it as a child, a teenager, a young adult, a young mother, and now—an empty nester. I'm telling you this because it was only while I was writing this cookbook that I finally discovered the secret to creating a luscious macaroni and cheese casserole that doesn't dry out in the oven. I have always preferred mac and cheese straight out of the saucepan for this reason, but this method is truly the best of both worlds: saucy and silky inside, melty bubbling cheese on the outside. The difference is in both the sauce and the method, and I cannot wait for this recipe to be part of your life!

3 cups whole milk

3 tablespoons salted butter, at room temperature, plus more for the baking dish

2 egg yolks

1½ pounds sharp cheddar cheese, grated (6 cups)

6 ounces low-moisture mozzarella cheese, grated

½ cup grated Parmesan cheese

8 slices American cheese (I used Kraft Singles Deluxe), cut into quarters

½ teaspoon paprika

1 teaspoon kosher salt, plus more as needed

1 teaspoon ground black pepper, plus more as needed

1 pound elbow macaroni, cooked al dente and drained (reserve 1 cup pasta water)

6 ounces low-moisture mozzarella cheese, cut into very small dice

1. Preheat the oven broiler with a rack in the bottom half of the oven.

2. In a medium saucepan, heat the milk until just under a gentle boil. Remove from the heat and stir in the butter to melt it.

3. Whisk the egg yolks in a small bowl, then temper them by slowly drizzling in about 3 large spoons of the hot milk mixture, whisking constantly.

4. Pour the tempered eggs into the saucepan, whisking constantly.

5. In a blender or food processor, combine 3 cups of the cheddar, the grated mozzarella, Parmesan, and quartered American cheese slices.

6. Sprinkle in the paprika, salt, and pepper.

7. Pour the hot milk mixture into the blender . . .

8. And blend it on high for 30 seconds, until all the cheese is melted . . .

9. And the sauce is totally smooth. It should be pretty thin and pourable, but will still have a nice silkiness.

10. Pour the macaroni into a large bowl . . .

11. Pour all the sauce on top . . .

12. And stir to mix.

13. The pasta should be very saucy; splash in a little pasta water as needed. Taste a spoonful of the mac and cheese and add more salt and pepper to taste!

14. Butter a 9 × 13-inch baking dish and add half of the saucy macaroni.

15. Add half of the remaining cheddar . . .

16. And half of the diced mozzarella.

17. Pour in the rest of the macaroni . . .

18. And top with the rest of the cheddar and diced mozzarella.

19. Broil until the cheese is bubbling and starting to turn brown, about 10 to 12 minutes, watching to make sure it doesn't burn. Serve immediately while it's hot and saucy!

SCALLOPED POTATOES WITH HAM

MAKES 8 TO 12 SERVINGS

This very classic casserole was a necessity for me in the old days, when we'd have a bunch of leftovers after a big Easter ham dinner. It's creamy, cheesy, hearty, and wonderful, and I'm happy to say that the version I make now is finally (*chef's kiss*) perfect after many highs, lows, mishaps, and "meh" moments. The biggest challenge I've had with scalloped potatoes and ham through the years is how crazy-messy it looks when you first pull it out of the oven. The solution, it turns out, was so simple: Just set it on the counter as soon as you pull it from the oven and go find something to do. The resting time is 100 percent the secret to success, and the key to one of the best comfort-food casseroles you'll ever eat!

Salted butter, for the baking dish

1½ cups heavy cream

1½ cups half-and-half

1 yellow onion, finely diced

2 tablespoons fresh thyme leaves, minced (or 2 teaspoons dried)

½ teaspoon kosher salt

1 teaspoon black pepper

¼ cup all-purpose flour

3 pounds russet potatoes, unpeeled, scrubbed clean and sliced very thin

3 cups small-diced baked ham (from a whole ham or ham steak; sliced deli ham doesn't work as well)

2 cups grated sharp cheddar cheese

2 cups grated Monterey Jack cheese

1. Preheat the oven to 350°F. Butter a 9 × 13-inch baking dish.

2. In a medium saucepan, combine the heavy cream and half-and-half. Fully heat the mixture over medium heat but do not let it boil.

3. Add the onion, thyme, salt, and pepper to the hot mixture . . .

4. And whisk to combine, then reduce the heat to medium-low and simmer for a few minutes to let the flavors meld.

5. Add the flour and whisk to combine, then remove the pan from the heat.

6. Layer one-third of the potato slices in the buttered dish.

7. Sprinkle one-third of the ham on top . . .

8. And one-quarter of each cheese.

9. Pour one-third of the cream mixture on top . . .

10. Then repeat the layers twice more. Sprinkle the final one-quarter of the cheeses after the last cream layer.

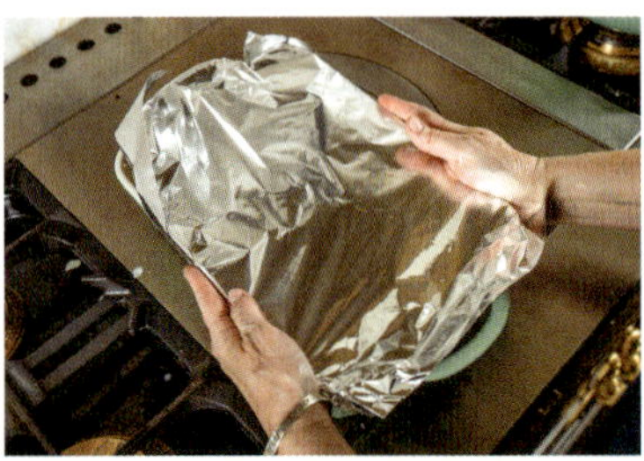

11. Cover the dish with foil and bake for 40 minutes . . .

12. Then remove the foil and bake until bubbling and golden, about 20 more minutes.

Important: Allow the casserole to sit for at least 15 minutes before serving to let the sauce settle and thicken. Cut into squares or scoop out with a big serving spoon!

"That girl is a cowboy."

Look at those layers!

Even better than
the original!

MEATY, CHEESY LASAGNA

MAKES 12 SERVINGS

I made the same lasagna recipe for thirty-five years, even before I ever met Ladd. It's so darn good, it actually caused him to eventually propose to me. Powerful lasagna, I tell ya! However, as I have changed and grown and evolved (and gotten bored; happens to most home cooks eventually!), I have also worked on changing and growing and evolving my lasagna. This isn't something I entered into unadvisedly or lightly, as changing a sacred dish in my family can be a perilous proposition. Everyone likes things the way they've always liked them! Still, I surged on, and the lasagna I wound up with is splendid in every way, while also honoring the original. I changed the sausage, used better tomatoes, sloshed in some wine, swapped in fresh mozzarella for the low-moisture stuff, and—notably—I altered the engineering a bit to create visible, discernible layers that are more structural than my original, which was always delicious but fell apart once it landed on the plate. But one of the primary tweaks is that instead of the good ol' American cottage cheese I used in my original version, I made my own ricotta for an absolutely glorious texture and flavor. I don't tend to make things from scratch just for the sake of doing it, but in this case, it's absolutely worth the effort! If you've loved my O.G. lasagna through the years, I hope you'll do me a solid and give this one a whirl. It might be the beginning of a whole new lasagna era in our friendship!

1 pound ground beef

1½ pounds Italian sausage

6 garlic cloves, minced

Two 6-ounce cans tomato paste

½ cup red wine (or beef stock or chicken stock)

Kosher salt

Ground black pepper

One 28-ounce can whole peeled San Marzano tomatoes

4 tablespoons minced fresh parsley, plus more for garnish

4 tablespoons minced fresh basil leaves

2½ cups ricotta, homemade (see page 128) or store-bought

2 large eggs

1 cup grated Parmesan cheese

Heavy cream or milk, as needed

One 10-ounce package lasagna noodles, cooked until just under al dente, drained, and laid flat to keep their shape until assembly

1 pound fresh mozzarella, cut into 12 slices

1. Place the ground beef and Italian sausage in a large pot or Dutch oven over medium-high heat . . .

2. And cook until the meat is totally browned, crumbling it as you go. Drain off half the excess grease.

3. Add the garlic and the tomato paste, stirring it into the meat. Cook for 3 minutes to fry the tomato paste and deepen the flavor.

4. Pour in the wine . . .

5. And stir together. Let it cook for 2 more minutes . . .

6. Then add 2 teaspoons each of salt and pepper . . .

7. The tomatoes . . .

8. And 2 tablespoons each of the parsley and basil.

9. Stir to combine, breaking up the tomatoes into chunks. Reduce the heat to low and let the sauce cook uncovered for 45 minutes, stirring occasionally. Turn off the heat and preheat the oven to 375°F.

10. In a medium bowl, combine the ricotta and eggs.

11. Add ½ cup of the Parmesan, the remaining 2 tablespoons parsley and basil, ½ teaspoon salt, and 1 teaspoon pepper.

12. Stir to combine. The mixture should be spreadable; if it seems a tad dry, splash in a tablespoon or two of heavy cream or milk.

13. To assemble the lasagna, layer four noodles in a deep 9 × 13-inch pan, overlapping as you go. Add just under half the meat mixture . . .

14. And spread it into an even layer.

15. Add a layer of all the mozzarella slices . . .

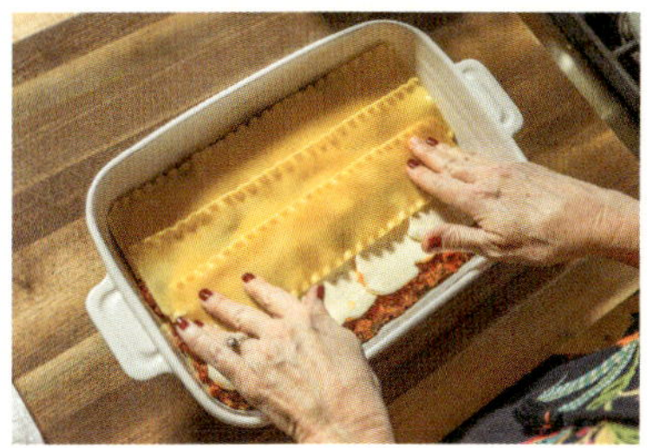

16. Another layer of four noodles . . .

17. And all the ricotta mixture, spreading it to the edges of the pan with the back of a spoon.

18. Add the final layer of four noodles . . .

19. And the rest of the sauce, spreading it into an even layer.

20. Sprinkle the top with the remaining ½ cup Parmesan . . .

21. Then cover with foil. Bake for 20 minutes, then remove the foil and bake for another 15 minutes . . .

22. Until very hot and bubbling.

23. Let it sit for 15 minutes to settle down before sprinkling it with parsley and cutting it into squares.

24. Serve it to very hungry humans!

Storage tips

- *To refrigerate: Assemble the lasagna, cover it with foil, and refrigerate it, unbaked, for up to 2 days. Remove it from the fridge 1 hour before baking it.*
- *To freeze: Assemble the lasagna in a disposable foil lasagna pan. Cover it with plastic wrap, then wrap it tightly in foil. You can freeze it for up to 6 months. To bake, simply thaw the lasagna in the fridge (this can take as long as 2 days), then remove the plastic wrap before baking. Or you can bake from a frozen state: Remove the plastic wrap, add the foil back on, and bake for 1 hour at 325°F, then remove the foil and bake for 35 minutes at 375°F.*

HOMEMADE RICOTTA

MAKES ABOUT 2½ CUPS

For the longest time, I mistakenly assumed that making ricotta was a complicated process. But once I tried it with a friend one bright and sunny afternoon a few years ago, I was mad at myself for waiting so long! I encourage you to try this once. It's as simple as can be, and the only special "equipment" you need is a piece of cheesecloth. I love it in lasagna, but it's also glorious spread on toast with raspberry jam or honey. Plus, there's something so satisfying about just whipping up a batch of homemade cheese. Makes me feel like a domestic goddess, except for the fact that my laundry room is a catastrophe. But back to the ricotta: Hope you make it soon!

8 cups (½ gallon) whole milk

1 teaspoon kosher salt

Juice of 2 lemons (generous ¼ cup)

1. Add the milk and salt to a medium pot over medium-high heat.

2. Bring to a gentle simmer, stirring occasionally, until it reaches a temperature of about 200°F.

3. Turn off the heat and squeeze in the lemon juice, taking care not to let any seeds drop in.

4. Give it a stir; it will start to show signs of separating and curdling pretty quickly!

5. Let the mixture sit until the ricotta curds have totally separated from the whey, 8 to 10 minutes. Science is amazing!

6. Place a cheesecloth-lined strainer over a bowl or pitcher and spoon in the ricotta.

7. Let it sit and drain for 5 to 10 minutes; 5 minutes will mean a slightly creamier ricotta while 10 minutes will dry it out more.

8. You can use the ricotta as is, but I like to transfer it to a food processor or blender for about 45 seconds to give it a smoother consistency!

9. Spoon the ricotta into an airtight container and store it in the fridge for up to 5 days.

So easy to make at home,
and so good!

Ladd's favorite casserole, even better than before!

CHICKEN SPAGHETTI

MAKES 8 TO 10 SERVINGS

My mom's chicken spaghetti is a triumph, and really requires no fiddling or tweaking. It's hearty and wonderful, and it has stood the test of time for fifty-plus years—and the recipe has consistently been in the top ten recipes on my website for almost two decades. All of this said, a year ago I decided to challenge myself to figure out how to make my mom's chicken spaghetti even better, if that was even possible. This is the result of my quest, and while I could never use the word "better" to describe it (because how can you make something better that's already perfect?), I will say that it is spectacular and very worth the extra effort, even just once before you go back to the original. It's very true to my mom's version, with a few tweaks: homemade cream of mushroom soup (oh my!), a mix of cheeses, and a glug of sherry. It will definitely do!

4 cups Homemade Chicken Stock (page 136) or store-bought stock or broth

12 ounces uncooked spaghetti, broken into thirds

2 cups Homemade Condensed Cream of Mushroom Soup (page 133) or two 10-ounce cans store-bought

2 cups shredded cooked chicken (see page 216) or rotisserie chicken

½ cup finely diced onion

1 green bell pepper, finely diced

1 red bell pepper, finely diced

1 teaspoon Lawry's seasoned salt

½ teaspoon kosher salt, plus more to taste

½ teaspoon ground black pepper, plus more to taste

¼ teaspoon cayenne pepper, or to taste

3 cups grated sharp cheddar cheese

1 cup grated Monterey Jack cheese

½ cup dry sherry (or more chicken stock)

1. Bring a large pot of salted water to a boil and add 2 cups of the chicken stock. Dump in the spaghetti and cook it until al dente.

2. Drain the spaghetti and pour it into a large bowl.

3. Add the cream of mushroom soup . . .

4. The chicken . . .

5. And the onion and bell peppers.

6. Add the seasoned salt, kosher salt, black pepper, and cayenne . . .

7. 1½ cups of the cheddar and the Monterey Jack . . .

8. And the sherry and the remaining 2 cups chicken stock.

9. Stir everything until it's totally combined and saucy. Taste it and add more kosher salt, black pepper, or cayenne if needed!

10. Pour the mixture into a 9 × 13-inch baking dish . . .

11. And top it with the remaining 1½ cups cheddar.

12. Bake until hot and bubbling, 35 to 40 minutes. Let it sit for 10 minutes before serving! Serve it by the big ol' spoonful.

Storage tips

- *To refrigerate: The casserole can be assembled, covered, and refrigerated, unbaked, for up to 2 days. Remove it from the fridge 30 minutes before baking.*
- *To freeze: Use a disposable foil baking dish. Cover in plastic wrap, then foil, and freeze for up to 6 months. Thaw the casserole in the fridge for 24 hours before baking. To bake it from the frozen state, remove the plastic wrap and put the foil back on. Bake for 1 hour at 325°F, then remove the foil and bake for another 40 minutes at 350°F.*

Sofia loves Aunt Paige!

HOMEMADE CONDENSED CREAM OF MUSHROOM SOUP

MAKES ABOUT 2 CUPS

My mom's chicken spaghetti is legendary, and it calls for two cans of slightly weird and incredibly unfancy cream of mushroom soup. Though the canned stuff can sometimes be the subject of derision, I find it to be one of the most consistent pantry ingredients in the world, and it's pretty much unmatched when it comes to achieving that Sunday potluck creamy casserole vibe that reminds us of our grandmas. But every now and then, if you want to have a little from-scratch fun, I encourage you to try a batch of homemade! As is the case with all the old recipes from my mom, grandma, and other wonderful women in my life, I would never say that chicken spaghetti is better with this homemade condensed soup. But I *would* strongly and enthusiastically encourage you to try it sometime. It's kinda wonderful! (And it's not just for casseroles; it happens to make for a dreamy pot of soup—see the sidebar on page 134!)

8 ounces cremini mushrooms

2 tablespoons salted butter

2 tablespoons olive oil

½ medium onion, diced small

1 garlic clove, minced

1 teaspoon fresh rosemary leaves, minced

1 teaspoon fresh thyme leaves, minced

2 tablespoons all-purpose flour

2½ cups Homemade Chicken Stock (page 136) or store-bought stock or broth

½ teaspoon kosher salt

½ teaspoon ground black pepper

⅔ cup heavy cream

1 teaspoon Worcestershire sauce

1. Finely dice, then chop, the mushrooms so they're in very small pieces.

2. In a medium skillet, melt the butter with the olive oil over medium-high heat. Add the mushrooms, onion, garlic, rosemary, and thyme . . .

3. And cook, stirring occasionally . . .

4. Until the mushrooms are deep golden, the onion is soft, and all the liquid has cooked off.

5. Sprinkle the flour on top . . .

6. And cook for about 2 minutes, stirring constantly.

7. Pour in the stock . . .

8. Add the salt and pepper . . .

9. And continue cooking, stirring occasionally, until the soup is starting to get thick, about 5 minutes.

10. Pour in the heavy cream . . .

11. And add the Worcestershire.

12. Then continue cooking, stirring occasionally, until thick, about 5 minutes more.

13. Scrape the condensed soup into a pint jar (sometimes I use 2 jars if I don't want to fill them too full), allow it to cool, screw on the lid, and store in the fridge for up to 1 week. (Or you can use it right away if you need!)

CREAM OF MUSHROOM SOUP

To turn the condensed soup into cream of mushroom soup, simply combine the condensed soup base, 3 cups chicken stock, and 1 cup half-and-half in a saucepan and bring to a simmer. (Make it even richer by using 2 cups broth and 2 cups half-and-half.) Serve in small bowls; it's nice and rich.

Perfect for casseroles!

HOMEMADE CHICKEN STOCK

MAKES ABOUT 3 QUARTS

It would never be practical for me to exclusively use homemade chicken stock in my recipes, because I go through too much of it in my day-to-day cooking life and I never mind the stuff in the carton. But anytime I have bones leftover from boiling chicken for the meat, or from a rotisserie chicken that I've used for shredded chicken, it's a no-brainer to make stock from them! (I just pop them in plastic bags in the freezer and let them accumulate.) It has such a beautiful homemade consistency and flavor that I don't think the store-bought version could ever have, and while it's not a requirement when making soups and casseroles, it sure is nice when you can swing it! Using already-cooked chicken bones *and roasting them before making the stock* will result in richer color and deeper flavor than just chucking raw bones in the pot. That said, any chicken bones will work—just cook the stock for several hours and magical results are guaranteed!

5 pounds chicken bones, cooked or raw (some meat attached is fine)

4 large carrots

1 bunch celery

2 yellow onions, halved

8 garlic cloves, peeled

1 bunch parsley stems

1 bay leaf

1 tablespoon black peppercorns

1 tablespoon kosher salt (optional), or more to taste

1. Preheat the oven to 450°F.

2. Arrange the chicken bones on a sheet pan . . .

3. And roast them until dark golden, about 20 minutes.

4. Transfer them to a large Dutch oven or soup pot.

5. Cut the carrots and celery into large chunks . . .

6. And add them to the pot along with the onions, garlic, and parsley stems.

7. Add the bay leaf, peppercorns, and salt, if using. (I leave mine unsalted so I have more flexibility with recipes, but you can salt it if you want to enjoy the stock as a stand-alone soup.)

8. Cover everything with cold water and bring the stock to a simmer over medium heat.

9. Reduce the heat to low and simmer for 4 hours with the lid off, which will help the stock reduce a bit and intensify the flavor.

10. After 4 hours, turn off the heat and spoon the bones and veggies into a fine-mesh strainer over a large bowl.

11. Remove them when the strainer is full and discard them (or, if you're like me, snack on those carrots!)

12. Return the strainer to the bowl and pour the rest of the stock through the strainer.

13. Force through the last of the liquid, then let the stock cool to room temperature and place the bowl in the fridge for 3 hours. (If you like the stock to be fattier, transfer it into jars and refrigerate.)

14. Once the fat has risen to the top and solidified, scrape off the excess and discard it. Transfer the stock into jars and refrigerate for up to 2 weeks, or freeze it in freezer-safe containers for up to 6 months. (You can also freeze it in ice cube trays for convenient small portions.)

Note: Depending on the makeup of the bones you use, the stock can be gelatinous once chilled, as you can see in the photo above. This is perfect and normal, and the gelatin is good for your bones (literally!). When heated, the stock will return to a liquid state.

INSANELY GOOD BEEF ENCHILADAS

MAKES 5 GENEROUS TWO-ENCHILADA SERVINGS, OR UP TO 15 SINGLE-ENCHILADA SERVINGS (SEE NOTE, PAGE 141)

As a lover (devourer!) of Mexican and Tex-Mex food, I have a long list of favorite dishes I'd never want to part with. Variety is key, and I love all the flavors and colors and sauces and spice. I think I'd have to put beef enchiladas in the top five, if not top three, if not the top spot (depending on the day and whether a pan of these drippy, wonderful enchiladas is in front of me). This is a refined, tested, and perfected version of a recipe I've made for thirty years now, with a deeper, richer sauce and more cheese than should ever be allowed in one casserole dish. So good on a Friday night with a cold beer!

ENCHILADA SAUCE

6 tablespoons vegetable oil

3 tablespoons all-purpose flour

3 tablespoons ground New Mexican red chile powder

3 cups Homemade Chicken Stock (page 136) or store-bought stock or broth

One 28-ounce can tomato puree

2 teaspoons dried Mexican oregano (or regular oregano)

1 teaspoon ground cumin

1 teaspoon kosher salt

FILLING

2 tablespoons olive oil

1 medium yellow onion, finely diced

4 garlic cloves, minced

1 jalapeño, seeded and finely diced

1½ pounds lean ground beef

1 teaspoon kosher salt, plus more as needed

1 teaspoon ground black pepper, plus more as needed

ASSEMBLY

Ten 6-inch yellow corn tortillas

3 cups grated sharp cheddar cheese

3 cups grated pepper Jack cheese

2 chopped green onions, for garnish

Sour cream, for serving

1. First, make the enchilada sauce: Heat the vegetable oil over medium heat, then sprinkle in the flour.

2. Whisk until smooth, then cook until the mixture starts to bubble, about 2 minutes.

3. Sprinkle in the chile powder . . .

4. And cook, whisking constantly, for 1 minute, making sure not to let the mixture burn.

5. Pour in the stock, whisking constantly . . .

6. Then add the tomato puree . . .

Extraordinary enchiladas!

7. Along with the oregano, cumin, and salt. Stir and let the mixture come to a gentle boil, then reduce the heat and let it simmer for 20 minutes, stirring occasionally.

8. Make the filling: In a separate large pot, heat the olive oil over medium-high heat and sauté the onion, garlic, and jalapeño until the onion starts to turn translucent, about 3 minutes.

9. Add the ground beef and cook it, crumbling as you go . . .

10. Until cooked. Season with the salt and pepper, then taste to adjust the seasonings.

11. By now the sauce should be nice and thick! Turn off the heat under both pans and preheat the oven to 375°F.

12. Assemble the enchiladas: Spoon 1 cup of the enchilada sauce into a 9 × 13-inch pan.

13. Wrap the tortillas in a damp kitchen towel and place them on a microwave-safe plate. Microwave for 45 seconds, until the tortillas are warm and pliable.

14. Quickly dunk a tortilla in the sauce . . .

15. Then place it on a plate and add equal amounts of the meat and cheeses, about ¼ to ⅓ cup each. You want the tortillas full, but you also want to be able to roll them up!

16. Roll the tortilla as tightly as you can . . .

17. And place it seam side down in the pan.

18. Repeat with the rest of the tortillas and filling . . .

19. Sprinkle any leftover meat mixture on top . . .

20. And scrape the contents of the assembly plate evenly over the top as well. We aren't wasting any of this gloriousness!

21. Pour over the rest of the sauce . . .

22. Then spread it out to the edges of the pan and top the sauce with the rest of the cheeses.

23. Bake the enchiladas until the cheese is melted and the edges are starting to bubble, 25 minutes.

24. Sprinkle the green onions on top and serve immediately with sour cream on the side.

Note: These enchiladas are so rich that one enchilada could pass as a portion if you want to serve more people. Alternatively, you can stretch out the ingredients to make more enchiladas (up to 5 more) if you wish! Just fill each tortilla a little less full and pour less sauce on the first pan. Bake the extra five in a separate small square pan (about 8 × 8 inches), or bake all 15 in a larger baking dish.

WHITE CHICKEN ENCHILADAS

MAKES 6 TWO-ENCHILADA SERVINGS OR 12 SINGLE-ENCHILADA SERVINGS

As an alternative to rich, red beef enchiladas, these creamy and extremely cheesy (I'm not kidding; you will be shocked at the amounts below) enchiladas will totally do! When I have the time and patience, I love to roast my own poblanos, which are in abundance in both the filling and the sauce. What I love most about this recipe, which has evolved and become more amazing over time, is just how indulgent it is . . . and to repeat my point above, how cheesy it is. Seriously, there's cheese in the chicken mixture, in the sauce, and melted on top of the casserole. Some might refer to the amount as over-the-top and ridiculous, and if they do, I'll know I'm doing something right.

4 poblano peppers (or 8 to 10 good-quality canned roasted chiles)

CHICKEN FILLING

2 tablespoons olive oil

1 medium yellow onion, small diced

5 garlic cloves, minced

1 jalapeño, seeded and finely diced

1 teaspoon ground cumin

¼ teaspoon ground coriander

1 teaspoon kosher salt

1 teaspoon ground black pepper

2½ cups shredded cooked chicken (see page 216) or rotisserie chicken

½ cup Homemade Chicken Stock (page 136) or store-bought stock or broth

½ cup heavy cream

2 cups grated Monterey Jack cheese

SAUCE AND ASSEMBLY

2 tablespoons salted butter

2 tablespoons all-purpose flour

2 cups Homemade Chicken Stock (page 136) or store-bought stock or broth

1 cup sour cream

3½ cups grated Monterey Jack cheese

1 teaspoon ground cumin

¼ teaspoon ground coriander

1½ teaspoons kosher salt

Ground black pepper

Twelve 6-inch yellow corn tortillas

Cilantro leaves, for serving

1. Preheat the oven broiler and arrange the rack at the highest spot. Place the poblanos on a sheet pan . . .

2. And broil until they are blistered and blackened, about 6 to 8 minutes. Remove the peppers from the oven and turn the heat to 350°F.

3. Use tongs to transfer the peppers to a zip-top plastic bag. Seal the bag and let them steam for 15 minutes.

4. Use a knife to scrape the skin off the peppers . . .

Chicken, cheese, and
chilies galore!

5. Then scrape out the seeds and chop the peppers! (Note: If you can get good canned roasted chiles, you can start at this step.)

6. Now make the chicken filling! In a large pan, heat the olive oil over medium heat. Add the onion, garlic, and jalapeño . . .

7. And stir and cook the veggies for 5 minutes. Sprinkle in the cumin, coriander, salt, and pepper and stir and toast the spices for 1 minute.

8. Add half the chopped poblanos and the chicken.

9. Stir, then add the ½ cup chicken stock and heavy cream.

10. Stir and continue cooking for 3 minutes to allow the cream to thicken.

11. Transfer the mixture to a bowl to cool and return the pan to the stove over medium heat.

12. Make the sauce: In the same pan, melt the butter, sprinkle the flour on top . . .

13. And whisk until smooth. Cook the roux for 3 minutes . . .

14. Then whisk while stirring in the 2 cups chicken stock . . .

15. And cook until the sauce is thick and bubbling, 4 to 5 minutes.

16. Turn off the heat and stir in the other half of the poblanos.

17. Add the sour cream and stir until totally mixed.

18. Add 1 ½ cups of the Monterey Jack, the cumin, coriander, salt, and pepper to taste and stir until the cheese is totally melted.

19. Back to the cooled chicken mixture! Stir in the 2 cups Monterey Jack. Have I mentioned there's cheese in this casserole?

20. Wrap the tortillas in a damp kitchen towel and place them on a microwave-safe plate. Microwave for 45 seconds, until the tortillas are warm and pliable.

21. Time to assemble! Spread ½ cup of the sauce in a 9 × 13-inch baking pan.

22. Spoon a scant ¼ cup of the chicken mixture onto a tortilla.

23. Roll it as tight as you can and place it seam side down in the sauce.

24. Then keep going with the rest of the tortillas and filling!

25. Pour the rest of the sauce over the top (oh my!).

26. Spread it evenly and (here we go again!) top with the remaining 2 cups cheese.

27. Bake the enchiladas until the cheese is melted and bubbling around the edges, with a few golden spots, 25 to 30 minutes. Serve one or two enchiladas on each plate and sprinkle with cilantro!

Note: These are very rich, and one enchilada is a sufficient serving for most, especially with a side salad or with rice and beans. (That said, don't let me stop you from eating two!)

MILLION-DOLLAR SPAGHETTI

MAKES 8 TO 10 SERVINGS

This casserole is a celebration of my three favorite pasta sauces. And actually, once it finishes baking, it has probably created a couple of additional pasta sauces on its own! Spaghetti baked with pesto, Alfredo, and marinara with a big layer of cheese on top could almost seem like a cop-out if you use store-bought sauces (though I would not only never judge anyone for doing so, I would also not be afraid to do it myself in a pinch), but when all three sauces are made from scratch . . . oh, man. The flavor explosions! The fantastic textures! Such a wonderful, satisfying pasta bake on its own, served with a side salad, or accompanying chicken or steak. Its delicious simplicity made it soar onto my list of essential recipes, and I have zero doubt in my mind that you will love this!

1 pound spaghetti, cooked according to the package directions and drained (penne works, too)

1 cup Best-Ever Pesto (page 107)

2 cups Alfredo sauce (see page 209, steps 1 through 6)

4 cups Homemade Marinara Sauce (page 148) or good, chunky store-bought marinara (or the spaghetti sauce on page 188 for a meaty version!)

3 cups grated low-moisture mozzarella cheese

Chopped parsley and basil leaves, for garnish

1. Preheat the oven to 425°F.

2. Place the spaghetti in a deep 9 × 13-inch baking dish. Add the pesto . . .

3. And toss it all together until the pesto is totally coating the spaghetti! (I could stop right here and eat this whole pan. Yum!)

4. Pour the Alfredo sauce on top. It should seep in and around the noodles.

5. Add the marinara sauce in a layer . . .

6. And sprinkle on the mozzarella.

7. Bake until the cheese is melted and the edges are bubbling and starting to crisp, about 20 minutes. Sprinkle on plenty of parsley and basil and serve piping hot!

The best of
three worlds!

HOMEMADE MARINARA SAUCE

MAKES ABOUT 2 QUARTS

It feels a little funny to share a homemade marinara sauce recipe with you, considering store-bought jarred marinara sauce is most definitely my favorite pantry staple. Good sauce from the store can be so, so good (not to mention handy), and as I write this I have no fewer than seven jars (and various brands!) on my shelves. Still, I love the times I make a pot of this homemade sauce: It's bursting with flavor and has the most fantastic texture, with a pleasant sweetness that comes from both good canned tomatoes and a whole lot of carrots. It's everything marinara should be!

¼ cup olive oil

1 medium yellow onion, finely diced

6 garlic cloves, minced

2 large carrots, peeled and very finely diced

2 tablespoons tomato paste

Two 28-ounce cans whole peeled tomatoes (San Marzano are preferred!)

½ teaspoon kosher salt, plus more to taste

½ teaspoon ground black pepper, plus more to taste

1 teaspoon sugar, plus more to taste

¼ cup minced fresh parsley

2 tablespoons minced fresh oregano leaves

Cooked pasta, for serving

1. In a large pot over medium heat, combine the olive oil, onion, garlic, and carrots.

2. Stir the veggies to combine and cook, stirring occasionally, until they start to soften, about 5 minutes.

3. Add the tomato paste . . .

4. And stir it into the vegetables. Let it cook for 2 minutes . . .

5. Add the cans of tomatoes . . .

6. Then use a potato masher or meat chopper to break the tomatoes into bits.

Good marinara is *sooo* good!

7. Add the salt, pepper, and sugar . . .

8. And the parsley and oregano . . .

9. Stir everything together, reduce the heat to low, and simmer, uncovered, and stirring occasionally, until the carrots are very soft, about 1½ hours. Give it a taste and add more salt, pepper, or sugar, depending on your tastes!

10. After the cook time, you can partially puree the sauce with an immersion blender if you'd like it to be smoother. I leave it just as it is—it's nice and chunky. Serve it immediately over pasta (or use it in Million-Dollar Spaghetti, page 146!), or let it cool completely and transfer it to jars or other containers. The marinara will keep in the fridge for up to 2 weeks, or you can freeze it in freezer bags for up to 6 months.

Can't a woman put her feet up and rest every once in a while?

SENSATIONAL STUFFED SHELLS

MAKES ABOUT 8 SERVINGS

The kid in me loves any shell-shaped pasta, from teeny ones to big ol' jumbos, and even though there's already a lasagna recipe and two spaghetti casseroles in this cookbook, I really think this glorious favorite deserves a spot, too! The ricotta filling gets melty and soft in the oven, and while a good marinara is my go-to sauce for this, you can sub in a rich, meaty sauce instead. Stuffed shells, I love ya!

Salted butter, for the baking dish

4 cups Homemade Marinara Sauce (page 148) or store-bought marinara

1 tablespoon crushed Calabrian chili paste (sold in a jar; optional)

4 cups Homemade Ricotta (page 128, recipe doubled) or store-bought ricotta

2 large eggs

1½ cups grated Parmesan cheese

1 teaspoon kosher salt

1 teaspoon ground black pepper

1 teaspoon red pepper flakes

¼ cup chopped fresh parsley, plus more for garnish

3 cups grated Havarti or mozzarella cheese (or a mix of both)

24 jumbo pasta shells, cooked al dente and drained

1. Preheat the oven to 375°F. Butter a 9 × 13-inch baking dish.

2. In a medium saucepan, heat the marinara over medium heat. Stir in the Calabrian chili paste, if using, then turn off the heat.

3. In a large bowl, combine the ricotta and eggs . . .

4. And 1 cup of the Parmesan, the salt, pepper . . .

5. The red pepper flakes and parsley . . .

6. And 2 cups of the Havarti and/or mozzarella.

7. Mix until completely combined . . .

8. Then spoon it into a gallon-size plastic zipper bag (or a large piping bag), twisting the open end several times.

9. Snip the end of the bag and pipe the ricotta mixture into each pasta shell until full but not overflowing.

10. Place the stuffed shells diagonally in the prepared baking dish, with the open sides facing up.

11. Spoon the sauce over the shells, leaving little areas here and there where the shells and cheese can peek through.

12. Top with the remaining 1 cup Havarti and/or mozzarella and sprinkle with the remaining ½ cup Parmesan.

13. Transfer the casserole to the oven . . .

14. And bake until the cheese is melted and the edges are brown and bubbling, 25 to 30 minutes. Sprinkle with parsley and serve gooey and warm!

ADD PROTEIN!

Beef: Brown 1 pound ground beef in the pan before stirring in the marinara. The sauce will be rich and meaty!

Sausage: Brown 1 pound crumbled Italian sausage instead of the beef.

Chicken: Chop 2 cups shredded cooked chicken into small bits and stir it into the ricotta mixture. The filling will be bursting with chicken!

Perfect for a potluck!

I didn't mean for the beef chapter to be one of the biggest in this book. Then again, I didn't mean for it *not* to be. Did that make sense? I sure hope so. Anyway, it should come as no surprise that the beef section of my virtual recipe box is as bulging as my husband's biceps. This is fitting, of course, considering Ladd, more than anyone, has informed the development, refinement, and perfecting of these beautiful beef dishes. I've served the majority of them to my husband, the kids, and the cowboys for nearly three decades, and they run the gamut from slow braises to fancy cuts to ground beef heroes. Where's the beef, you ask? It's all right here!

My most beloved recipe
for twenty-five years.

THE MOST PERFECT POT ROAST

MAKES 10 SERVINGS

In the almost twenty-year history of my cooking website and cookbooks, there is no recipe more loved than my Perfect Pot Roast. It can be a challenging dish to master in one's early cooking life (it sure was for me!), but once the code is cracked, the culinary heavens open up and it's smooth sailing (pot roast-wise) from there on out. I'm so happy to share this recipe with you. It's a top ten in my life, it is actually foolproof, and thanks to a couple of minuscule tweaks of my original recipe—just a simple addition of both tomato paste and red wine, which send the richness through the roof—it is even more perfect than before. Enjoy this with the people you love!

3 tablespoons olive oil

One 4- to 5-pound whole chuck roast (choose a nicely marbled roast!)

1 tablespoon kosher salt, plus more to taste

2 teaspoons ground black pepper, plus more to taste

2 yellow onions, peeled and halved

6 to 8 carrots, trimmed and cut into 2-inch chunks

1 mounded tablespoon tomato paste

1 cup red wine (or more beef stock)

3 cups Homemade Beef Stock (page 160) or store-bought stock or broth

3 thyme sprigs, or more to taste

3 rosemary sprigs, or more to taste

Mashed potatoes (see page 284), for serving

Chopped parsley, for serving

1. Preheat the oven to 275°F.

2. Heat a large heavy Dutch oven over medium-high heat and add the olive oil. Season both sides of the pot roast with the salt and pepper, then place it in the pot to sear.

3. Let the roast cook for 2 to 3 minutes, or until browned and crisp around the bottom edges. Turn it over to the other side to sear for another 2 to 3 minutes . . .

4. And remove the roast to a plate.

5. Lay the onions in the pot cut side down, then sprinkle in the carrots.

6. Let the veggies sear on the surface until they get some brown edges, turning a bit for even browning, about 3 minutes.

7. Add the tomato paste and stir it around to fry for 1 minute . . .

8. Then pour in the wine . . .

9. And the stock.

10. Stir everything together, then slide the beef back into the pot on top of the veggies. (Be sure to let all juices from the plate drip into the pot!)

11. Arrange the herb sprigs around the meat . . .

12. Then cover the pot and roast in the oven until the roast is falling-apart tender. (Pull it apart with two forks to check.) This can take anywhere from 3 to 4½ hours, depending on the weight and the piece of meat.

13. Remove the herb stems from the pot.

14. Optional (and see the Tip opposite): If there is an excess layer of oil on top after the pot has sat for a few minutes, you can use a shallow spoon to remove some.

15. Just add the oil to the same plate as the herb stems.

16. Use two forks to shred the meat.

17. It should shred very easily without requiring any force at all. (If it seems tough or doesn't pull apart easily, it hasn't cooked long enough! Return it to the oven for another 45 minutes and that should do the trick.) Keep shredding, keeping it mostly in larger chunks . . .

18. With some smaller shreds. Taste and add a little more salt if it needs it, then cover the pot and keep it warm until serving.

19. I like to serve by spooning mashed potatoes in a wide, shallow bowl . . .

20. Adding some meat, onion pieces, and carrots . . .

21. Then spooning over some of that delicious cooking liquid!

22. Sprinkle a little chopped parsley over each serving.

POT ROAST WISDOM

Question: "I don't know what I'm doing wrong. I've tried and tried to make pot roast and no matter what I do, it's always tough and overcooked!"

After interacting with so many people about recipes over the past two decades, this is certainly one of the most common cooking questions I've been asked. Tough and "overcooked" pot roasts are the source of so much frustration, and as a regular home cook myself, I remember the days when this stumped me, too. Truth is, I actually love getting this question, because there happens to be an immediate solution to the dilemma! I can't solve many of the world's big mysteries, but this is one I've got a handle on.

Answer: If your pot roast is tough, it isn't overcooked; it actually hasn't cooked long enough!

It's true, friends. If you take the lid off your pot after cooking the roast and encounter a tough, impossible-to-shred piece of meat, you simply need to put the lid back on and keep cooking it. The meats used for pot roast (typically chuck or bottom round) have a high amount of connective tissue, which contains collagen. It is scientifically necessary to cook the meat low and slow for enough time to dissolve the collagen and turn it into gelatin. This gives the pot roast that luscious melt-in-your-mouth, fork-tender quality you want, and the time each piece of meat takes can vary up to an hour or more. So stick with it and cook it for an additional 30 minutes at a time until the meat falls apart. The liquid amount should be fine, but feel free to add more beef broth to the pot if it looks like it's reducing/evaporating too much.

Tip: When it comes to removing excess oil from the pot roast, the best method I've found is making the roast the day before I want to serve it and storing it in the fridge overnight. After the meat is shredded, pour the contents of the Dutch oven over a fine-mesh strainer set over a large bowl to separate the cooking liquid. Store the liquid and the meat/veggies in separate containers in the fridge overnight. The next day, when you're ready to serve, remove the solidified fat cap from the liquid. (You don't have to remove every last bit, just some big chunks will do!) Then reheat the liquid, meat, and veggies together over medium-low heat until it's all warmed. You can also add a little beef broth if more liquid is needed.

HOMEMADE BEEF STOCK

MAKES ABOUT 3 QUARTS

As is the case with Homemade Chicken Stock (page 136), I use so much beef stock in my everyday cooking life that exclusively using homemade isn't practical. But after first trying this stock method, which I learned from my culinary friend and co-worker Trey, I realized just how exquisitely delicious a good, rich stock can be. When I'm making a roast or stew or special soup, it's always made a little better with a jar of this beautiful beefy liquid. Get yourself some beef bones and make a batch!

4 pounds miscellaneous beef bones (ask the butcher at your supermarket)

6 ounces tomato paste

2 yellow onions, peeled and quartered

1 garlic bulb, halved crosswise to expose the cloves

6 carrots, scrubbed clean

6 celery stalks

4 rosemary sprigs

4 thyme sprigs

1 bunch parsley stems

2 bay leaves

1 tablespoon black peppercorns

1. Preheat the oven to 475°F.

2. Set the bones on a sheet pan or other work surface. Smear each bone with some of the tomato paste . . .

3. And rub the tomato paste all over the bones so that they're fully coated.

4. Transfer the coated bones to a heavy roasting pan along with the onion wedges . . .

5. And the halved garlic bulb.

6. Roast the bones until very deep in color, 25 to 30 minutes.

7. Transfer the bones, onions, and garlic to a large pot, making sure to include any drippings from the pan.

Roasted bones make all the difference!

8. Cut the carrots and celery into big chunks . . .

9. And add them to the pot with the rosemary, thyme, and parsley stems.

10. Add the bay leaves and sprinkle in the peppercorns . . .

11. And cover everything with water. Bring to a gentle simmer over medium heat.

12. When the stock has simmered for 15 minutes, skim any foam and bubbles that have accumulated on the surface. Simmer the stock for 4 hours, uncovered.

13. Look at that deep, rich color! Turn off the heat and remove some of the bones and veggies to make it easier to strain the stock. (Let all the stock drip off them before you remove them!)

14. Pour the stock into a large bowl through a fine-mesh strainer . . .

15. And force any remaining stock through the strainer.

16. Let the stock cool, cover the bowl with foil, and refrigerate for at least 4 hours to allow the fat to solidify on top.

17. Use a spoon or spatula to scrape the fat cap from the bowl. (Leaving some fat behind is fine!)

18. Remove and discard the fat . . .

19. Then ladle the stock into jars. Store the stock in the fridge for up to 2 weeks, or in freezer-safe containers for up to 9 months.

MEATLOAF, MASTERED

MAKES 8 TO 10 SERVINGS

What's in a name? That which we call meatloaf by any other name would taste as dang good. (Is that Shakespeare?) I have loved meatloaf all my life, even before I knew the word "meatloaf" was kind of weird. I often wonder how much more popular meatloaf would have been through the decades if the name had been less literal and more evocative, something like *Chateaubriand*. One can only imagine. But whatever the name, meatloaf is one of life's real comfort food pleasures and treasures.

As simple a concept as meatloaf is, it really does require some finessing and thought to really get it right. This recipe reflects my own years-long effort to make my meatloaf truly great (not to mention foolproof). If I could serve you a slice right now, I would . . . but since I can't (at least not tonight!), please do yourself a favor and make this as soon as possible.

MEATLOAF

6 slices Soft White Sandwich Bread (page 55) or good store-bought white bread

1 cup whole milk

2 pounds ground beef (85/15)

4 large eggs

1 heaping cup freshly grated Parmesan cheese

½ cup minced flat-leaf parsley

2 teaspoons ground black pepper

¾ teaspoon kosher salt

¼ teaspoon seasoned salt

10 slices thin/regular bacon, with 1 inch trimmed off the ends (refrigerate or freeze these pieces for later use!)

TOPPING AND SAUCE

¾ cup ketchup

6 tablespoons brown sugar

1 teaspoon dry mustard

2 to 3 dashes Worcestershire sauce

2 to 3 dashes hot sauce, or more to taste

1. Preheat the oven to 375°F. Line a sheet pan with foil and set a wire rack in the pan.

2. Make the meatloaf: Place the bread in a medium bowl and pour the milk on top. Set it aside for a few minutes for the bread to absorb the milk.

3. In a large bowl, combine the ground beef and eggs . . .

4. The Parmesan, parsley, pepper, kosher salt, and seasoned salt.

5. Smash up the bread a bit to ensure it's entirely moistened by the milk . . .

6. Add it to the bowl with the meat . . .

7. Then mash up the mixture until it's totally mixed. Don't be afraid to use your hands!

8. Transfer the meat to the prepared sheet pan and form it into a loaf around 5 inches wide by 12 inches long. (This will ensure it's not too tall or thick.)

9. Place a piece of bacon on the very end of the meatloaf, tucking the ends of the bacon underneath the meatloaf.

10. Repeat with the rest of the bacon, then tuck the sides in a little more so that the bacon is taut. Bake for 55 minutes.

11. While the meatloaf is in the oven, make the topping and sauce—the best part! In a small bowl, combine the ketchup, brown sugar, mustard, Worcestershire, and hot sauce.

12. Stir until combined and give it a taste. Add more hot sauce if you want more spice!

13. Remove the meatloaf when the 55 minutes is up . . .

14. And spread on two-thirds of the sauce, brushing some on the sides. You want it pretty thick on the top of the meatloaf.

15. Bake the meatloaf until the internal temperature reaches 160 to 165°F, another 20 to 25 minutes. The sauce should still look thick on top and a little caramelized around the edges. You can also broil the meatloaf for 3 minutes or so to caramelize the top more deeply!

16. Let the meatloaf rest for 10 minutes, then slice it and serve it with remaining sauce for dipping.

Serve with

- *The Creamiest, Dreamiest Mashed Potatoes (page 284)*
- *The Creamiest Mac and Cheese (page 119)*
- *Really Great Grits (page 297)*
- *Any starchy side*

Variation

- *Serve slices on bread for a meatloaf sandwich!*

Pure, delicious
comfort food!
The Creamiest,
Dreamiest Mashed
Potatoes (page 284)

The way to my family's heart.

CHICKEN-FRIED STEAK

MAKES 6 SERVINGS

There is no more perfect meal for a cowboy (or cowgirl, or cowpoke!) than this. It's a once-a-month meal (at the most) for my family, and when you see my plate at the end of this recipe, you'll understand why. It's truly iconic: Chicken-Fried Steak, and this is my favorite way to make it over the past few years.

CHICKEN-FRIED STEAK

3 pounds cube steak (see Note)

Kosher salt and ground black pepper

2 cups buttermilk, homemade (see page 5) or store-bought

2½ cups all-purpose flour

2 teaspoons seasoned salt

¾ teaspoon paprika

¼ teaspoon cayenne pepper

Vegetable oil, for frying

3 tablespoons salted butter, plus more as needed

GRAVY

Salted butter and oil, as needed

⅓ to ½ cup all-purpose flour, as needed for desired consistency

4 cups whole milk, plus more as needed for thinning

1 tablespoon ground black pepper

Kosher salt, to taste

The Creamiest, Dreamiest Mashed Potatoes (page 284) or The Most Perfect Biscuits (page 16), for serving

Note: Cube steak has been put through the tenderizing machine twice by the butcher. Alternatively, you can buy tenderized round steak, then pound it with the tenderizing side of a meat mallet to tenderize it more.

1. Season both sides of the cube steaks with kosher salt and black pepper, then place the steaks in a large bowl and pour the buttermilk on top.

2. Toss the steaks in the buttermilk until thoroughly coated. (There should be very little buttermilk left in the bowl!) Let sit for 30 minutes.

3. In a shallow dish, combine the flour, seasoned salt, paprika, cayenne, 1 tablespoon kosher salt, and 2 teaspoons black pepper . . .

4. And stir to mix well.

5. In a large heavy skillet over medium heat, heat 1 inch of oil and add the butter.

6. When the oil/butter mixture is hot, bread a piece of the steak by dipping it in the flour mixture four times: first side, second side, then first and second sides again. You want the breading to be very thick, so that you can no longer see the wet buttermilk.

7. Lay the breaded meat in the oil and butter . . .

8. Then repeat to bread more of the meat, filling the skillet.

9. Cook the steaks on both sides until the breading is deep golden, about 3 minutes per side. Tend to the meat the whole time it's cooking, as you might need to move the pieces around the pan to avoid burning from hot spots.

10. Remove the steaks to a pan lined with paper towels, then cook another batch of meat. Add more oil and butter to the pan if it starts to dwindle a bit.

11. Remove the last of the meat, let it drain on the paper towels, and turn the heat to medium-low.

12. Time to make the gravy! Make sure there's about ¼ cup of remaining grease in the skillet. If there isn't enough, add equal amounts of oil and butter to get to ¼ cup. If there's too much, pour off a little. Then sprinkle in the flour! Start by sprinkling on 3 tablespoons or so . . .

13. Then immediately whisking it into the grease. When it's incorporated, sprinkle in more flour. If you whisk in the flour and it's too dry/crumbly, add more oil and butter. If it's too greasy looking, sprinkle in a little more flour, a tablespoon at a time. All told, you'll wind up using ⅓ to ½ cup flour.

14. You want to wind up with a smooth paste (roux) that is neither dry nor overly greasy! Cook the roux for 5 to 8 minutes, however long it takes to turn dark golden brown. If you use plain flour for your gravy (which I often do), it will look very pale at first. You want to cook until it's deep and nutty.

15. Pour in the milk, whisking constantly. The gravy will immediately start to thicken when you first pour it in, but will calm down the more milk you add.

16. After the milk is whisked in, sprinkle in the pepper.

A meeting of the agricultural minds.

17. Cook the gravy, stirring or whisking constantly, until bubbling and thick! If it gets too thick too soon (within 5 minutes), splash in more milk. The gravy is forgiving; you can keep adding splashes of milk to get the consistency perfect. The whole gravy process can take up to 20 minutes. Before serving, taste it and add more salt as needed.

18. Place one of the fried steaks next to mashed potatoes or biscuits, then spoon a generous amount of gravy over both. (If you use biscuits, lay the two halves cut side up and top with the gravy.)

19. There's really no getting around the fact that this is the only acceptable amount of gravy for this plate, and that is why this is a once-a-month meal in my house. Sprinkle with more black pepper and enjoy!

MARLBORO MAN SANDWICH

MAKES 6 SANDWICHES

This beefy, oniony sandwich is absolutely essential . . . according to Ladd. It's essential to his happiness, it's essential to his well-being, and it's essential for his taste buds. He loves this sandwich beyond measure, and if it were up to him, it would be on the menu once a week. Through the years, I have tended to get distracted by other more exciting (and, in my opinion, elevated) beef sandwich recipes, but whenever I feel like Ladd needs a little boost, I jot "cube steak" down on my grocery list. The Marlboro Man sandwich is not and will never be elevated. And that's exactly why Ladd Drummond (and every cowboy I know) loves it.

2 pounds cube steak

2 teaspoons seasoned salt

1 teaspoon kosher salt

2 teaspoons ground black pepper

1 cup (2 sticks) salted butter

2 large yellow onions, sliced thick

½ cup Worcestershire sauce, plus more as needed

2 tablespoons Tabasco sauce, plus more to taste

6 good white deli rolls, split open

1. Slice the steak against the grain into 1-inch strips.

2. Season the pile with the seasoned salt, kosher salt, and pepper . . .

3. And toss to coat.

4. Heat a large skillet over medium-high heat and melt 4 tablespoons of the butter. Add one-third of the meat in a single layer . . .

5. And let it cook for 2 minutes without disturbing it. Turn it to the other side and let it cook for 1 minute. You want to get as much color on the meat as you can without overcooking it, which will make it tough.

6. Cook the rest of the meat in two additional batches, adding 1 tablespoon additional butter with each batch, removing the meat to a plate as you go.

7. Melt 4 more tablespoons of the butter in the same skillet and turn the heat to medium.

Ladd's favorite sandwich!

8. Add the onions . . .

9. And cook for 5 minutes, stirring constantly, until they're starting to soften and turn golden. (You still want them to have a little texture and bite.)

10. Add the Worcestershire . . .

11. The Tabasco . . .

12. And the browned meat.

13. Reduce the heat to low and stir the meat, onions, and sauce together so that everything is well coated.

14. Add 2 more tablespoons of butter and let it melt in the sauce, stirring frequently.

15. In a separate skillet, melt 1 tablespoon of butter and brown one of the rolls. Repeat with the rest. (Or you can brown all the rolls with the rest of the butter if you have a skillet large enough! You can also spread the butter on the rolls and brown them under the oven broiler.)

16. Taste a piece of meat and adjust the salt, pepper, Worcestershire, and/or Tabasco according to your tastes! I usually add more of both sauces at the end. Give it one more stir and turn off the heat.

17. To build each sandwich, pile some meat and onions on the bottom half of the roll . . .

18. Retrieve some of the sauce . . .

19. And spoon it over the meat and onions, letting it soak into the roll.

20. Top it with the other half of the roll and hand it to a hungry human!

Variations

- *Add 8 ounces sliced mushrooms with the onions.*
- *Add sliced green and red bell peppers with the onions.*
- *Place slices of provolone on top of the sandwich and broil it to melt before the top bun goes on.*

The empty nesters!

CHUCK'S SLOPPY JOES

MAKES 8 SERVINGS

I wrestled with including this recipe in this book, which I consider a complete volume of my favorite recipes on Earth, the recipes I'd never want to be without. On one hand, Sloppy Joes are a crowd-pleasing Middle American comfort food classic that has fed more teenagers and cowboys in my house than I could even estimate. On the other hand, Sloppy Joes are . . . sloppy. Messy. Probably the most un-fancy dish I can think of. Do they really fall under the category of "essential?" But then I remembered one important thing: My father-in-law, Chuck, absolutely loved these Sloppy Joes, and always told me that he thought they were the best Sloppy Joes he'd ever had. Done, finished, conversation over. This recipe will forever mean the world to me for that fact alone—and guess what? They happen to be utterly delicious!

2½ pounds ground beef

1 medium yellow onion, diced

5 garlic cloves, minced

1 green bell pepper, diced

3 tablespoons tomato paste

2 teaspoons kosher salt

2 teaspoons ground black pepper

1 teaspoon dry mustard

1 tablespoon chili powder, plus more to taste

2 tablespoons packed brown sugar

½ teaspoon red pepper flakes, plus more to taste

5 or 6 dashes Worcestershire sauce, to taste

1½ cups ketchup

1 cup hot water

8 soft burger buns, split open

Kettle-cooked potato chips, for serving

1. In a large skillet, cook the ground beef over medium-high heat until it's totally browned, crumbling it as you go. Drain off most of the fat.

2. Sprinkle in the onion, garlic, and bell pepper . . .

3. Then add the tomato paste, salt, black pepper, dry mustard, and chili powder. Lots of flavor!

4. Add the brown sugar and red pepper flakes . . .

5. And stir to thoroughly mix everything together. Cook for 5 minutes to allow the vegetables to begin to soften.

6. Add the Worcestershire . . .

Perfect for a crowd!

7. And the signature ingredient: the ketchup!

8. Stir to mix everything together . . .

9. Then pour in the hot water. Stir, reduce the heat to low, and let simmer for 20 minutes, stirring occasionally, until the sauce has deepened in color and thickened a bit.

10. Lay out the buns and let everyone serve themselves by spooning the Sloppy Joe mixture onto the bottom bun.

11. Smush the top bun on and dive in. Don't worry about how messy things are about to get! Serve the Sloppy Joes with chips.

Mauricio gets the Sweetest Dad award!

SIMPLE, PERFECT CHILI

MAKES 6 TO 8 SERVINGS

Chili is such a deeply personal thing, from the beans (or no beans!) to the seasonings to the spice to the fixin's on top. I've made what I call "Simple, Perfect Chili" for going on three decades now, and I make it when I need a pot of "brown, hot, and plenty of it!" (shout-out to *City Slickers*) food that is very consistently delicious. And delicious it absolutely is, not to mention easily adapted: I don't like beans in my chili but Ladd does, so I'll grab myself a bowl before dumping them in. Ladd doesn't like a ton of spice, but I do, so I'll add dashes of hot sauce over mine. Ladd likes his alongside a piece of cornbread. I'll crumble and stir cornbread into mine. (Then top it with about ten other things!) Anyway, this is the chili that started it all, and it's still going strong in my house!

2 pounds ground beef

2 generous tablespoons chili powder, or more if desired

1 teaspoon ground cumin

1 teaspoon dried oregano

1 teaspoon kosher salt

¼ teaspoon cayenne pepper, or more if you'd like more heat

5 garlic cloves, chopped

One 8-ounce can tomato sauce

¼ cup masa harina

One 15-ounce can kidney beans, drained and rinsed

One 15-ounce can pinto beans, drained and rinsed

Grated sharp cheddar cheese, for serving

Chopped red onion, for serving

Cornbread (optional; see page 300), for serving

Tortilla chips

1. In a large pot, cook the ground beef over medium-high heat until fully browned, crumbling it as you go. Spoon out the excess grease. Add the chili powder, cumin, oregano, salt, cayenne, and garlic . . .

2. And stir to combine. Cook the spices in the meat for 3 minutes, stirring occasionally.

3. Add the tomato sauce . . .

4. Then add 2 cans of water.

5. Stir the chili . . .

6. Then put the lid on the pot, turn the heat to low, and simmer for 1 hour, so the flavors deepen. Peek at the chili from time to time and stir in a cup or two of water if it seems to be getting too dry.

7. When the hour is up, mix together the masa harina and ½ cup of warm water in a small bowl.

8. Stir it into a smooth paste . . .

9. Then pour it into the pot . . .

10. And stir it to combine.

11. Add 1 more cup of water! The water really helps the chili become beautifully saucy.

12. Finally, stir in the beans.

13. Stir in 1 more cup of water (or more if you like it saucier) and let the chili simmer for 10 minutes for the beans to heat up and the masa to cook a bit. Taste and add more salt if needed.

14. Serve it in bowls and add grated cheddar and red onion (and any other topping you'd like). The chili is delicious with cornbread!

How to serve

THINGS TO TOP CHILI WITH

- *Any grated cheese: Monterey Jack, pepper Jack, Oaxaca*
- *Sliced avocado or prepared guacamole*
- *Hot, melty queso dip*
- *Crumbled saltine crackers*
- *Pico de gallo*
- *Crumbled cornbread (see page 300)*

THINGS TO TOP WITH CHILI

- *Cheeseburgers (see pages 191 and 195)*
- *Hot dogs*
- *Nachos*
- *Cooked spaghetti or macaroni*
- *Fritos (Frito pie!)*
- *Taco salad*

The Very Best Cornbread
(page 300)
Beefy, saucy, and oh so tasty!

RICH AND CHUNKY BEEF CHILI

MAKES 6 SERVINGS

There's simple, perfect chili made with ground beef, as seen on page 177. But when I have the time, I think there's nothing more delectable than a chunky beef chili made with a smooth red chile sauce and simmered for what feels like an eternity, because it smells so amazing as it cooks. I use dried chiles, which are found in most supermarkets, to make the incredible red sauce that becomes the flavor foundation for the dish, and my gosh . . . I can't say enough about what it all does to my tastebuds. This is really as much stew as it is chili, and if you are a fan of both beef and zesty Tex-Mex flavors, this will become a new obsession for you. It's worth every minute! Why have one favorite chili recipe when you can have two?

2 dried guajillo chiles (about ½ ounce), stems removed

2 dried ancho chiles (about 1 ounce), stems removed

2 tablespoons vegetable oil

One 3- to 4-pound chuck roast, cut into 1-inch chunks

Kosher salt and ground black pepper

1 large white onion, diced

6 garlic cloves, grated

4 cups Homemade Beef Stock (page 160) or store-bought stock or broth

2 teaspoons ground cumin

2 teaspoons dried Mexican oregano (or regular oregano)

2 tablespoons yellow cornmeal

4 canned chipotle peppers in adobo sauce

2 tablespoons adobo sauce

2 tablespoons apple cider vinegar

FOR SERVING

Sliced jalapeños

Sour cream

Cotija cheese

Lime wedges

Cilantro leaves

1. First, make the red sauce: In a medium skillet, toast the chiles over medium-high heat, turning occasionally, until they're fragrant and beginning to turn darker, 4 to 5 minutes.

2. Pour in water to cover the chiles (about 2 cups), then bring to a boil . . .

3. And turn off the heat. Let the chiles sit for 10 to 15 minutes to soften.

4. Place the softened chiles in a blender . . .

5. And pour in 1 cup of the cooking liquid.

6. Securely attach the lid and blend the chiles until you have a smooth puree. Set it aside while you get started on the meat. (Note: You can make this sauce a day ahead of time and store it in the fridge to save time!)

Rich and chunky!

7. In a heavy Dutch oven, heat the vegetable oil over medium-high heat. Add enough beef to make a single layer. Season with salt and pepper . . .

8. Then sear the meat on all sides until dark, about 4 to 5 minutes. Remove the meat to a sheet pan or plate and continue cooking the meat in batches . . .

9. Until it's all seared.

10. Reduce the heat to medium-low, add the onion and garlic . . .

11. And cook, stirring constantly, until the onion is starting to brown, about 3 minutes.

12. Pour in 1 cup of the stock . . .

13. And stir, scraping any browned bits off the bottom of the pan.

14. Add the cumin and oregano . . .

15. And the cornmeal! (It adds a subtle flavor and helps to thicken the chili.)

16. Stir and cook for 1 minute to release the fragrance of the seasonings.

17. Return the meat and any pan or plate juices . . .

18. And add the red sauce . . .

19. The chipotle peppers and the adobo sauce . . .

20. And the remaining 3 cups beef stock. If necessary, add just enough water to cover the meat.

21. Place the lid partially on the pot, leaving an inch or two gap, then simmer, for 1 hour 15 minutes, stirring occasionally.

22. Uncover and continue cooking, stirring occasionally, until the meat is very tender and the chili has thickened, about 30 more minutes.

23. Stir in the apple cider vinegar, then taste and add more salt as needed.

24. Serve big bowlfuls or small cups, depending on appetites. (It's very rich and flavorful!)

25. Top with jalapeño slices, sour cream, and Cotija cheese. Serve with lime wedges and cilantro!

Lucky Ladd!

REALLY AMAZING RIGATONI AND MEATBALLS

MAKES 6 TO 8 SERVINGS

There are certain dishes in certain families that cause certain reactions when they land on the dining table. This is *certainly* one of those dishes in mine. A big serving bowl of pasta with meat-a-balls says "I'm home" like few things do, and this version has been finessed and improved through the ages and stages of our crew. For years I fried my meatballs before letting them simmer in the sauce, but I've walked away from that step! I've found that dropping them into the sauce right after forming them and letting them very slowly simmer to doneness results in the most gloriously tender meatball and a sauce so flavorful, it's almost impossible to believe it. I love, love, love this recipe (and I hope you love times three it, too!).

MEATBALLS

4 large slices good crusty bread, such as sourdough or Italian loaf

12 ounces ground beef

12 ounces ground pork

¾ cup freshly grated Parmesan cheese, plus more for serving

¼ cup whole milk

¼ cup minced parsley, plus more for serving

2 garlic cloves, minced

2 large eggs

¼ teaspoon kosher salt

1 teaspoon ground black pepper

SAUCE AND PASTA

½ cup olive oil

1 yellow onion, finely diced

4 garlic cloves, minced

½ teaspoon red pepper flakes

1 cup red wine, such as Cabernet Sauvignon or Burgundy (or beef stock or broth)

Two 28-ounce cans crushed tomatoes

1 teaspoon sugar

12 fresh basil leaves, chopped, plus more for serving

Kosher salt and ground black pepper

2 pounds rigatoni, cooked al dente and drained

1. Preheat the oven to 200°F.

2. Lay the bread slices on a sheet pan and toast them until the bread is totally dry and crisp, about 30 minutes. (Alternatively, you can leave them to dry on the countertop for 24 hours, but I'm usually not thinking that far in advance!)

3. Break the bread into chunks and put it in a food processor or blender.

4. Pulse the bread until it is broken up into a mixture of smaller crumbs and larger bits. Set aside and get started on the sauce!

5. Make the sauce: In a large pot, heat the olive oil over medium-high heat. Add the onion, garlic, and red pepper flakes . . .

Tender, luscious
meatballs!

6. And stir and cook the onion until it starts to soften, about 2 minutes.

7. Pour in the red wine . . .

8. And let it cook, stirring occasionally, until reduced by about half, 3 to 4 minutes.

9. Add the crushed tomatoes and sugar . . .

10. Then stir and turn the heat to medium-low to simmer for 15 minutes.

11. Make the meatballs: Place the ground beef and ground pork in a large bowl and pour in the breadcrumbs.

12. Add the Parmesan, milk, parsley, and garlic . . .

13. Then crack in the eggs and add the salt and pepper.

14. Mix the mixture thoroughly with your hands or a spatula. Hands work best in terms of smushing everything together!

15. Use a kitchen or ice cream scoop or ½-cup measure to grab a portion of the meat mixture . . .

16. Then form it into a ball. Keep going with the rest of the meat mixture . . .

17. Then drop the meatballs into the sauce.

18. Very gently move the meatballs around in the sauce to make sure they are all coated.

19. Drop in the basil . . .

20. And (again, gently!) stir it in.

21. Reduce the heat to low and let the meatballs simmer in the sauce until they're fully cooked, about 30 minutes. (Stir the meatballs twice during this time.) Taste a little bite of the sauce and stir in a little extra salt if needed.

22. Serve the meatballs and sauce over the cooked pasta in a serving bowl for family-style serving, or just serve individual portions. Top with grated Parmesan and extra parsley and basil!

Easy, breezy Alex!

MARVELOUSLY MEATY SPAGHETTI SAUCE

MAKES 8 TO 10 SERVINGS

A good meaty pasta sauce is an essential for every home cook, and this will be my favorite forever! This incredibly hearty sauce was shared with me by my passionate food friend, Jess. Positively bursting with both meat and veggie flavor, it's amazingly versatile! Serve it over any pasta, layer it in lasagna, or spoon it over slices of garlic bread for an Italian version of Sloppy Joes. Best of all, this is a really easy sauce that doesn't taste easy at all. It celebrates everything that's wonderful about a food processor, taking the chop work out of the equation—all you need is a bit of patience and willingness to stir. (Oh, and a hearty appetite sure helps.)

8 ounces pancetta, diced small

6 large garlic cloves, smashed and peeled

2 tablespoons extra-virgin olive oil, plus more for serving

1 medium yellow onion, cut into chunks

1 large celery stalk, cut into 1-inch pieces

1 medium carrot, peeled and cut into 1-inch pieces

1 pound ground beef

1 pound ground pork

3 bay leaves (fresh if you can find them!)

1 cup dry white wine

1 cup whole milk

One 28-ounce can whole peeled tomatoes

2 tablespoons tomato paste

1 cup Homemade Beef Stock (page 160) or store-bought stock or broth

1 tablespoon kosher salt, plus more to taste

Ground black pepper

Red pepper flakes

1 pound bucatini (or other) pasta, cooked al dente and drained, for serving

Freshly grated Parmesan cheese, for serving

Chopped parsley, for serving

1. Combine the pancetta and garlic in a food processor and process for 1 to 2 minutes, until you have a very fine paste.

2. In a large Dutch oven, heat the olive oil over medium-high heat. Add the pancetta mixture . . .

3. And cook, stirring often, until the fat starts to render and the pancetta starts to brown, 5 to 7 minutes.

4. In the food processor (you don't need to clean it!), combine the onion, celery, and carrot.

5. Pulse until the mixture is finely chopped, scraping down the sides once if necessary.

6. Add the veggie mixture to the pancetta and cook, stirring occasionally, until the onion is translucent and the vegetables start to turn golden, about 5 minutes.

Simple and divine!

7. Add the beef and pork . . .

8. And cook for 10 minutes, until the meat is browned, crumbling the meat and stirring frequently. Spoon out and discard about half the fat and liquid.

9. Add the bay leaves and wine, then stir for 3 more minutes, scraping the bottom of the pot to release all the flavorful bits.

10. Next comes the milk! You really won't know it's in here, but it makes such a difference in the finished sauce.

11. Back to our BFF, the food processor. Add the tomatoes and puree until smooth, about 1 minute.

12. Add the tomato paste, tomatoes, stock, and salt.

13. Stir until combined. Bring the sauce to a strong simmer, then reduce the heat to low and simmer for 2 hours, uncovered, stirring occasionally.

14. Remove the bay leaves, then taste and adjust the seasonings, adding salt and pepper as needed. (Depending on the sweetness of the carrots, you might need a little more salt than you'd think!) To spice things up, stir in some red pepper flakes.

15. To serve, fill a bowl with pasta and drizzle it with a little olive oil.

16. Top it generously with sauce and grate on some Parmesan!

17. Sprinkle with fresh parsley and serve.

BIG, THICK BURGERS

MAKES 2 BURGERS

I am fickle when it comes to burgers, constantly toggling between preferring them thick or thin. The problem I encounter is that I love lots of toppings on my burgers, particularly thick ones, so the finished beefy structure winds up being more like a skyscraper. And actually, this isn't a problem at all . . . a big, hard-to-get-in-your-mouth burger can be an absolute delight, especially when the burger patty itself holds its own, flavor-wise, against all the other elements in the build. After many decades of making everything from mediocre burgers to memorable ones, this is my very favorite way to make one that's gosh darn marvelous. The flavor is in the beef, not on it, which makes every single bite perfect!

1 tablespoon olive oil

1 tablespoon salted butter

1 small white onion, diced very small (you can also grate the onion on a cheese grater to make it super fine)

3 garlic cloves, minced

2 teaspoons steak seasoning

1 pound ground beef (85/15)

4 or 5 dashes Worcestershire sauce

½ teaspoon kosher salt

½ teaspoon ground black pepper

4 slices bacon

4 slices cheddar cheese

2 oversize burger buns, split open

Ketchup, for serving

Whole-grain mustard, for serving

2 large pieces green leaf lettuce

4 tomato slices

½ cup sliced pickles

Thin French Fries (page 287), for serving

1. In a medium skillet, heat the olive oil and butter over medium heat. Add the onion and garlic.

2. Cook for 5 minutes, stirring often, to soften, then sprinkle in the steak seasoning.

3. Continue cooking for 3 more minutes, stirring constantly, until the onion is soft. Remove from the heat and let cool for 10 minutes.

4. Place the ground beef in a large bowl and add the onion.

5. Break up the meat a bit and start mixing in the onion, then add the Worcestershire, salt, and pepper.

6. Thoroughly mash the mixture together until the onion is totally part of the beef and the seasonings are well mixed in.

7. Cook the bacon in a cast-iron skillet over medium-high heat until just crisp. Remove the bacon to a plate lined with paper towels. (Leave the bacon grease in the pan and the heat on!)

8. Form half of the meat mixture into a thick round, about 5 inches wide, using your thumb to make an indentation in the center. (This will keep the patty from plumping too much while it cooks.)

9. Place the patty in the skillet and repeat with the rest of the meat.

10. Reduce the heat to medium and cook the patties for 5 minutes on the first side, moving them slightly in the pan to make sure they don't stick and burn. Flip them and let them cook on the other side for 4 to 5 minutes, until they're no longer pink in the middle. (If the patties feel pretty firm without a lot of give, they're well cooked!)

11. When they have about 2 minutes of cooking time left, lay 2 slices of cheddar on each patty and get the buns ready.

12. For each burger, I like to put ketchup on the bottom bun and mustard on the top.

13. To make each sandwich, lift a patty with a slotted spatula . . .

14. And place it smack-dab on the ketchup.

15. Break the bacon slices in half and arrange 4 halves on top of the cheese.

16. Top the bacon with lettuce and tomato, then cover the mustard with a layer of pickles. (If you don't like pickles, please start liking pickles!)

Serve with Thin French Fries! (Feel free to use a knife and fork.)

A magnificent mouthful!
Thin French Fries (page 287)

Thick French Fries
(page 287)
The crispy edges
are divine.

SUPER-THIN DOUBLE BURGERS

MAKES 2 DOUBLE BURGERS

Ladd has always preferred two wafer-thin burger patties to one thick one, so I had to include this second burger option in my volume of essential dishes that define our lives. These are basically smash burgers, and we've been in love for years. There's nothing easier in the world; you just need a super-hot skillet and something metal to flatten the patties with, whether it's a designated burger press or a flat metal spatula (even a tiny iron skillet will work). The secret is to smash the heck out of the patties the second you get them in the skillet in order to lock in the almost see-through thinness. From there, the surface of the patties gets browned and crisp and the flavor absolutely goes through the roof. Have fun with these! I've made them for seven of us at a time before and used a few skillets and burners simultaneously. My kitchen still hasn't recovered from that ordeal, but it sure was fun and delicious!

12 ounces very cold ground beef (80/20)

1 tablespoon olive oil

1 tablespoon salted butter

Kosher salt and ground black pepper

4 slices American cheese

2 soft burger buns, split open

Thick French Fries (page 287), for serving

1. Heat a large heavy skillet over medium-high heat. Divide the meat into four equal portions.

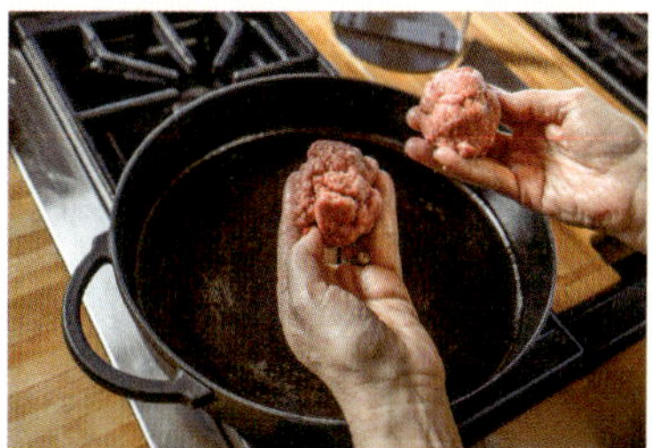

2. Add the olive oil and butter to the skillet and form two portions of the meat into balls.

3. Place them in the skillet, then smash them both as flat as you can get them with a burger press. (I have also used a metal spatula; just smash a patty flat with the spatula and use a metal measuring cup to help push the metal even flatter.)

4. As soon as you've got them flattened, sprinkle a little salt and pepper on each patty. Let them cook for 1½ minutes . . .

5. Then flip them to the other side.

6. Immediately lay a slice of cheese on each patty and let them cook for another minute.

7. Lift one of the patties with a spatula (preferably the slightly smaller one, if there is a size discrepancy) and place it on top of the second patty.

8. Use the spatula to grab both patties . . .

9. And place them on a bottom bun.

10. Put the top bun on immediately . . .

11. And serve with thick-cut French fries! Repeat with the other burger and have a double-burger date.

Note: Lay out the condiments—ketchup, mayonnaise, mustard, pickles—and let each person top their own. They can lift the top bun and go for it! But I like to get those top buns on right away so they soften and get infused with that burger steam and flavor right out of the pan.

I still love a man in a hat! (Especially if he's my man.)

PRIME RIB AU JUS

MAKES 8 TO 10 SERVINGS

It doesn't get any better than prime rib, I'm just going to state for the record right now. I've made it for holidays and special occasions for decades now, and anytime I'm serving it, the whole fam damily sits up a little straighter in their dining chairs, knowing they're in for a treat. My method has been refined and perfected over the past ten years especially, and I've identified two steps that should be considered essential when making prime rib: First, I salt it and let it sit in the fridge for almost a day before roasting it, which allows the seasoning to permeate the meat more effectively (and it is a big hunka meat!). Second, I always make sure to remove it from the fridge an hour before I put it in the oven. That small step has made all the difference in how evenly it cooks and has all but eliminated the too-done edges and too-raw center I'd experienced from time to time. Put this very indulgent dinner on your list this year. (And psst. The leftovers are even better—see page 201!)

One 4- to 5-pound boneless prime rib (I prefer boneless because it takes less time to cook and cooks more evenly than bone-in)

4 tablespoons kosher salt, plus more as needed

3 tablespoons coarsely ground black pepper, plus more as needed

2 cups red wine, such as Cabernet Sauvignon or Burgundy

6 bouillon cubes

2 teaspoons Worcestershire sauce

2 teaspoons soy sauce

1. Place the beef on a parchment-lined sheet pan and sprinkle 1½ tablespoons of the salt on the underside. Rub it in a bit so that it sticks to the meat.

2. Flip the meat over and sprinkle on another 1½ tablespoons of the salt, rubbing it all over the surface. Stick it in the fridge, uncovered, for 18 hours. (If you don't have the fridge space for the sheet pan, you can wrap the beef in plastic wrap or place it in a plastic zipper bag to make it easier to store! It's ideal for it to be uncovered but not required.)

3. Remove the beef from the fridge 1 hour before you're ready to roast it. Sprinkle ½ tablespoon of the salt and 1½ tablespoons of the pepper on the underside . . .

4. Then sprinkle the remaining ½ tablespoon salt and 1½ tablespoons pepper on the top. Rub the seasoning in as much as you can to make sure most of it sticks.

5. When you're ready to roast the beef, arrange the oven rack in the bottom third of the oven and preheat the oven to 500°F.

6. Place the beef on a rack in a heavy roasting pan with the fat side up. Roast for 15 minutes, then reduce the oven temperature to 375°F and roast for an additional 30 to 40 minutes. Use a meat thermometer to watch the temp! For meat on the rare side, look for 120°F, or 135°F for more medium-rare to medium.

7. Remove the prime rib to a cutting board to rest while you make the jus. (It's important for it to rest for a good 15 minutes before slicing!)

8. If there are a lot of burned peppercorns in the roasting pan, carefully remove them with tongs or a paper towel. Turn on the heat under the pan to medium-high.

9. Pour in the red wine, whisking constantly to mix it with the beef drippings.

10. Let the mixture cook for 10 minutes, whisking occasionally, until it's reduced a bit.

11. Drop the bouillon cubes into 8 ounces of hot water and let them dissolve . . .

12. Then pour the flavorful broth into the pan.

13. Add the Worcestershire and soy sauce and stir it in . . .

14. Then cook for another 5 to 10 minutes, whisking occasionally, to deepen the flavors and reduce slightly.

15. Cut the prime rib into ½-inch-thick slices and serve it with jus on the side. Heaven!

Perfect sides to serve with prime rib

- *The Creamiest, Dreamiest Mashed Potatoes (page 284)*
- *The Creamiest Mac and Cheese (page 119)*
- *Crispy Oven-Roasted Potatoes (page 281)*
- *Really Great Grits (page 297)*
- *Charred Broccolini (page 320)*
- *Whiskey-Glazed Carrots (page 303)*

A special-occasion masterpiece!

The eighth wonder
of the world!

FRENCH DIP

MAKES 2 SANDWICHES

I'm not sure I'd go to the twenty-four-hour trouble to make prime rib and au jus just so I could make these sandwiches, but . . . actually, scratch that. Yes, I would absolutely go to the trouble of making it. A good French dip is one of life's true delights—and this one is "jus" spectacular! More often than not, I make French dips following a holiday meal of prime rib; it's the very best use of it, in my opinion! If you happen to have one of those fancy-schmancy meat slicers that can give you super-thin slices of the beef, even better. But for me, a sharp knife and a little determination is all I need. And it saves on counter space!

2 tablespoons salted butter

2 good deli rolls, split open

4 slices Swiss cheese

1 cup jus (from Prime Rib au Jus, page 197), warmed

½ pound Prime Rib (from Prime Rib au Jus, page 197), sliced very thin

1. Preheat the oven broiler.

2. In a large skillet over medium-low heat, melt the butter. Toast the rolls, cut side down, until golden and crisp around the edges.

3. Lay the rolls cut side up on a sheet pan and top each half with Swiss. (I lay them at a diagonal to cover more of the bread.)

4. Broil until the cheese is melted.

5. For each sandwich, dish up ½ cup of the jus. Set a cup on a plate with the bottom half of a bun.

6. Pile on half of the sliced beef and top with the top bun. Press it slightly to make sure the sandwich is secure. Slice the sandwich in half and dunk it in the jus before each bite!

SHORT RIB BEEF STEW

MAKES 6 TO 8 SERVINGS

It should come as no surprise that I'm a huge fan of slow-cooked cuts of beef. Pot roast is an obvious go-to, but I find it's very, very hard to beat a well-made, simple beef stew. Stew is *especially* irresistible when short ribs are the beefy foundation; my gosh! For those who aren't familiar, I always describe short ribs as the most glorious pot roast on the planet . . . which can be a little confusing if I'm saying that in the context of a beef stew recipes. I think I'm even confusing myself now. Anyway, suffice to say, this rich beef stew is one for the books. The root vegetables, paprika, and a bottle o' beer help make it fantabulous!

2 to 3 pounds beef short ribs (bones are preferred)

Kosher salt and ground black pepper

3 tablespoons olive oil

1 tablespoon salted butter

1 large yellow onion, diced

4 garlic cloves, minced

3 tablespoons tomato paste

One 12-ounce bottle lager beer

4 cups Homemade Beef Stock (page 160) or store-bought stock or broth

1 tablespoon Worcestershire sauce

1½ teaspoons sugar

¾ teaspoon paprika

2 large carrots, peeled and cut into ½-inch cubes

2 parsnips, peeled and cut into ½-inch cubes

1 medium turnip, peeled and cut into ½-inch cubes

2 tablespoons cornstarch (optional)

Really Great Grits (page 297) or The Creamiest, Dreamiest Mashed Potatoes (page 284), for serving

1. Generously season all sides of the short ribs with salt and pepper.

2. Heat a large pot over high heat and add the olive oil and butter. When it's hot, add the short ribs . . .

3. And sear them on all sides until the surface is deep in color, 7 to 8 minutes. Remove them to a plate. (You can sear the ribs in batches if need be!)

4. Reduce the heat to medium, add the onion and garlic.

5. Stir and cook until the onion starts to soften, about 3 minutes.

6. Add the tomato paste . . .

Really Great Grits
(page 297)

7. And cook, stirring often, for 3 minutes.

8. Pour in the beer . . .

9. Along with the beef stock . . .

10. And the Worcestershire.

11. Add the sugar, paprika, 1 teaspoon salt, and 1 teaspoon pepper and stir.

12. Return the short ribs to the pot.

13. Reduce the heat to low, place the lid on the pot, and simmer until the short ribs are extremely fall-apart tender, about 2 hours. Some will have fallen off their bone by now, but if some are still attached, don't worry—the meat should slide right off!

14. Remove the short ribs to a sheet pan, remove the bones and any chunks of cartilage (you can use them to make stock!), and shred the meat with 2 forks. Cover it loosely with foil and set aside.

15. Add the carrots, parsnips, and turnip to the pot and simmer, uncovered, until the vegetables are tender and the liquid is reduced a bit, about 25 minutes.

16. When the veggies are tender, add the shredded meat to the pot.

17. Stir, then taste and add more salt or pepper as needed. You can serve the stew immediately, or proceed with the steps below if you want the stew to be a little thicker.

18. Optional: To thicken the stew, bring it to a gentle boil, then mix the cornstarch with ¼ cup warm water. Pour it in . . .

19. And let it boil for 1 minute to thicken.

20. Turn off the heat and let the stew sit 10 minutes before serving.

21. Serve the stew in a wide bowl over cheese grits or mashed potatoes.

Note: Some cooks might consider a cornstarch slurry to be a bit of a cheat, because one can technically thicken a stew by simply giving it more time for the liquid to reduce and thicken on its own. But in small amounts, I have zero problem with it, especially if it helps you get this stew on the table faster!

Variation

- *You can use 2 to 3 pounds of chuck roast instead of short ribs! Just cut it into large chunks and sear it as directed (see step 3).*

"Cowboy, take me away!"

Chicken

For a family that lives smack-dab on an Oklahoma cattle ranch, we sure do love our chicken. To me, chicken has always been the basis of the very best comfort food recipes in my repertoire. It's mild in flavor, tender in texture, and it takes on whatever flavors you want. I love both white and dark meat equally, and I often buy big bulk packs of thighs, legs, and breasts to freeze in smaller portions. Chicken recipes remind me of the old days, when my grandmothers cooked it, fried it, and barbecued it like absolute pros. I pulled together some of my most tried-and-true dishes for this chapter, and they're tested to flavorful perfection. I love them all, and I hope you and your family love them more!

A Drummond kid fave!

MY FAMILY'S FAVORITE CHICKEN ALFREDO

MAKES 6 SERVINGS

When it comes to dishes that are geared for teenagers, I always think some form of chicken Alfredo has to be in the top ten. I remember a team dinner when my boys played football where it was on the menu; a mom had brought big foil roasting pans full of the classic creamy, cheesy pasta with chunks of chicken throughout. To my boys, Bryce especially, there is no more luxurious dinner on earth (and that's saying a lot, considering they live on a cattle ranch). When I make chicken Alfredo, I love keeping the chicken and pasta separate and celebrating the simple goodness of the Alfredo sauce (which, by the way, is great to make as a stand-alone sauce for any pasta situation! I'll show you how here). This one's for you, Brycie!

ALFREDO SAUCE

8 tablespoons (1 stick) salted butter

1 cup heavy cream

½ teaspoon kosher salt, plus more to taste

1 teaspoon ground black pepper, plus more to taste

3 cups freshly grated Parmesan cheese (I grate on a Microplane cheese grater so it's very fine in texture)

CHICKEN

Kosher salt and ground black pepper

½ cup all-purpose flour

3 thin chicken cutlets, about 4 to 6 ounces each

2 tablespoons olive oil

4 tablespoons (½ stick) salted butter

4 garlic cloves, smashed and peeled

12 ounces fettuccine, cooked according to the package directions and drained, 1 cup hot pasta water reserved

Minced fresh parsley, for serving

1. First, make the Alfredo sauce: In a medium saucepan, combine the butter and heavy cream over medium-low heat.

2. Let the butter melt into the cream, stirring occasionally, then sprinkle in the salt and pepper.

3. Whisk to combine and turn the heat to low.

4. Add the grated Parmesan in about four additions, whisking well after each one, until the cheese is totally melted and the sauce is smooth.

5. When all the cheese has been melted in, taste the sauce and add a tad more salt if needed, and as much more pepper as you like! Reserve the Alfredo sauce while you cook the chicken.

6. To cook the chicken, sprinkle 1 tablespoon salt and 1 tablespoon pepper on the flour and mix it with a fork.

7. Season both sides of the chicken with a little more salt and pepper . . .

8. Then lay them in the flour while you get the pan ready for frying.

9. In a large skillet, heat the olive oil and butter over medium-high heat.

10. Add the smashed garlic and stir it around for 3 minutes to allow the garlic to infuse the oil and butter.

11. Remove the garlic from the skillet. (You can discard it!)

12. Dredge both sides of the chicken in the flour mixture, shaking off the excess . . .

13. Then lay them in the skillet.

14. Cook them on the first side for about 4 minutes, gently moving them around the pan to make sure they don't burn.

15. Flip them to the other side, reduce the heat to medium-low, and cook until cooked through, about 3 minutes.

16. Remove the chicken to a board and set it aside. Pour off most of the excess grease in the skillet, leaving any of the small bits of chicken and about a tablespoon of the grease behind for flavor.

17. Turn the heat to low, pour in the Alfredo sauce, and stir as you heat the sauce to a gentle simmer.

18. Pour the drained pasta into the pan with the Alfredo sauce . . .

19. Then turn off the heat and use tongs to toss the pasta, coating it completely in the sauce. Splash in a little of the reserved pasta water if the sauce seems too thick.

20. Cut the chicken into ½-inch slices . . .

21. Pour the pasta onto a large platter . . .

22. Then arrange the chicken on top. Sprinkle with parsley and serve immediately!

Note: If you prefer the chicken to be coated in Alfredo sauce, simply stir the sliced chicken into the skillet with the pasta. Pour the whole thing onto the platter and sprinkle it with parsley.

Alfredo tweaks!

- *Stir 3 tablespoons prepared pesto (see page 107) into the Alfredo sauce after step 5.*
- *Add 8 ounces sliced mushrooms to the skillet after you remove the chicken. Stir and cook them for 10 minutes, sprinkling on salt and pepper toward the end. Pour in the Alfredo sauce and proceed with the recipe.*
- *Follow the mushroom step above with half a sliced yellow onion.*

CHICKEN POT PIE

MAKES 8 TO 10 SERVINGS

Chicken pot pie is a lifelong love of mine, and my recipe hasn't changed appreciably in the almost thirty years I've been making it from scratch. I point out "from scratch" because as a Gen Xer, I consumed approximately one million frozen chicken pot pies from the grocery store—you know, the kind with about 1½ bites of chicken and curious cubes of potatoes. For all their mass-produced-ness, I still thought those little chicken pot pies were amazing (and if I were to try one today, I'd probably still think so!). Given the above, I hope you'll believe me when I tell you that this recipe is basically the most outrageously delicious comfort food dish you'll ever put in your mouth. Through the years, I've experimented with store-bought pie crust, biscuit topping, and even puff pastry, but have wound up locking in homemade pie crust as the very best choice. It's flaky, it bakes up golden and glorious, and it doesn't absorb too much of the gravy/sauce, which I daresay is the very best (and most important) part of a pot pie. Can you tell I have spent thirty years obsessing over this recipe? I hope you take one bite and instantly understand why.

4 tablespoons (½ stick) salted butter

⅔ cup finely diced yellow onion

⅔ cup finely diced carrot

⅔ cup finely diced celery

¼ cup all-purpose flour

½ cup dry white wine

3 cups Homemade Chicken Stock (page 136) or store-bought stock or broth, plus more as needed

¼ teaspoon ground turmeric

¾ teaspoon kosher salt, plus more to taste

1 teaspoon ground black pepper, plus more to taste

2 teaspoons minced fresh thyme, or to taste

¼ cup half-and-half

2 to 2½ cups shredded cooked chicken (see page 216) or rotisserie chicken

Perfect Pie Crust (page 341) or All-Butter Pie Crust (page 344)

2 large eggs, whisked

1. Preheat the oven to 375°F.

2. In a large pot, melt the butter over medium heat. Add the onion, carrot, and celery . . .

3. And cook, stirring occasionally, until the veggies begin to soften and the onion starts to turn translucent, about 3 minutes.

4. Sprinkle the flour over the veggies . . .

5. And stir for another minute to let the flour cook a bit.

6. Pour in the wine . . .

The crust is as heavenly as the filling.

7. And stir for 2 more minutes to let it cook down and start to thicken the veggie mixture.

8. Next, add the stock! (See my note on page 137 about the chilled stock being nice and gelatinous.)

9. Add the turmeric, salt, pepper, and thyme.

10. Reduce the heat to medium-low, then stir and let the mixture thicken for about 5 minutes.

11. Stir in the half-and-half, then taste and add more salt and pepper if needed.

12. Next, add the chicken! If the mixture seems overly thick, splash in ½ to 1 cup of additional stock. (You want there to be plenty of gravy for the pot pie.)

13. Set a 2-quart baking dish (round, square, or oval) on a parchment-lined sheet pan, to catch any sauce overflow when baking. Pour the filling into the dish.

14. Roll out the pie crust so that it's an inch or so larger all around than the dish.

15. Place the dough on top of the dish and allow the extra to drape over the sides.

16. Trim off the excess so the overhang is uniform all around the dish . . .

17. Then brush a little of the egg wash on the underside of the edge . . .

18. To help it stick to the dish.

19. Cut three or four small slits in the center of the crust . . .

20. Then brush the egg wash all over the crust.

21. Bake until the crust is deep golden brown and the filling is starting to bubble, 25 to 30 minutes.

22. Let the pot pie sit for 15 minutes before serving, to allow everything to settle. Serve by the big ol' spoonful!

Sisters on the sea!

RAVISHING ROAST CHICKEN

MAKES 4 TO 6 SERVINGS

Perfect roasted chicken has been elusive throughout my cooking life, and I spent years trying to figure out the best method for getting a golden, crispy skin and a juicy interior. In almost every attempt, I began by slathering softened butter directly on the surface or smearing it under the skin. But in the past couple of years, I have unlocked the power of presalting the chicken for many hours before roasting, as well as letting it sit uncovered before roasting in order to get the skin as dry as possible before the chicken goes in the oven. Wow—what a difference it makes! The skin gets so golden and crisp, and you brush the chicken's own drippings on the skin at the end for the perfect amount of shine. You'll love this method!

I've gotten into a regular rotation of salting a chicken in the morning and sticking it in our garage fridge to sit until dinnertime rolls around. (There have been some funny moments of Ladd having to reach around a naked bird in order to grab his daily Dr Pepper, but that's another story for another time. It gets weird out here.)

1 whole chicken (about 4 pounds), giblets removed

2 tablespoons kosher salt

2 teaspoons ground black pepper

1 lemon, cut in half, plus more halved lemons for serving

20 garlic cloves, smashed and peeled

1 small bunch fresh thyme

2 tablespoons olive oil

1 large yellow onion, peeled and sliced into 4 thick rounds

1 cup Homemade Chicken Stock (page 136) or store-bought stock or broth

1 bunch fresh parsley (optional), for serving

1. Place the chicken on a wire rack set over a sheet pan. Sprinkle ½ tablespoon of the salt all over the surface, making sure to get it on the legs and wings.

2. Sprinkle another ½ tablespoon of salt inside the cavity, moving the chicken around to get it evenly distributed. Let the chicken sit uncovered in the fridge for a minimum of 4 hours—preferably up to 12 hours. During that time, the salt will be absorbed and disappear on the surface of the chicken.

3. When you're ready to roast the chicken, preheat the oven to 400°F. Pat the chicken dry if it has any moisture on the surface, then season the cavity with 1 teaspoon of the pepper and 1 teaspoon of the salt, then stuff it tightly with the lemon halves, garlic, and half of the thyme sprigs. The seasonings and aromatics should be bulging out of the cavity!

The skin is my
favorite part!

4. Cross the bottom of the drumsticks and wrap kitchen twine around the legs twice in a figure-8 pattern.

5. Tie a tight knot and let it sit while you get the other ingredients ready.

6. Pour the olive oil into a 12-inch cast-iron skillet, then lay the onion slices in the oil and arrange the rest of the thyme sprigs on top.

7. Place the chicken on top, breast side up, and sprinkle the remaining 2 teaspoons salt and 1 teaspoon pepper all over the surface.

8. Pour the stock or broth into the skillet, then place the skillet in the oven and roast the chicken until a thermometer inserted into the thigh registers 170°F, about 1 hour 15 minutes.

9. Right after you remove the chicken, use a heatproof brush to brush the chicken with the drippings in the bottom of the pan. This'll give it a gorgeous shine!

10. Place it on a platter with lemon halves and parsley sprigs, if using, and let it rest for 20 minutes, then carve it and serve it with the onions and pan juices!

11. Or let it cool until it can be easily handled, then use your hands to pull the meat off the bones and shred it for soups and casseroles. Save the bones for Homemade Chicken Stock (page 136)!

SLOW-ROASTED CHICKEN

MAKES 4 TO 6 SERVINGS

It might seem a little odd to include two different roast chicken recipes back to back in a cookbook. But when comparing this method to that of its more traditional cousin (see page 216), well . . . they really are apples and oranges! This chicken is absolutely fantastic when you have a little extra time and don't feel like doing a whole lot of prep. The chicken cooks very low and very slow, and the result is a soft, succulent roast chicken that pulls apart so easily that it requires no carving! And the slow-roasted veggies that partly braise in the chicken drippings? *Swoon!* I wish I'd known about this method decades ago, as it's really become my favorite way to cook chicken (as long as I'm not in a hurry). I'll happily keep both roast chicken recipes in my repertoire for now, but this is currently capturing my heart!

½ cup olive oil

4 garlic cloves, finely minced

2 tablespoons finely chopped parsley

1 tablespoon minced fresh thyme leaves

1 tablespoon minced fresh rosemary leaves

Grated zest of 1 lemon

1 teaspoon kosher salt

1 teaspoon ground black pepper

4 large carrots, scrubbed clean and cut into 1-inch chunks

1 large yellow onion, peeled and cut into 6 wedges

6 Yukon Gold potatoes, unpeeled, quartered

1 whole chicken (about 4 pounds), giblets removed, patted dry

1. Preheat the oven to 300°F with a rack in the middle of the oven.

2. In a small bowl, combine the olive oil and garlic . . .

3. The herbs and lemon zest . . .

4. And the salt and pepper.

5. Stir everything until it's well mixed.

6. In a large cast-iron skillet, spread the carrots, onion, and potatoes into a single layer.

7. Add 3 tablespoons of the herb mixture to the veggies . . .

8. And toss them to coat. Spread the veggies out again.

9. Lay the chicken on top of the veggies, breast side up. Top with the rest of the herb mixture.

10. Use a brush to spread the herb mixture all over the surface of the chicken, in all the crevices.

11. Now it's time to slow-roast this bad boy! Roast for 3 hours, occasionally using a baster or brush to baste the chicken with its juices.

12. Let the chicken rest for 20 minutes, basting it once during that time. Serve it right on the table with two serving forks; the chicken should pull apart very easily! (And the veggies/potatoes in this pan are absolute heaven!) Save the bones for Homemade Chicken Stock (page 136).

Paige is Ladd's favorite cowboy.

A slow-roasted
version of the classic!

CRISPY CHICKEN CUTLETS

MAKES 6 CUTLETS

When it comes to delicious family dinners, there are few things more versatile than a good crispy chicken cutlet. You can put them in different kinds of sandwiches, you can slice them to top salads, or you can just squeeze on lemon juice and serve them with whatever sides you fancy. The only thing is, really, really good crispy cutlets aren't necessarily easy to achieve; more often than not, they're a little on the bland side and require a lot of sauce or dressing (or cheese!) to give them purpose.

This recipe solves that issue entirely! It's another miracle shared with me by my good food friend Jess (actually, Jess's mom! The best recipes always come from moms), and they blow any other chicken cutlet I've ever tasted out of the water. Everything is simple and straightforward, but it's the texture and flavor of the breadcrumb mixture that makes all the difference. You'll understand as you read on, but I promise you one thing: This chicken will become an instant favorite. I can't make it often enough!

6 chicken cutlets, about 4 to 6 ounces each

2 tablespoons kosher salt

Ground black pepper

½ cup all-purpose flour

4 large eggs, whisked

2 cups packaged seasoned breadcrumbs

2 slices good-quality white bread, crumbled into small bits (I use my hands, or pulse in a blender or food processor; the bread needs to be coarse like sourdough, not soft or mushy)

1½ cups freshly grated Parmesan cheese (using the large holes of a box grater)

2 tablespoons dried parsley

1 tablespoon dried basil

8 garlic cloves, grated

Vegetable oil, for shallow-frying

8 tablespoons (1 stick) salted butter

1 lemon, cut into wedges, for serving

Chopped fresh parsley, for serving

1. First, flatten the chicken: One at a time, lay a cutlet between two pieces of parchment paper (or one large piece, folded over the chicken). Using a heavy mallet, pound the cutlet to an even thickness of about ¼ inch.

2. Season both sides of the flattened cutlets with the salt and pepper to taste.

3. Lay out three dishes for breading: one for the flour, one for the whisked eggs, and one for the seasoned breadcrumbs.

4. To the breadcrumb dish, add the fresh breadcrumbs . . .

A million different uses!

5. And the Parmesan.

6. Mix to combine, then add the parsley, basil, and garlic . . .

7. And thoroughly mix it with a fork (or your hands, which work great!). You want to make sure the garlic is evenly distributed.

8. Working one at a time, dredge the cutlets in the flour and shake off the excess . . .

9. Dunk them in the egg and let the excess drip off . . .

10. Then lay them in the breading mixture, pressing to get the mixture to stick well on both sides. Keep going until all the cutlets are breaded.

11. Heat a large skillet over medium heat and add about ⅛ inch of oil. When it's hot, melt 4 tablespoons of the butter in the oil.

12. Cook three cutlets at a time until they're golden and crisp on both sides, 3 to 4 minutes per side. Move the cutlets around gently as they cook and check to make sure the breading is not burning. You can turn down the heat slightly as needed.

13. Remove the cutlets to a pan lined with paper towels, then fry the second batch, adding the remaining 4 tablespoons butter (and a splash more oil if needed) to the skillet before frying. Serve them with lemon wedges and a sprinkle of parsley!

Other ideas!

- *After the cutlets are cooked, remove the paper towel from the sheet pan, top each cutlet with a spoonful of marinara and a slice of mozzarella, and broil them for 2 minutes to melt the cheese. Serve with pasta and marinara sauce or on a crusty bun with warm marinara for dipping.*
- *Slice the cutlets and serve them on top of any salad.*
- *Make crispy chicken bacon ranch sandwiches with burger buns, cutlets, ranch, and slices of bacon.*
- *Slice and serve on top of My Family's Favorite Chicken Alfredo (page 209) as a crispier chicken option.*
- *Toss arugula with a little oil and vinegar and pile it on top of cutlets for a Milanese-inspired situation.*

CHICKEN TORTILLA SOUP

MAKES ABOUT 8 SERVINGS

Of all the chicken soup recipes out there in the wild blue yonder, I think a really good chicken tortilla soup is, well, about as good as it gets. This one is packed with chicken and tortillas, not to mention flavor everywhere you turn! Such a great soup for a weeknight dinner, but the fixin's are so much fun, it's also perfect for company. This has been a favorite soup of mine for more than twenty-five years, and if "essential" means I wouldn't ever want to be without it, then yes! It's definitely an essential recipe for me.

- 1½ teaspoons ground cumin
- ½ teaspoon chili powder
- ½ teaspoon garlic powder
- 1 teaspoon kosher salt
- 3 thin chicken cutlets, about 4 to 6 ounces each, cut in half crosswise
- 2 tablespoons olive oil
- 1 medium yellow onion, diced
- 1 green bell pepper, diced
- 1 red bell pepper, diced
- 3 garlic cloves, minced
- 3 tablespoons tomato paste
- 4 cups Homemade Chicken Stock (page 136) or store-bought stock or broth
- 4¼ cups hot water
- One 10-ounce can classic Ro-Tel (diced tomatoes and green chilies)
- 3 tablespoons yellow cornmeal
- 5 small corn tortillas

TOPPINGS

- Diced red onion
- Grated Monterey Jack cheese
- Diced fresh tomato
- Avocado slices
- Cilantro leaves

1. In a small dish, mix together the cumin, chili powder, garlic powder, and ½ teaspoon of the salt.

2. Sprinkle half of the spice mix on the chicken and turn the pieces to coat both sides.

3. In a medium pot, heat the olive oil over medium-high heat. Add the chicken in a single layer.

4. Cook the chicken until the surface is deep golden on both sides, about 2 minutes per side. (It does not need to be fully cooked through at this point.)

5. Remove the chicken to a plate.

6. Add the onion, both bell peppers, the garlic, and the other half of the spice mix.

7. Cook the veggies until they soften and turn golden, about 5 minutes, stirring often. There should be some browned bits in the bottom of the pot from the chicken. Yum!

8. Add the tomato paste and stir it against the bottom of the pot for 1 minute for it to start to fry . . .

9. Then add the chicken stock . . .

10. Along with 4 cups of the hot water and the can of Ro-Tel.

11. Return the chicken to the pot . . .

12. Then cover the pot, reduce the heat to low, and simmer for 15 minutes to allow the flavors to develop and the chicken to finish cooking.

13. Remove the chicken from the pot and shred it with two forks into bite-size chunks.

14. Mix the cornmeal with the remaining ¼ cup hot water and stir for 1 minute to create a paste. Pour it into the soup, give it a stir . . .

15. Then return the chicken to the pot. Let the soup simmer for 5 minutes to let the cornmeal thicken the soup a little.

16. Slice the tortillas into thin strips . . .

17. And, right before serving, stir two-thirds of the strips into the soup, reserving the rest for topping.

18. Serve the soup with more tortilla strips and all the toppings!

A perfect chicken soup!
(Don't skip the toppings.)

CHICKEN AND NOODLES

MAKES 6 TO 8 SERVINGS

When it comes to the things I love in the world (and I love a lot of things), it's sometimes difficult for me to assign my top favorites. Movies, for example—I have so many I adore and would drop everything to watch. Food is another one: I have dozens and dozens of dishes that I would stick on my top ten list, depending on the day, my mood, and the occasion. One exception, however, is this glorious comfort food dish, which my grandma made for me countless times throughout my childhood. It has never, and will never, drop out of my true top ten favorite recipes of all time, both because of how it tastes and how it makes me feel. It's more stew than soup, but really, it defies definition. Ga-Ga always used frozen home-style noodles (and so did I for years; they're wonderful!) and added (get this) a couple of drops of yellow food coloring to achieve that golden chicken stew color. I have in recent years started making homemade noodles—you won't believe how simple it is—and traded the food coloring for a little turmeric, which brings both the color Ga-Ga sought and an unmistakable earthiness and warmth. I hate to play favorites, as I said above. But this is my favorite.

1¼ cups plus 2 tablespoons all-purpose flour, plus more for rolling out the dough

1½ teaspoons kosher salt, plus more to taste

2 large eggs

1 tablespoon salted butter

1 tablespoon olive oil

2 large carrots, peeled and diced small

2 celery stalks, diced small

1 medium yellow onion, diced

4 garlic cloves, minced

½ teaspoon ground black pepper

¼ teaspoon ground turmeric

2 tablespoons chopped fresh oregano

6 cups Homemade Chicken Stock (page 136) or store-bought stock or broth, plus more as needed

⅓ cup half-and-half

2 to 3 cups shredded cooked chicken (see page 216) or rotisserie chicken

2 tablespoons minced fresh parsley

1. First, make the dough for the noodles: Combine the 1¼ cups of flour and ½ teaspoon of the salt in the bowl of a stand mixer fitted with the paddle attachment.

2. Crack in the eggs. Turn the mixer on low and mix for 3 minutes, until it starts to come together . . .

3. Add a tiny amount (¼ to ½ teaspoon) of very cold water if it looks like the mixture is still dry. Be careful not to add more water than needed or the dough could get too sticky and wet.

4. When the dough comes together in a ball, let the mixer run for 1 more minute to knead the dough. If it seems too sticky, sprinkle in ½ teaspoon flour.

Homemade noodles make this even better!

5. Remove the dough from the mixer, form it into a ball, and let it rest at room temperature for 15 minutes. (You can make the dough up to 24 hours in advance and chill it, wrapped in plastic. Just remove it from the fridge 1 hour before you need it so it comes room temperature.)

6. Meanwhile, heat a Dutch oven over medium heat and melt the butter with the olive oil. Add the carrots, celery, onion, garlic, the remaining 1 teaspoon salt, and the pepper.

7. Cook the veggies until the onion turns translucent, about 5 minutes, stirring occasionally.

8. Sprinkle in the turmeric . . .

9. And the 2 tablespoons of flour.

10. Stir constantly to coat the veggies in the flour, letting the flour cook just a bit. You'll see the turmeric start to turn the veggies a gorgeous golden color!

11. Sprinkle in the oregano . . .

12. And pour in the stock.

13. Stir and bring the mixture to a gentle boil, then cover the pot, reduce the heat to medium-low, and let it simmer until slightly thickened, about 15 minutes.

14. While the soup simmers, get the noodles ready: Spread some flour on a cutting board . . .

15. Then roll out the dough as thin as it will go. The size that you roll it out to is less important than the thinness; try to roll it out to about ⅛ inch.

16. Use a pizza cutter or knife to slice thin (¼-inch) strips in the dough. Don't worry about them being perfectly straight; just keep them a somewhat uniform width.

17. When the dough is all sliced, make two perpendicular cuts to create shorter noodles.

18. Sprinkle on a little flour and separate the noodles, dropping them in a pile as you go. You can grab several at a time, just try not to stretch them out as you pick them up.

19. Lightly toss the noodles to make sure they are all separate and not sticking together. You can sprinkle on a couple of teaspoons more flour to keep them from sticking.

20. Turn the heat to medium-high and drop small handfuls of the noodles into the pot, keeping them separated as you drop them in.

21. Let the stew come to a gentle boil and cook the noodles for 3 minutes, during which time they'll plump up a bit. The liquid should thicken a little bit more as well, due to the flour on the noodles. (You want it to be a little on the thick side, but not as thick as a stew.)

22. Splash in the half-and-half and stir it to combine . . .

23. Then add the chicken! If you like to have more of an even ratio of noodles to chicken, add about 2 cups of chicken. If you want it to be very chicken-forward, add 3 cups or more!

24. Sprinkle in fresh parsley . . .

25. Then turn off the heat and serve it immediately. Note that the noodles will continue to plump a bit and thicken as they sit in the pot. You can splash in a little more chicken stock or broth if you need to thin slightly!

CRUNCHY BUTTERMILK FRIED CHICKEN

MAKES ABOUT 14 PIECES

I have a confession to make, and my reputation as a ranch wife and down-home country cook is at stake: I can take or leave fried chicken. It's weird, I know, but as much as I've tried to understand it, I really can't explain this anomaly. To me, there are just so many more interesting, fun, luscious, drippy, flavorful things I'd rather eat. On the other hand, every single member of my family thinks fried chicken is one of life's real delicacies. Welcome to my world! Years ago, I faced this reality and was confronted with two choices: First, I could send my beloved family to KFC an hour away and tell them to enjoy themselves, maybe send me a postcard. Or second, I could figure out how to make fried chicken that was tasty enough for even me to crave and foolproof enough that I wouldn't dread the process. So I took the "when in Rome" approach and made enough batches of fried chicken to (finally) get kinda good at it! This recipe is the messy and crunchy fruit of all my fried chicken labors, and yes—it is freaking fantastic!

Note: This chicken marinates in buttermilk and spices for several hours, then it rests for 1 hour after breading. So, plan ahead—but the result is worth it!

CHICKEN MARINADE

3 cups buttermilk, homemade (see page 5) or store-bought

1 cup juice from a jar of pickles

2 tablespoons packed brown sugar

1 tablespoon paprika

3 tablespoons kosher salt

1 tablespoon ground black pepper

3 to 3½ pounds bone-in chicken pieces (I like drumsticks and thighs)

FOR FRYING

2 cups all-purpose flour

1 cup cornstarch

2 teaspoons baking powder

1 tablespoon paprika

1 tablespoon onion powder

1 tablespoon garlic powder

1 tablespoon kosher salt

1 teaspoon ground black pepper

2 pounds lard or vegetable shortening, for frying (I prefer lard!)

The Most Perfect Biscuits (page 16), for serving

Salted butter and honey, for serving

1. First, marinate the chicken: Place an extra-large (2-gallon) plastic zipper bag in a large bowl to help support it, then combine the buttermilk, pickle juice, brown sugar, paprika, salt, and pepper.

2. Hold the top of the bag while you smush and mix the ingredients until well combined.

3. Drop the chicken pieces into the bag . . .

The Most Perfect Biscuits
(page 16)
Takes a little time,
but so worth it!

4. Then smush around the chicken so it's all coated in the buttermilk mixture. Seal the bag and place it in the fridge for at least 4 hours, or up to 12 hours. (Note: You can absolutely marinate the chicken in a large bowl if you have the fridge space for it. The plastic bag makes it easier to wedge in among the contents of your fridge!)

5. When you're ready to fry, in a shallow dish, mix together the flour, cornstarch, baking powder, paprika, onion powder, garlic powder, salt, and pepper.

6. Remove 1 piece of chicken at a time . . .

7. And dredge it in the flour mixture, pressing hard on all sides to make sure it adheres to the chicken.

8. Repeat with the rest of the chicken, placing it on a wire rack over a sheet pan. If there are any pieces with bare spots, give them another dredge to make sure everything is well breaded. Let the chicken sit at room temperature for 1 hour, so that it loses its chill a bit. This will help it fry more evenly and will also give the breading a better texture.

9. Preheat the oven to 350°F. Add the lard to a shallow cast-iron pan or skillet over medium-high heat . . .

10. And let it melt. Heat it to a temperature of 325°F.

11. Fry the chicken in batches of 4 or 5 pieces, adjusting the heat to maintain a temperature of 300 to 325°F and turning the pieces as needed so they don't burn. Each batch should take 8 to 10 minutes; lower the heat slightly if the breading appears to be getting too brown too quickly.

12. Remove the pieces to a rack set over a sheet pan as you cook them. After you're done, check one of the larger pieces and see if there is any visible pink. If so, or if you want to make sure all the chicken is hot for serving, put the pan in the oven and bake the chicken for 10 minutes more, until the meat is cooked through. Serve with biscuits, butter, and honey!

CHICKEN NUGGETS

MAKES ABOUT 16 NUGGETS

Wait—don't touch that dial! This is not your average chicken nugget recipe. But before I give you details, can I just take a moment to acknowledge how important chicken nuggets have been to my family through the years? From frozen dinosaur-shaped nuggets when my kids were tiny to quick stops at McDonald's on our way to football games; from beer-battered nuggets I made during their college years to versions coated in various cereal crumbs (we still serve a version at the Merc!), the humble chicken nugget has played quite a role in our family's life.

After many years of figuring out new ways to fry chunks of chicken tenders or breasts, the lights went on when I started making nuggets from a ground chicken mixture instead. What a game changer! The result is a little more like the fast-food style of nugget: crisp on the outside and soft, tender, and easy to eat. I have never gone back to using chicken breast chunks. As for serving them, I'm a ketchup or barbecue sauce kind of girl, but according to my kids, ranch is the only correct way to go.

NUGGET MIXTURE

1 pound ground chicken

1 large egg

1 tablespoon heavy cream

1½ teaspoons seasoned salt

1 teaspoon garlic powder

1 teaspoon paprika

½ teaspoon kosher salt

½ teaspoon ground black pepper

FOR FRYING

¼ cup cornstarch

¼ cup all-purpose flour

½ teaspoon kosher salt

½ teaspoon ground black pepper

2 eggs

1½ cups seasoned panko bread crumbs

Vegetable oil, for frying

FOR SERVING

Kosher salt

Ree's Favorite Ranch (page 238), Heavenly Homemade Barbecue Sauce (page 246), honey mustard, or any dipping sauce you like

1. Make the nugget mixture: In a large bowl, combine the ground chicken, egg, and heavy cream.

2. Add the seasoned salt, garlic powder, paprika, kosher salt, and pepper.

3. Stir until well mixed. The mixture will be pretty soft and sticky! (It will also be a little weird at this stage, but trust the process!)

4. When ready to fry, make a breading station with three bowls: In one bowl combine the cornstarch, flour, kosher salt, and pepper. Stir with a fork to mix.

5. Whisk the eggs in a second bowl . . .

6. And pour the panko into the third.

Crispy, tender little wonders!
Ree's Favorite Ranch (page 238)

7. Using a 1-ounce scoop, add one scoop of the chicken mixture at a time to the seasoned flour mixture.

8. Roll it to coat it in the mixture, then lightly pat it into a nugget-shaped patty.

9. Quickly coat both sides with the egg . . .

10. Then place it in the bowl of panko, turning it to coat both sides.

11. Keep going with the rest of the ingredients until all the chicken is used.

12. Pour about 1 inch of oil into a heavy pot and heat over medium-high heat until the temperature reaches about 360°F. Carefully drop in a few of the nuggets . . .

13. And fry them until the bottoms are golden and crisp, 2½ to 3 minutes, moving them around the pan gently to make sure they don't burn.

14. Carefully flip the nuggets and let them cook for about 1½ minutes more, until golden and crisp all over.

15. Remove the nuggets to a pan lined with paper towels.

16. Continue to cook the rest in batches. Sprinkle with a little extra kosher salt before serving with ranch, barbecue sauce, ketchup, honey mustard, or any dipping sauce you like!

REE'S FAVORITE RANCH

MAKES ABOUT 3 CUPS

No ranch compares to this—at least for me! This recipe has barely changed since I started making it when my babies were babies, and I love it every bit now as I did then. What has changed is how much more quickly we go through it now than we did in the old days, when I was naive enough to think ranch dressing was for salads and carrot sticks. Little did I know my kids would one day consider it their most essential condiment for pizza, fries, chicken nuggets, burgers, and even steak bites. Kids these days! (I couldn't agree more about pizza, though. Life-changing!)

1 cup mayonnaise, homemade (see page 67) or store-bought (I use store-bought)

½ cup sour cream

⅓ cup buttermilk, homemade (see page 5) or store-bought (I use store-bought)

1 garlic clove, grated on a Microplane zester

¼ cup finely chopped fresh parsley

1 tablespoons finely minced fresh chives

2 tablespoons finely minced fresh dill

1 teaspoon Worcestershire sauce

¼ teaspoon paprika

⅛ teaspoon cayenne pepper

A few dashes hot sauce

½ teaspoon kosher salt, plus more as needed

1 teaspoon freshly ground black pepper

1 teaspoon distilled white vinegar

1. In a medium bowl, combine all the ingredients.

2. Whisk until everything is well mixed, then taste and add more salt, pepper, or any of the other ingredients you feel it might need! Customize it as you like—see the list of add-in ideas at right!

3. Transfer the dressing to a jar or bowl and store it covered in the fridge for at least 4 hours before serving in order to let the flavors develop. The dressing can be stored in the fridge for up to 1 week.

Other flavor add-ins

- *Grated zest of 2 lemons for a lemony ranch*
- *1 more teaspoon freshly ground pepper for peppercorn ranch*
- *1 to 2 tablespoons adobo sauce from a can of chipotle peppers for chipotle ranch*
- *2 tablespoons finely minced cooked bacon for bacon ranch*
- *1 to 2 tablespoons pesto, homemade (see page 107) or store-bought, for a nice pesto ranch*
- *1 to 2 tablespoons sun-dried tomato pesto and 2 tablespoons minced fresh oregano for a tangy Italian ranch*

Chicken Nuggets
(page 235)
Goes with absolutely
everything!

I've been cooking for the humans in my life for decades at this point(!), and I tend to get so hopelessly caught in a loop of cooking beef and chicken that I almost have to set reminders on my phone to remember to make a pork dish every now and then. Pork can sometimes (okay, often!) be a little lackluster: tough or flavorless or just blah. The flip side of this is that when pork is good, it is so very, very good! For years I've made the same go-to pork dishes for my fam—from simple chops to slow braises—and there is nothing remotely blah about any of them. For this cookbook, however, I reexamined all of them and as delicious as they were to begin with, I think they're even better now. Dear pork, I know I don't always show it, but I love ya!

CLASSIC BBQ PULLED PORK

MAKES ENOUGH PORK FOR 16 TO 18 SANDWICHES

I'm not necessarily a big barbecue girl . . . until I am. What I mean is, I don't generally crave barbecue foods like the other (extremely carnivorous) members of my family do. However, if I have the opportunity to eat a fantastically delicious pulled pork sandwich, whether it's at a church potluck, a summer cookout, or a barbecue restaurant in Texas, I will probably want to eat five of them. Good pulled pork is definitely a weakness for me, and after years and years of attempting different oven versions, I can say that this one is definitely *the* one.

Note: Like all good pulled pork, this one needs a lot of time in the oven to fulfill its mission, but even before that stage, I let this one sit in the spice rub for a whole 24 hours. Stick with it! You'll be so, so happy you did.

¼ cup packed brown sugar

1 tablespoon chili powder

1 tablespoon paprika

2 teaspoons garlic powder

2 teaspoons kosher salt

1 teaspoon ground black pepper

1 teaspoon cayenne pepper

One 9- to 10-pound bone-in pork shoulder roast (also called pork butt)

4 large white onions, peeled and halved

Barbecue sauce, homemade (see page 246) or your favorite bottled sauce

FOR SERVING

Soft hamburger rolls

Barbecue sauce

Sliced white onions

Pickles

1. In a small bowl, stir together the brown sugar, chili powder, paprika, garlic powder, salt, black pepper, and cayenne.

2. Place the pork shoulder on 2 pieces of overlapping plastic wrap, then sprinkle half the spice mix on the fat side.

3. Rub the spice mix all over the surface and sides of the pork.

4. Flip the pork over, sprinkle on the rest of the spice mix, and rub it onto the whole surface of the pork.

5. Gather up the sides of the plastic wrap and tightly wrap the pork. (Use a little more wrap if needed to tightly enclose it!) Place the pork in the fridge and refrigerate it for 12 hours minimum; 24 hours is best!

Heavenly Homemade
Barbecue Sauce
(page 246)

6. When you're ready to cook the pork, preheat the oven to 300°F. Place the onions in a large heavy Dutch oven.

7. Unwrap the pork from the plastic (look at that gorgeous color!) . . .

8. And place it on top of the onions.

9. Cover the pot and roast the pork until fork-tender and absolutely falling apart, about 7 hours.

10. When the pork is ready . . .

11. Transfer it to a sheet pan . . .

12. Along with the wildly caramelized onions!

13. And remove the large bone and any other smaller bones (they should easily come loose) and discard them.

14. Shred the meat with two forks, adding the onions here and there so they get shredded with the meat.

15. Shred the meat to your liking! I like it pretty fine because it's easier to make a bunch of sandwiches, but you can leave in some larger chunks if you prefer.

16. Use a shallow serving spoon to strain off as much of the fat from the liquid in the pot as you like, then pour about half of the drippings over the pork.

17. Pour on 1½ cups of the barbecue sauce . . .

18. And use tongs to toss and coat the pork. Take a taste and add more barbecue sauce or drippings as you wish!

19. Transfer the meat to a large pan. (I like to use disposable foil pans for easy reheating and/or transport!)

20. And drizzle 1 cup of the barbecue sauce over the top.

21. Serve the pork with soft buns, more barbecue sauce, sliced onions, and pickles!

This is their happy face.

HEAVENLY HOMEMADE BARBECUE SAUCE

MAKES 2 CUPS

Necessity is the mother of invention, and while I did not invent barbecue sauce, I never made it from scratch until one dark and stormy night on the ranch when the kids were little. I was making oven barbecue chicken for dinner and realized I was plumb out of my favorite barbecue sauce (Head Country is the brand, by the way! It's still my favorite). After pitching a small fit and considering feeding everyone sugary cereal for dinner, I grabbed a few pantry ingredients (ketchup, brown sugar, and molasses) and decided to patch together a from-scratch version of barbecue sauce instead. I can't remember what else I added to that first batch, but it did the trick. In the many years since, I have tweaked and perfected my homemade sauce to sweet, spicy, smoky, slurpy perfection. I absolutely adore this sauce, and while I still love my standby fave from the supermarket, I make this homemade version every chance I get!

2 tablespoons olive oil

1 onion, diced small

2 garlic cloves, minced

1½ cups ketchup

½ cup molasses

½ cup packed brown sugar

¼ cup minced canned chipotle peppers in adobo sauce

¼ cup apple cider vinegar

1 tablespoon Worcestershire sauce

2 teaspoons soy sauce

1 teaspoon kosher salt

½ teaspoon ground black pepper

1. In a medium saucepan, heat the olive oil over medium heat. Add the onion and garlic . . .

2. And cook, stirring occasionally, for 3 minutes to soften the onion.

3. Add the ketchup, molasses, brown sugar . . .

4. The minced chipotles and apple cider vinegar . . .

5. And the Worcestershire, soy sauce, salt, and pepper.

6. Stir the mixture . . .

7. Then bring it to a gentle boil. Reduce the heat to low and simmer for 20 minutes, stirring occasionally.

8. The sauce will slightly thicken and darken during that time. It can be used right away, or let it cool to room temperature . . .

9. And transfer it to jars or other containers. (I usually split the sauce up into 2 or 3 jars.) The sauce will keep in the fridge for up to 10 days.

Optional

After the sauce cools, you can puree it with an immersion blender (or in a regular blender) until smooth. I like the chunks, but it's delicious smooth, too!

Homemade BBQ sauce = Heaven!

SPICY DR PEPPER PULLED PORK

MAKES 18 SERVINGS

This may not look much different from the other pulled pork in this cookbook (see page 242), but please trust me . . . it is a unique pulled pork experience all its own. While my classic pulled pork is more geared toward barbecue lovers, this one is mysteriously smoky and sweet, primarily because it's cooked in Dr Pepper, which is the official pop of all cowboy types. There's room in my life (and yours!) for both pork recipes, and you'll get into a rhythm of which one suits which setting. Have a cool drink standing by if you make this one, though. The spice will wake you up!

Note: This is another very long-braising recipe, by the way, so plan ahead. Obviously, it's worth every second it has to stay in the oven.

PORK

1 large yellow onion

One 6-pound boneless pork shoulder (also called pork butt)

2 tablespoons packed brown sugar

One 11-ounce can chipotle peppers in adobo sauce

2 cans Dr Pepper

2 tablespoons kosher salt

2 tablespoons ground black pepper

FOR SERVING

Street taco tortillas

Finely shredded cabbage (I used a mix of green and red, but either is fine!)

Lime wedges

Thinly sliced jalapeños

1. Preheat the oven to 300°F.

2. Slice the onion . . .

3. And lay the slices in a large Dutch oven. Lay the pork shoulder on top of the onion and top with the brown sugar . . .

4. Then dump the chipotles and their liquid over the brown sugar . . .

5. And pour the Dr Pepper over the chilies!

6. Sprinkle on the salt and pepper . . .

7. Then place the lid on the pot and roast the pork for a solid 6 hours! Twice during this time, take the pot from the oven and (carefully!) flip the pork over to ensure even cooking. I usually use a large serving fork and a pair of strong tongs to do this. Just be careful—it's very hot at this stage!

8. After 6 hours, remove the pot from the oven.

9. Use two forks to pull the pork apart. It should fall apart without much effort at all. If it still seems tough, return the lid to the pot and stick it back in the oven for another 45 minutes.

10. Shred the meat in the pot, letting any liquid in the pan become part of the meat! It's spicy and smoky and sweet and amazing. Serve it right out of the pot or transfer it to a serving bowl and serve it with tortillas, shredded cabbage, lime wedges, and sliced jalapeños for tacos!

Dr Pepper makes it magical!

Other ways to use the pork

- *In sandwiches, topped with slaw, jalapeño slices, and a squeeze of lime juice*
- *Piled on top of Really Great Grits (page 297)*
- *Spooned over The Creamiest, Dreamiest Mashed Potatoes (page 284)*
- *Stirred into hot queso dip and served with tortillas chips*
- *Served as a main protein alongside any starch or veggie!*

Sautéed Green Beans
(page 313)
My favorite way to
eat pork chops!

FRIED PORK CHOPS

MAKES 4 SERVINGS

This recipe for simple-but-sensational fried pork chops is most essential to Ladd and our youngest son, Todd. I've made them for the whole family (and the whole cowboy family as well!) forever, but never more frequently than in the two years Todd was home as an only child after all his siblings had flown the coop. During that window, Ladd, Todd, and I were a happy little family of three, and they'd devour these chops no matter what time of day (or how often) I made them. They're a delight with fried eggs at breakfast, they're awesome with green beans at dinner, and because they're thin and have a built-in bone for a handle, they have proved to be the most perfect portable lunch (or snack!) for Ladd during all his ranch work shenanigans. Take one peek at the simplicity of the ingredient list. Just one more reason to give these a try ASAP!

8 thin bone-in breakfast chops (the thinnest ones you can find)

Kosher salt and ground black pepper

1 cup all-purpose flour

1 teaspoon seasoned salt

¾ cup vegetable oil, for frying

4 tablespoons (½ stick) salted butter

1. Season both sides of the pork chops with salt and pepper . . .

2. Then, in a large bowl, mix together the flour, 1 teaspoon kosher salt, 1 teaspoon pepper, and the seasoned salt until the spices are well distributed.

3. In a heavy 12-inch skillet, heat the oil over medium heat, then melt in the butter.

4. When the butter is sizzling, dredge 1 pork chop in the flour mixture to coat both sides, shaking off the excess . . .

5. And lay it in the pan. Continue with 3 more chops . . .

6. And cook until the surface is golden and crisp around the edges on both sides, about 2½ minutes per side. Move the chops around the pan gently to ensure they don't burn.

7. Remove the chops to a platter and repeat to cook the rest of them. Serve immediately with your favorite sides!

BARBECUE PORK TENDERLOIN

MAKES 6 TO 8 SERVINGS

We dine on so much beef and chicken in our house that I can go weeks completely forgetting about pork. Even when we do eat pork, it's usually a simple fried pork chop situation or something like pulled pork, which feeds a crowd. But any time I make a really good dinner of sliced pork tenderloin, I ask myself why I don't bust it out more often. Pork tenderloin is so easy to eat (it's tender, hence the name), and it's a mild-tasting blank canvas for whatever flavors you want to bring into the mix. This version includes one of my two very favorite elements—abundant charred barbecue flavor (without having to light a fire!) and a cool, colorful topping to make it fun. A gorgeous dinner!

PINEAPPLE SALSA

½ pineapple, cored and diced small

3 jalapeños, minced

1 poblano pepper, diced small

1 large red bell pepper, diced small

Grated zest and juice of 1 lime

1 tablespoon agave syrup

¼ cup chopped cilantro

1 teaspoon kosher salt

½ teaspoon ground black pepper

PORK

2 tablespoons smoked paprika

1 tablespoon packed brown sugar

1 teaspoon garlic powder

1 teaspoon onion powder

1 teaspoon kosher salt

1 teaspoon ground black pepper

2 whole pork tenderloins (about 1¼ pounds each)

2 tablespoons olive oil

1½ cups barbecue sauce, homemade (see page 246) or your favorite bottled sauce

1. If you're planning to cook the pork right away, preheat the oven to 400°F. Line a sheet pan with foil.

2. Make the pineapple salsa so it has time for the flavors to develop. In a medium bowl, combine all the salsa ingredients . . .

3. And stir to mix. Cover it and let it sit in the fridge while you cook the pork. It'll be extra delicious! Feel free to make the salsa up to 8 hours ahead. A great way to save time if you're serving this to guests!

4. Season the pork: In a small bowl, combine the smoked paprika, brown sugar, garlic powder, onion powder, salt, and pepper.

5. Stir until all the spices are totally mixed together.

Incredible flavor
everywhere you turn!

6. Lay the tenderloins on a small baking sheet or platter. Pour on half the seasoning mixture and rub it all over the surface of the pork . . .

7. Then flip the pork and repeat with the rest of the seasoning. (If you have the time, wrap the tenderloin in plastic wrap and refrigerate for up to 4 hours to let the seasoning penetrate the pork. When ready to cook, preheat the oven to 400°F and line a sheet pan with foil.)

8. In a large skillet, heat the olive oil over medium-high heat. Add the tenderloins . . .

9. And sear the pork on all sides until nicely browned, about 5 minutes total.

10. Transfer the pork to the lined pan and transfer it to the oven.

11. Roast the pork for 5 minutes, then remove it and brush about ¼ cup of the barbecue sauce on each tenderloin.

12. Return it to the oven for 5 more minutes, then remove it and brush each tenderloin with another ¼ cup of the sauce.

13. Do this one more time, then turn on the oven broiler. After brushing on the third addition of sauce, broil the pork for 1 to 2 minutes, until the top starts to bubble and caramelize.

14. Place the tenderloins on a cutting board and drizzle on any sauce from the pan. Let them rest a few minutes before slicing.

15. Slice the tenderloins into ½-inch-thick rounds . . .

16. Then transfer them to a serving platter and spoon half the salsa on top. Serve with the rest of the salsa on the side.

CAJUN PORK TENDERLOIN

MAKES 6 TO 8 SERVINGS

Ahh, what a glorious dinner this is! It's a celebration of both pork tenderloin and zippy Cajun flavors, and the sauce alone is positively drinkable. Beer plays a role in both the pork and the sauce, and the result is absolutely restaurant-worthy. Easy enough for a weeknight dinner, but definitely elegant enough for your VIP guests! You'll never look at boring old pork tenderloin the same way again.

Two 1-pound pork tenderloins (about 1¼ pounds each)

½ cup olive oil, plus more for drizzling

2 tablespoons Cajun seasoning

2 teaspoons kosher salt, plus more as needed

1 teaspoon ground black pepper

1 bottle amber lager

1 tablespoon honey

1 tablespoon Creole mustard

2 tablespoons cold salted butter

2 tablespoons minced chives

1. Place the pork on a sheet pan or a platter and pour 2 tablespoons of the olive oil over each one. Roll them in the oil to coat both sides.

2. Sprinkle each tenderloin with 2 teaspoons of the Cajun seasoning, 1 teaspoon kosher salt, and ½ teaspoon pepper. Rub the seasoning into the pork and let it sit at room temperature for 15 minutes. (If you have time, wrap them in plastic wrap and let them sit in the fridge for 4 hours.) Preheat the oven to 375°F.

3. In a large skillet, heat the remaining ¼ cup oil over medium-high heat. Add the tenderloins and sear them on all sides until golden brown all over, about 5 minutes total. Turn off the heat but do not clean the skillet. (You'll need it in a bit!)

4. Transfer the pork to a 9 × 13-inch baking dish . . .

5. And pour half the beer over the tenderloins.

6. Cover the pan with foil and roast the pork for about 20 minutes, until it reaches an internal temperature of 145°F. Remove the tenderloins from the oven and let them rest while you make the sauce.

7. Heat the skillet you used for the tenderloins to medium-high heat. Add the honey . . .

8. And the Creole mustard.

9. Stir and start to scrape up any browned bits in the pan . . .

10. Then add the remaining 4 teaspoons Cajun seasoning . . .

11. And the rest of the bottle of beer.

12. Remove the pork to a cutting board to rest . . .

13. Then pour about half the juices from the baking dish into the skillet.

14. Stir to mix everything together, then bring it to a boil. Let the sauce cook and reduce for 6 to 8 minutes . . .

15. Until it has reduced by about half and is deeper in color.

16. Turn off the heat and add the butter to the pan . . .

17. Along with 1 tablespoon of the chives. With the heat off, stir to melt the butter into the sauce.

18. Cut the tenderloins into ½-inch-thick slices, arrange them on a serving platter, and spoon about ⅓ cup of the sauce over each one. Sprinkle with the remaining chives, and serve with extra sauce on the side.

Serve with

- *The Creamiest, Dreamiest Mashed Potatoes (page 284)*
- *Really Great Grits (page 297)*
- *The Creamiest Mac and Cheese (page 119)*
- *Whiskey-Glazed Carrots (page 303)*
- *Sautéed Green Beans (page 313)*
- *Drop Biscuits (page 19)*

Whiskey-Glazed
Carrots (page 303)
The sauce is
absolutely divine!

Seafood

I'd like to introduce you to what is officially the smallest chapter in this cookbook. But don't get me wrong: I love seafood; my family loves seafood; my friends, neighbors, Romans, and countrymen love seafood. But all I can tell you is that we live in landlocked Oklahoma, and it just ain't a big thing here. So I hope you will hear me when I tell you that in order for me to include a seafood recipe in a cookbook of my most beloved, classic dishes, it sure has to be a winner. So here are—count 'em, folks—*five* (I had to make room for lots of desserts) of my absolute favorite "surf" recipes, with a yummy sauce to boot. From a simple (but freaking outstanding) shrimp cocktail to a nostalgic delight from an old cafeteria in my hometown, this is the best fish I've got to offer, folks. I hope you enjoy the heck out of it!

PERFECT SHRIMP COCKTAIL

MAKES 6 TO 8 SERVINGS

It might seem odd for me to have a recipe for shrimp cocktail, considering one can easily grab them in the refrigerated section of a supermarket or warehouse club! Store-bought shrimp cocktails are totally fine for what they are, but their ubiquity has made me forget just how sublime a truly well-made platter of precisely cooked shrimp and sinus-clearing cocktail sauce really is! The size of the shrimp is important: I use colossal size and cook them until just barely opaque to make sure they're utterly tender. The cocktail sauce is of equal importance: I have a high ratio of prepared horseradish in mine to make sure anyone who eats it is awake and present! But the step I think is most often missed when making shrimp cocktail is the water it's cooked in. Boiling a mix of citrus and aromatics before adding in the shrimp to cook them adds such a delicious (and very subtle) flavor that brings out the natural yumminess of the shrimp. Warehouse club shrimp cocktails are fine! But this? This is the finest.

COCKTAIL SAUCE

1 cup ketchup

¼ cup prepared horseradish, plus more to taste

2 teaspoons Worcestershire sauce

1 teaspoon kosher salt

1 teaspoon ground black pepper

2 tablespoons fresh lemon juice

SHRIMP AND COOKING LIQUID

1 medium yellow onion, peeled and quartered

2 lemons

1 large celery stalk, broken into thirds

1 small bunch fresh parsley (about 10 sprigs)

2 bay leaves

1 tablespoon black peppercorns

2 pounds colossal (13/15 count) EZ-peel shrimp (this is shrimp that still has the shells attached, but they are split and easy to remove)

FOR SERVING

Abundant ice, for cooling and serving the shrimp

Lemon wedges

1. First, make the cocktail sauce so the flavors can start to deepen: In a medium bowl, combine the ketchup, horseradish, Worcestershire, salt, pepper, and lemon juice.

2. Stir to mix all the ingredients, then cover the bowl and refrigerate until the shrimp are ready.

3. Cook the shrimp: In a large pot, combine the onion quarters, the juice of 2 lemons (plus the squeezed lemon halves after they've been juiced), the celery, parsley, bay leaves, and peppercorns.

4. Bring the cooking liquid to a boil over medium-high heat, then reduce the heat to medium-low and let it simmer for 20 minutes to deepen in flavor. Prepare an ice bath with ice and a little water in a large bowl and have it standing by.

Not your average shrimp cocktail!

5. Add the shrimp to the pot, cooking in batches if needed . . .

6. And cook just until the shrimp are pink and opaque but not tightly curled (which would be overcooked), about 2 minutes.

7. Immediately plunge the shrimp into the ice bath to stop the cooking process, then proceed with cooking the rest of the shrimp if needed.

8. Pour off some of the water and bulk up the ice in the bowl if needed to adequately chill all the shrimp.

9. Peel the shrimp, leaving the tails on, and serve them in shallow bowls over ice. I like to do two or three different bowls if I'm serving a crowd. (If you want to be more casual, let your guests peel the shrimp themselves! Just have an empty bowl nearby so they have a place to throw the shells.)

10. Serve with the cocktail sauce and lemon wedges!

Variation

- *Serve the shrimp with Tasty Seafood Sauce (page 269) instead of (or in addition to) the cocktail sauce.*

PARTY IDEAS!

Make a Bloody Mary mix of vodka, tomato juice, Worcestershire, prepared horseradish, and salt and pepper to your liking. Stir and pour the mixture into shot glasses, then add a single shrimp to each glass with the tail hooked over the rim.

Or make full-size Bloody Marys by pouring the mixture into ice-filled glasses and adding a skewer of 2 to 3 to each glass so that the shrimp are sticking out of the top.

Bloody Marys and these shrimp just go together!

LOBSTER MAC AND CHEESE

MAKES ABOUT 6 SERVINGS

I'm not sure there's anything more indulgent than a luscious, creamy, cheesy baked pasta with little bites of lobster meat throughout. Lobster mac and cheese is one of the greatest dishes on earth, and this small-but-mighty casserole is perfect for any special occasion. Share it with a few friends as a main dish with a salad, or serve it as a side with gorgeous steaks. This is indeed as creamy as it is cheesy (you'll understand when you see the ingredient list!), with a delightful crisp topping that is the perfect little touch. Alex's favorite dish forever and ever . . . for good reason! It's a treasure.

2 tablespoons salted butter, plus softened salted butter for the baking dish

¼ cup panko breadcrumbs

¼ teaspoon red pepper flakes

1 cup plus 2 tablespoons grated Parmesan cheese

2 or 3 small to medium lobster tails, cooked in boiling salted water for 5 minutes and cooled (or about 6 ounces cooked lobster meat)

4 cups (1 quart) heavy cream

8 ounces mascarpone cheese, softened

1 cup grated Gruyère cheese

¼ cup grated white cheddar cheese

Pinch of kosher salt

Generous pinch of ground black pepper

12 ounces medium shell pasta, cooked al dente

1. Preheat the oven to 400°F. Butter a 2-quart baking dish.

2. To make the crumb topping: Melt the butter in a small skillet over medium-low heat, then add the panko, pepper flakes, and 2 tablespoons Parmesan.

3. Cook the crumbs until they are deep golden, stirring constantly, 4 to 5 minutes. (They'll get a little darker than this!)

4. Next, if you cooked the lobster tails yourself, remove the meat: Use kitchen shears to slice down both sides of the membrane covering the meat.

5. Peel back the membrane . . .

6. Then grip the meat and peel it away from the shell. Chop the meat into small pieces and set it aside.

7. In a large saucepan, heat the heavy cream over medium heat, stirring occasionally.

The creaminess is
through the roof!

8. When the cream is simmering, add the mascarpone . . .

9. And whisk until the mascarpone is melted.

10. One at a time, add the Gruyère and white cheddar, stirring well after each addition to allow them to melt.

11. Stir in the salt and pepper and turn off the heat . . .

12. Then pour in the pasta . . .

13. And sprinkle in the remaining 1 cup Parmesan.

14. Stir until everything is melted and very creamy.

15. Add most of the lobster, reserving a few pieces for the top of the casserole, and stir it in.

16. Pour the pasta into the buttered baking dish.

17. Sprinkle the crumb topping over the pasta . . .

18. Then arrange the reserved lobster on top.

19. Bake the casserole just until the cheese barely starts to bubble around the edges, 8 to 10 minutes.

Note: Lobster is pricey so I call for a moderate amount of meat in this recipe, but feel free to up the amount for a much more lobster-forward experience.

TENDER, FLAKY BAKED SALMON

MAKES 8 TO 12 SERVINGS

I went for years without appreciating (or, to be honest, even liking) salmon. Eventually, sometime in my forties, two things turned this around for me: One, my cookbook editor (hi, Cassie!) visited Oklahoma and brought me proper lox and bagels from New York City. And two, cookbook author Pam Anderson, of whom I was a huge fan, came to visit the ranch years ago and showed me how she cooks salmon. It's such an unusual method and will give you pause . . . but the result is salmon as salmon is supposed to be enjoyed! Just barely cooked through, still tender and soft, but nice and flaky. It's a wonder!

1 side of salmon, about 3½ pounds, skin on and trimmed (many come trimmed, or you can ask your butcher or fishmonger to trim it for you)

2 tablespoons olive oil

1½ teaspoons kosher salt

½ teaspoon ground black pepper

1 lemon

Parsley leaves, for serving

Tasty Seafood Sauce (page 269) or any tartar-like sauce (optional), for serving

1. Line a sheet pan with foil and place the salmon on the pan skin side down (diagonally, if needed to fit). Drizzle the salmon with the olive oil . . .

2. Then sprinkle on the salt and pepper.

3. Now here's where it gets cool! Place the salmon in the (cold) oven and turn on the oven to 400°F. Let the salmon slowly warm and cook for 25 minutes.

4. And this is what it should look like! You'll see the defined flakes of the salmon and the edges will be just starting to crisp.

5. Transfer it to a serving platter and squeeze on the juice of half a lemon. Cut the rest of the lemon into wedges and arrange them on the platter. Sprinkle on parsley leaves and, if you'd like, serve with your choice of sauce on the side. You can slice the salmon into portions, but it's better broken into big chunks with a serving fork.

Other ways to use the flaked salmon

- *Arrange it on top of salads.*
- *Serve it over rice with soy or teriyaki sauce.*
- *Stir flaked salmon with mayo, chopped celery, and finely diced red onion to make a salmon salad for sandwiches.*

Charred Broccolini
(page 320)
Tasty Seafood
Sauce (page 269)

Such a yummy all-purpose sauce!

TASTY SEAFOOD SAUCE

MAKES ABOUT 2 CUPS

This is a cross between a classic tartar sauce (like one would serve with fish and chips) and classic rémoulade sauce (a Creole sauce/dip used for fried seafood or sandwiches). I tried to mash up the two sauce names, but just wound up with names like *remoutar* and *tartarlade*. I don't like made-up words, so I'm just going to call this what it is, a tasty sauce or dip for everything from baked fish to fried shrimp. Hey, "tasty seafood sauce"—it has a nice ring to it!

1 cup mayonnaise, homemade (see page 67) or store-bought

1 tablespoon grainy mustard

1 teaspoon garlic powder

1 teaspoon onion powder

1 tablespoon minced fresh chives

2 tablespoons finely chopped capers

¼ cup finely chopped dill pickles

½ teaspoon kosher salt, plus more as needed

½ teaspoon ground black pepper, plus more as needed

Juice of 1 lemon

Couple dashes of hot sauce (optional)

1. In a medium bowl, combine the mayonnaise, mustard, garlic powder, and onion powder.

2. Add the chives, capers, pickles . . .

3. And the salt, pepper, and lemon juice.

4. Stir and taste the sauce, adjusting the seasonings and adding more of anything you wish! More pickles and capers will give you a chunkier sauce. You can add hot sauce at this stage if you wish.

Serve with

- *Tender, Flaky Baked Salmon (page 266): spooned over after flaking the fish*
- *Perfect Shrimp Cocktail (page 260): instead of (or in addition to) cocktail sauce*
- *Fabulous Fish Almondine (page 273): a little dab'll do ya*
- *French fries (see page 287): as a dip—you heard me!*
- *Big, Thick Burgers (page 191) or Super-Thin Double Burgers (page 195): as a spread on the bun*
- *Chicken Nuggets (page 235): as a zippy alternative to ranch*

SPICY SHRIMP SCAMPI

MAKES 6 SERVINGS

There are many, many versions of shrimp scampi out there—some with pasta, some without. The strict definition of scampi is simply shrimp cooked in a garlic, butter, and wine sauce. Who the heck even needs pasta with that level of simplicity at play? I took that more traditional approach with scampi not long ago, and I realized eating it with pasta all those years distracted from what it really is meant to be: a singular shrimp experience, which the garlic, butter, and wine support so gorgeously! I spike mine with Calabrian chiles, which are my new obsession, but they aren't needed unless you really like spicy. Serve this with nothing but bread on the side, which you can use to dab up the leftover juices in the pan.

1 pound jumbo (21/30 count) shrimp, peeled and deveined

⅓ cup olive oil

8 garlic cloves, 4 minced and 4 thinly sliced

Grated zest and juice of 1 lemon

1 heaping tablespoon plus 1 teaspoon Calabrian chili pepper paste

1 cup dry white wine

Kosher salt and freshly ground black pepper

2 tablespoons salted butter

2 tablespoons chopped parsley

Warm crusty bread, for serving

1. In a large bowl, combine the shrimp, olive oil, minced garlic, lemon zest, and a heaping tablespoon of Calabrian chiles.

2. Stir to coat the shrimp thoroughly, then let sit to marinate for 15 minutes. Just that small amount of time will make the shrimp so much more flavorful!

3. Heat a large skillet over medium-high heat. Without oiling the pan, add a batch of the shrimp in a single layer.

4. Cook the shrimp on both sides to get some good color around the edges, about 1 minute per side.

5. Dump the shrimp onto a plate . . .

6. Then repeat with the rest of the shrimp.

The most
addictive shrimp!

7. Add the sliced garlic to the pan and quickly stir it to keep it from burning, about 30 seconds.

8. Slowly pour in the wine, stirring and scraping the bottom of the skillet.

9. Squeeze in the lemon juice . . .

10. Add 1 teaspoon of the Calabrian chiles . . .

11. Add a pinch of salt and pepper to taste.

12. Stir and let the light, yummy sauce cook for 2 to 3 more minutes, so the sauce can reduce slightly.

13. Turn off the heat and add the shrimp to the skillet.

14. Make space in the center of the pan and add the butter.

15. Stir and let the butter melt, tossing the shrimp in the sauce as it melts.

16. Add the chopped parsley and stir, then serve immediately with chunks of warm, crusty bread!

FABULOUS FISH ALMONDINE

MAKES 6 SERVINGS

I have shared a fish almondine recipe in a cookbook before, because it is such a nostalgic dish for me. It was my main dish selection during my many trips to Luby's Cafeteria with my beloved grandmother Ga-Ga, and it will forever have a place in my heart. (By "it" I mean both Luby's and fish almondine!) If I could go back in time and eat one more go-through-the-line-with-your-tray-and-add-as-many-little-dishes-of-whatever-food-you-want lunch at Luby's with Ga-Ga, I would drop whatever I was doing and go immediately. I'd get mac and cheese, buttery spinach, and about seven other things plus Jell-O, and Ga-Ga and I would talk about her friends Dorothy and Delphia and Ruthie, and I'd talk to her about the boy I was dating or the man I was marrying or the baby I was having . . . I'm crying right now as I write this. So back to the fish almondine! This is not the most elegant, French-inspired version of the dish, but it's certainly the best I have to offer! It's blissfully easy and so, so good. I'll love it till the end of time.

⅓ cup all-purpose flour

1 teaspoon kosher salt, plus a couple of pinches here and there

½ teaspoon ground black pepper, plus a couple of pinches here and there

¾ teaspoon paprika

½ cup mayonnaise, homemade (see page 67) or store-bought

Grated zest and juice of 1 lemon, plus 1 lemon cut into wedges for serving

Six 6-ounce cod fillets

¾ cup panko breadcrumbs

6 tablespoons (¾ stick) salted butter, melted

⅓ cup sliced almonds

2 tablespoons minced parsley

1. Preheat the oven to 375°F. Line a sheet pan with parchment paper.

2. In a shallow dish, combine the flour, salt, pepper, and ½ teaspoon of the paprika.

3. Stir with a fork until well combined.

4. In a small bowl, combine the mayonnaise, lemon zest, a pinch of salt and pepper, and the remaining ¼ teaspoon paprika.

5. Stir until well mixed.

Perfect for entertaining!

6. Dredge each piece of cod in the flour mixture, shaking off the excess . . .

7. And lay them on the sheet pan.

8. Smear the top of each cod fillet with the mayonnaise mixture.

9. To make the panko topping, in a small bowl, combine the panko, melted butter, almonds, a pinch each of salt and pepper, and the minced parsley.

10. Stir until everything is well mixed and the panko crumbs are nice and buttery.

11. Divide the topping evenly among the cod fillets, covering the mayonnaise layer.

12. Bake the cod until the crumb topping is golden and the fish is opaque and flaky, 16 to 18 minutes.

13. Squeeze a little lemon juice over each fillet and serve with extra lemon wedges!

WHY COD IS MY FAVE

While I dabble in cooking different fish, from salmon to tilapia to haddock to sea bass, I would say cod makes up about 75 percent of my seafood-cooking life. It's a mild white fish, with thick, flaky layers, and it takes on the flavor of the recipe without losing its yummy, slightly nutty flavor. While it isn't the cheapest fish in the sea, its middle-ground pricing doesn't break the bank, and it's never too fancy. But if I'm being honest, I think the reason I love cod the most is that I used to eat it with my grandmother (see this recipe's headnote). I'm such a softie!

Potatoes & Sides

I used to be a vegetarian. It's true. From age eighteen until when I met Ladd at twenty-five, I ate no meat and subsisted almost primarily on vegetables, grains, and a ridiculous amount of cheese . . . with quite a bit of coffee Häagen-Dazs thrown in. To this day, even though I love and crave a good steak, I have never stopped loving the world of sides, and I'm not above making a whole meal out of them. Gimme all the potatoes, gimme all the green beans, gimme all the carrots (especially when they're swimming in butter, brown sugar, and whiskey. Trust me, you'll thank me in a few pages!). This smorgasbord of sides will make ya smile!

CRISPY HASH BROWN PATTIES

MAKES ABOUT TWELVE 5-INCH HASH BROWN PATTIES

These crispy, lacy potato patties are my husband, Ladd's, absolute weakness. They're also Ladd's wife's absolute weakness. (Hi.) I like to put a fried egg right on top of mine! But once you start serving these with steaks or burgers, they're going to become a regular part of your side dish rotation. A little hint of onion makes these incredibly flavorful, and they're remarkably easy to make. I encourage you to enter the homemade hash brown era of your life. You'll want to make it permanent!

3 medium russet potatoes (about 2¼ pounds), scrubbed clean but not peeled

1 medium yellow onion (about ½ pound), halved and peeled

¼ cup plus 1 tablespoon potato starch

1½ teaspoons kosher salt, plus more for serving

½ teaspoon freshly cracked black pepper, plus more for serving

Vegetable oil, for frying

1. Spread out a thin tea towel and shred the potatoes using the large side of a box grater.

2. Do the same with the onion. The onion basically disappears into the potato!

3. Gather up the sides of the towel . . .

4. And twist it closed in order to squeeze as much liquid out of the potatoes as you possibly can. This takes a few big squeezes, and a continual tightening of the twist to force out more liquid. (Hint: If you have a salad spinner, that also does a great job!)

5. When the potatoes are very dry, place them in a bowl and sprinkle the potato starch on top . . .

6. Then add the salt and pepper.

Great for breakfast or dinner!

7. Toss several times to ensure the seasoning and the potato starch are fully mixed with the potatoes.

8. In a heavy skillet (I like to use cast iron for this!) over medium heat, heat enough oil to cover the bottom of the pan. Working one or two at a time (depending on the size of skillet you use), drop ½ cup piles of potato mixture into the pan, gently flattening them to about ½ inch thick. (Don't press them flat, just push the shredded potatoes out to the edges to create a 5-inch round.)

9. Let the hash browns cook undisturbed until you can see the edges getting crisp and golden, 4 to 5 minutes.

10. Then flip them to the other side and let them cook until the underside is golden and crisp, 3 to 4 minutes more.

11. Add a little sprinkle of salt and pepper, then remove the hash browns to a pan lined with paper towels. Repeat to make the rest, adding a couple of tablespoons of oil at a time as needed. Serve the hash browns warm (but they're great at room temperature, too!).

Note: Hash browns can be kept on a sheet pan in a 200°F oven to keep warm while you fry additional batches!

CRISPY OVEN-ROASTED POTATOES

MAKES ABOUT 6 SERVINGS

These potatoes, which could be considered both roasted and fried (you'll understand as you read!), may take a little time, but they make the perfect holiday or Sunday dinner side, especially served with prime rib, beef tenderloin, or a juicy roasted chicken . . . or as a glorious snack with ketchup or roasted garlic mayo (see page 68). You can cook them in lard or shortening, but they are the very best if you use duck fat, which is blessedly available in many grocery stores these days. This recipe makes enough for about six, but I won't tell anybody if you make it serve one or two. They really are that good! A good roasted potato is a requirement on any essential recipe list, and this one will forever be on mine.

4 pounds russet potatoes, peeled and cut into 2-inch chunks

Kosher salt

⅔ cup duck fat (sold in jars), lard, or shortening

2 tablespoons cornstarch

2 teaspoons onion powder

½ teaspoon ground black pepper, plus more as needed

8 garlic cloves, unpeeled, lightly smashed

4 rosemary sprigs

2 fresh or dried bay leaves

Flaky salt, for finishing

1. Preheat the oven to 400°F.

2. Place the potatoes in a colander and run them under cold water for 2 minutes to remove the excess starch.

3. Bring a large pot of water to a boil over medium-high and add 1 tablespoon kosher salt. Add the potatoes . . .

4. And cook for 5 to 7 minutes, until they are still firm but have a thin layer of loose potato around the edges. I use the end of a sharp knife to test them; the end should easily pierce the surface of the potato but then hit resistance.

5. Drain the potatoes, then vigorously shake the potatoes in the colander several times. I learned this trick from the amazing J. Kenji López-Alt, and it's brilliant. The goal is to loosen the outer layer on the potatoes, which creates a craggy surface that will roast up nice and crisp! Keep shaking until a lot of loose potato bits are on the outside of the potatoes and set them aside for a few minutes to steam off some moisture.

6. Pour the duck fat into a large heavy roasting pan and place the pan in the oven to start to heat the fat, about 5 minutes.

7. Meanwhile, pour the potatoes onto a sheet pan and sprinkle on the cornstarch . . .

8. Along with 2½ teaspoons kosher salt, the onion powder, and the pepper.

9. Stir and toss the potatoes until they're all evenly coated in the cornstarch and seasonings.

10. When the duck fat and pan are very hot, carefully remove the pan from the oven and place it on a heatproof surface. Transfer the potatoes to the pan in an even layer. (They will start to sizzle immediately!)

11. Dip a heatproof brush in the hot fat and brush or dab the potatoes with it.

12. Tuck the garlic cloves, rosemary, and bay leaves in among the potatoes.

13. Roast the potatoes for 40 minutes, then remove the pan from the oven and use metal tongs to carefully turn the potatoes. Return to the oven and continue roasting for 40 minutes, turning again after 20 minutes . . .

14. Until all sides are golden brown and very crisp. (The potatoes will roast for about 1 hour and 20 minutes total.)

15. Remove the herb stems and transfer the potatoes (and any garlic) to a serving platter.

16. Sprinkle with flaky salt before serving.

Crispy and
delicious!

THE CREAMIEST, DREAMIEST MASHED POTATOES

MAKES 10 TO 12 SERVINGS

The name of this recipe says it all. These are without question the best mashed potatoes in the world, for two reasons: First, the creaminess is through the roof and every bite is a scrumptious journey through bliss. Second, they can be made ahead of time—up to three days—and baked to mashed potato perfection right before you want to serve them. This make-ahead step has saved me countless potato peel/cook/mash messes on key holidays over the years, and they are a top-ten essential recipe for every single member of my family. Try them at your next family gathering. They bring happiness and joy!

5 pounds Yukon Gold potatoes or russet potatoes*

1 cup (2 sticks) salted butter, cut into pieces, plus 5 optional tablespoons

One 8-ounce package cream cheese, at room temperature

¾ cup heavy cream

½ cup half-and-half, plus more as needed

2 teaspoons kosher salt, plus more as needed

1 tablespoon ground black pepper, plus more as needed

1 teaspoon seasoned salt, plus more as needed

Yukon Gold potatoes are a little waxier, so the mashed potatoes will be slightly firmer than with russets, which are a little fluffier and will result in a looser mashed potato. The beautiful thing is that there is no right or wrong answer! I use both interchangeably.

1. Peel the potatoes and cut them into quarters. Bring a large pot of water to a gentle boil over medium-high heat.

2. Add the potatoes to the water . . .

3. And let the water come to a boil. Cook until a fork easily slides into the potatoes with very little resistance, about 30 minutes. If they seem like they're still a little firm, cook for 5 to 10 more minutes.

4. Drain the potatoes and return them to the same pot. Reduce the heat to low.

5. Mash the potatoes over several minutes, allowing a lot of the steam to release as you mash them (the heat on the stove will help with this).

6. Turn off the heat and add the 1 cup butter . . .

The only mashed potatoes
you'll ever need!

7. Along with the cream cheese, heavy cream, and half-and-half.

8. Sprinkle in the kosher salt, pepper, and seasoned salt . . .

9. And mash to mix in the ingredients. As you mash, go slow and use more of a folding motion; you don't want the potatoes to get gummy, and being gentle is the best way to prevent this.

10. After everything is mashed, stir everything a few times to make sure all the potato chunks are mixed in. Taste the mashed potatoes and add more seasoning if they need it, and another splash of half-and-half if the potatoes seem too thick. The mixture should be a little looser than typical thick mashed potatoes. Don't worry if it looks a little lumpy; those bake away in the oven.

11. Pour the potatoes into a 9 × 13-inch baking dish . . .

12. Then smooth out the top. (Optional: Lay 5 tablespoons of butter evenly on top of the potatoes if you want to have little pools of melted butter on the finished casserole!)

13. Cover the dish with aluminum foil and refrigerate it for up to 3 days, if you're making the potatoes ahead of time. (If you're ready to bake the mashed potatoes, you can skip the refrigeration step!)

14. When you're ready to bake, preheat the oven to 375°F. (If the potatoes have been in the fridge, take them out an hour before baking.) Bake the potatoes for 25 minutes covered in foil, then remove the foil and bake for an additional 15 to 20 minutes, until the edges are bubbling and turning golden. Serve to a mashed potatoes–loving crowd!

FRENCH FRIES (THICK OR THIN)

MAKES 6 TO 8 SERVINGS

In my opinion, mediocre fries are still fantastic, so well-made fries are over-the-top insane! Throughout my life of making fries for all manner of cowboys, kids, and company, I've always used the double-frying method, which involves frying at a low temperature to cook the potatoes before raising the temp and frying them a second time until golden and crisp. It works whether you're doing thick fries, thin fries, and any fry in between. Once you've made them a couple of times, it becomes such a cinch, you're going to want to make them once a week, whether as a side or snack. Raise your hand if you agree that French fries are the definition of essential. (Raising both hands here . . .)

6 to 8 russet potatoes (2 to 3 pounds total), peeled

Beef tallow, lard, or vegetable oil, for frying

Sea salt

1. Cut the potatoes into ½-inch-thick sticks for thick fries or about ⅛-inch-thick strings for thin fries.

2. For either kind of fries, place the cut potatoes in a large bowl of cold water as you cut them. Pour off the water, then fill the bowl again with cold water. Let the potatoes soak at room temperature for at least 30 minutes or up to 2 hours in the fridge.

3. Remove the potatoes from the water and place them on a sheet pan lined with paper towels.

4. Use more paper towels to thoroughly dry the potatoes. Be sure all the water has been dabbed off!

5. In a large Dutch oven, heat the tallow over medium heat. You want to start frying when it reaches around 325°F.

6. For thick fries, working in small batches to avoid oil overflow, use a metal spider or slotted spoon to lower the potatoes into the oil. Fry them until they're tender but still totally pale, 3 to 4 minutes.

7. Remove the fries to a rack over a sheet pan and repeat with the rest of the potatoes.

8. Turn the heat to medium-high and raise the oil temperature to 375°F. Again, working in batches, lower the fries into the oil for the second stage of frying . . .

9. And cook them until deep golden and crisp on the surface, another 2 to 3 minutes. (Be sure to keep small kids away while you're deep-frying! It's a good idea to put the pan on the back burner, too.)

10. Remove them to a sheet pan with clean paper towels and repeat with the rest of the parfried fries! Sprinkle them generously with sea salt and serve them immediately!

11. The process is essentially the same for the thin fries! Remove them from the soaking water and place them on paper towels . . .

12. Pat them totally dry . . .

13. Fry them in batches in 325°F oil for 2 to 3 minutes . . .

14. Remove them . . .

15. Then fry them in 375°F oil until the fries are golden (and a little wild! That's what I love about them), 1 to 2 minutes.

16. Plenty of sea salt, then it's time for a fry party!!

Serve with

- *Homemade Mayonnaise (page 67) and ketchup*
- *Big, Thick Burgers (page 191) or Super-Thin Double Burgers (page 195)*
- *Meatloaf, Mastered (page 163)—oh my*
- *Prime Rib au Jus (page 197)*
- *Chuck's Sloppy Joes (page 174)*
- *Marlboro Man Sandwich (page 170)*

Truly the best
dinner rolls of all time!

PERFECT POTATO ROLLS

MAKES 24 DINNER ROLLS

These are my favorite dinner rolls in the universe, not to mention very foolproof, which I appreciate given I am not necessarily a talented bread maker. Potato rolls were originally created a couple of centuries ago when wheat was expensive and more scarce, but once you try one of these, you'll wonder if it was some kind of divine intervention. Hot baked potatoes are the foundation of the dough, and provide the initial warmth the dough needs to rise to gorgeous puffiness. The rest of the recipe just requires time, which I know you'll agree is totally and completely worth it. Serve these rolls as a dinner side, or you can use them for sandwiches or sliders if you're into that kind of thing!

2 medium russet potatoes, baked or microwaved until tender

1 cup whole milk

1 tablespoon fresh lemon juice

3 tablespoons honey

1 tablespoon grated garlic

5 tablespoons melted salted butter, plus softened salted butter for greasing the pan and serving

2 large eggs

1 package (2¼ teaspoons) instant yeast

1 tablespoon kosher salt

4½ to 5 cups bread flour, plus more for rolling out the dough

2 tablespoons olive oil

Sea salt, for sprinkling

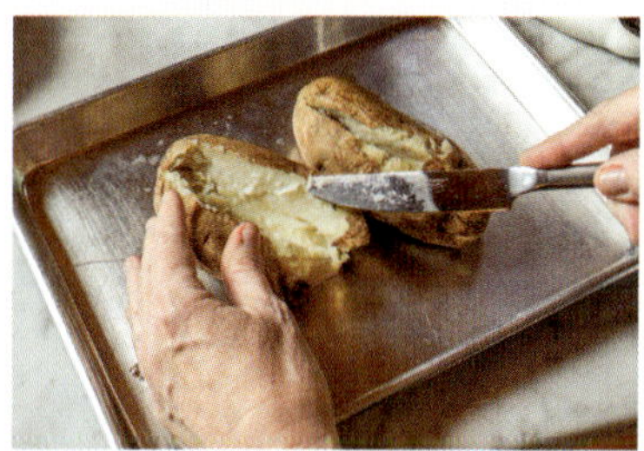

1. When they are still hot but can be handled, slice open the potatoes . . .

2. And squeeze (or scrape, holding them with a towel) the the potato flesh into the bowl of an electric mixer fitted with the dough hook attachment.

3. Turn the mixer on low for 10 to 15 seconds, just to break up the chunks a bit.

4. Leaving the speed on low, add the milk, lemon juice . . .

5. The honey . . .

6. The garlic . . .

7. The melted butter . . .

8. And 1 of the eggs.

9. Sprinkle in the yeast and the kosher salt, then let everything mix for 1 minute.

10. While the mixer is still going, add 4½ cups of the flour in several small additions (I use a serving spoon).

11. Increase the speed to medium and let it mix for 5 minutes. The dough should go from pretty shaggy and rough to pretty smooth and should pull away from the bowl. If it is very sticky and won't pull away from the bowl, add up to ½ cup more flour, 1 tablespoon at a time.

12. Remove the dough from the bowl and fold the outsides underneath to form a ball.

13. Smear the olive oil in a mixing bowl and place the dough inside. Cover the bowl with plastic wrap . . .

14. And place it in a relatively warm, draft-free place for 1 hour. It should become really puffy and double in size! If it hasn't risen much, give it another 45 minutes.

15. Smear some softened butter all over the inside of a 9 × 13-inch baking pan, then turn the dough out onto a lightly floured surface.

16. Use a bench scraper to divide half of the dough into twelve equal portions, then repeat with the other half of the dough.

17. Use the palm of your hand to vigorously roll each portion into a neat ball . . .

18. Then place the balls into the buttered baking dish.

19. Cover the pan with plastic wrap, set it aside . . .

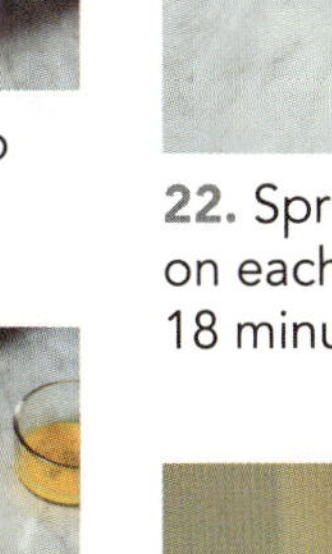

20. And let the rolls rise until they're really puffy and there is no space between them. Preheat the oven to 375°F.

21. Whisk the remaining egg with 1 tablespoon water and brush the egg wash all over the surface of the rolls.

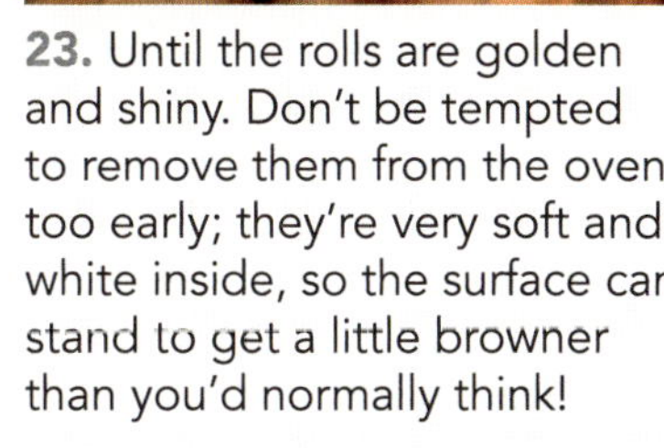

22. Sprinkle a little sea salt on each roll. Bake for 16 to 18 minutes . . .

23. Until the rolls are golden and shiny. Don't be tempted to remove them from the oven too early; they're very soft and white inside, so the surface can stand to get a little browner than you'd normally think!

Make them ahead of time and warm them, covered in foil, in a 200°F oven for 15 to 20 minutes!

My little potato roll!

POTATOES AU GRATIN

MAKES ABOUT 8 SERVINGS

As a home cook, I've always been a little unclear about the practical difference between scalloped potatoes (see page 121, sans ham) and potatoes au gratin. They both involve baking potatoes in some kind of creamy, cheesy sauce, and I've always considered them a little synonymous and interchangeable. To keep them separate in my mind through the years, I generally slice my scalloped potatoes and dice my au gratins, but either way is delicious! This very simple au gratin dish is super rich due to heavy cream, and it's well received at family meals 100 percent of the time. (That's a good record!) I make these potatoes to go with steaks, ham, pork, or even prime rib on a special occasion. They are tremendously yummy.

2 tablespoons salted butter, softened

4 large russet potatoes, scrubbed clean but not peeled

½ cup whole milk

2 tablespoons all-purpose flour

½ cup heavy cream

4 garlic cloves, finely grated

1 teaspoon kosher salt

½ teaspoon ground black pepper

½ teaspoon seasoned salt

1 tablespoon rosemary, finely minced

2 cups grated sharp cheddar cheese

Finely minced chives

1. Preheat the oven to 400°F. Smear the butter all over the bottom and sides of a 2-quart baking dish.

2. Cut the potatoes into a large dice . . .

3. And place them in the dish.

4. In a small pitcher, combine the whole milk and flour.

5. Whisk until totally combined . . .

6. Then add the heavy cream . . .

7. Along with the garlic, kosher salt, pepper, and seasoned salt. Whisk to combine.

8. Add the rosemary and whisk it in . . .

A luscious potato side dish!

9. Then pour the mixture over the potatoes. It will look like they're swimming in the cream mixture, and that's just what you want! Magic happens while it bakes.

10. Top with 1 cup of the cheddar . . .

11. Then cover with foil and bake for 30 minutes.

12. Remove the foil, sprinkle on the remaining 1 cup cheddar and bake for 20 to 25 minutes more . . .

13. Until the potatoes are fork-tender and the edges are browned. Let it sit for 15 minutes for the cream sauce to settle and thicken, then sprinkle on the chives just before serving.

Serve with

- *Prime Rib au Jus (page 197)*
- *Ravishing Roast Chicken (page 216) or Slow-Roasted Chicken (page 219)*
- *Meatloaf, Mastered (page 163)*
- *Fried Pork Chops (page 251)*
- *Barbecue Pork Tenderloin (page 252) or Cajun Pork Tenderloin (page 255)*

Sofia is the coolest baby ever.

REALLY GREAT GRITS

MAKES 10 TO 12 SERVINGS

Grits are so hard to explain to those who didn't grow up eating them, and more often than not, I've let my grits do most of the talking. A good side dish of creamy, cheesy grits is truly sublime, and the strict definition really doesn't wind up mattering much. Besides, a strict definition is actually difficult to come by: Grits are similar to polenta, made from corn like polenta, but wind up looking more like a porridge. And by the way, what is the strict definition of porridge? This is why it's complicated to focus on the "what" when it comes to grits. So I'll just take my regular approach of saying "Just trust me. Try this once." You'll be so glad you did!

1 teaspoon kosher salt, plus more to taste

2 cups quick-cook stone-ground grits (see Note on page 299)

1 teaspoon onion powder

1 teaspoon garlic powder

½ teaspoon ground black pepper, plus more to taste

½ teaspoon cayenne pepper

1½ cups heavy cream

3 egg yolks, whisked

¾ cup (1½ sticks) salted butter, cut into pieces

3 cups grated sharp cheddar cheese

A few dashes of hot sauce (optional)

2 tablespoons minced chives, for garnish

1. In a medium saucepan, bring 6 cups water to a boil over medium-high heat and add the salt . . .

2. And while whisking gently, pour in the grits, continuing to whisk until they're incorporated.

3. Turn the heat to low and add the onion powder, garlic powder, black pepper, and cayenne.

4. Whisk to mix in the seasonings . . .

5. Then pour in 1 cup of the heavy cream and whisk to combine.

6. Cook for 5 minutes, whisking occasionally. The grits will continue to cook a little bit with the heavy cream, which makes them extra delicious!

These grits will change your life!

7. Slowly add a ladleful of the hot grits to the egg yolks, whisking to quickly incorporate them, so the yolks are tempered and don't harden and cook. Continue whisking while you add a second ladle of grits.

8. Pour the tempered yolks into the grits, whisking constantly . . .

9. Then turn off the heat and add the butter, cheddar, and the remaining ½ cup heavy cream.

10. Whisk gently until the butter and cheese are totally melted. Taste a spoonful and add more salt or black pepper as needed. You can also add some hot sauce at this point if you like a little more heat and flavor.

11. Serve the grits right out of the saucepan and sprinkle each serving with chives, or pour them into a serving bowl . . .

12. And sprinkle the chives all over.

13. Serve the grits immediately while very warm. Note that the grits will begin to firm up as they sit. If you want to have a little more flexibility, keep them in the saucepan and you can always thin them with a little hot water if they start to become too firm.

Note: You can use stone-ground grits as well, but you'll need more water and a longer cooking time.

Serve with

- *The Most Perfect Pot Roast (page 157) instead of mashed potatoes*
- *Meatloaf, Mastered (page 163) Yum! Great combo!*
- *Crunchy Buttermilk Fried Chicken (page 232)*
- *Fried Pork Chops (page 251)*
- *Cajun Pork Tenderloin (page 255)*
- *Ravishing Roast Chicken (page 216) or Slow-Roasted Chicken (page 219)*

THE VERY BEST CORNBREAD

MAKES 8 TO 10 SERVINGS

This is the best cornbread on the planet. I say that knowing how very personal cornbread probably is to each and every one of you. Some like it cakey, some like it sweet, some like it coarse, yada yada yada. But for me, this is what cornbread was really meant to be: simple and very corn-forward, with impossibly crisp edges and a crumbly texture that begs you to tear it apart over chili or soup. I use this cornbread, which my mom has made my whole life, whether I'm incorporating it into Thanksgiving stuffing or serving it with a pot of beans. But my go-to way to eat it is warm, with a smear of softened butter and a generous drizzle of honey. I can't think of anything better in the world!

1 cup yellow cornmeal

½ cup all-purpose flour

1 tablespoon baking powder

1 teaspoon kosher salt

1 cup buttermilk, homemade (see page 5) or store-bought

½ cup whole milk

1 large egg

½ teaspoon baking soda

4 tablespoons (½ stick) salted butter, melted, plus 2 tablespoons

1. Preheat the oven to 425°F.

2. In a large bowl, stir together the cornmeal, flour, baking powder, and salt.

3. Measure the buttermilk and milk into a measuring cup and add the egg.

4. Add the baking soda . . .

5. And stir with a fork until well combined.

6. Stirring constantly, pour the milk/buttermilk mixture into the dry ingredients . . .

7. And stir gently until the batter just comes together . . .

My mom's cornbread is
the gold standard!

8. Then slowly stir in the melted butter.

9. Heat a 10- to 12-inch cast-iron skillet over medium heat and melt the remaining 2 tablespoons butter.

10. When the butter is sizzling, pour in the batter. It should sizzle a bit too when it hits the pan!

11. Smooth out the top of the batter, then let it sizzle on the stove for 1 minute.

12. Place the pan in the oven and bake the cornbread until it is golden brown and pulling away from the pan a bit, 18 to 20 minutes. Cut into squares and serve warm with softened butter.

Serve with

- *Simple, Perfect Chili (page 177) or Rich and Chunky Beef Chili (page 180)*
- *Short Rib Beef Stew (page 202)*
- *Crunchy Buttermilk Fried Chicken (page 232)*
- *Classic BBQ Pulled Pork (page 242) or Spicy Dr Pepper Pulled Pork (page 248)*
- *A drizzle of honey!*

Grandparenting is my happy place.

WHISKEY-GLAZED CARROTS

MAKES 6 TO 8 SERVINGS

I love cooked carrots and don't necessarily have to coat them in a boozy, sticky-sweet glaze in order to enjoy them . . . but it sure doesn't hurt! These are my O.G. whiskey carrots—I think I first shared them on my website almost eighteen years ago—and one of the few recipes in this cookbook I didn't alter at all. I tried. I wanted to. I looked for way to improve them. But they've stood the test of time for a reason, and I hope you love them!

½ cup (1 stick) salted butter

2 pounds carrots, peeled and cut into thick rounds

4 garlic cloves, finely chopped

½ cup Jack Daniel's or other whiskey

½ cup packed brown sugar

1 teaspoon kosher salt, plus more as needed

⅓ cup pure maple syrup

2 tablespoons minced chives

1. In a large skillet, melt 1 tablespoon of the butter over high heat. Add the carrots . . .

2. Then cover the skillet and cook for 4 minutes without stirring.

3. Remove the lid and add the garlic . . .

4. Then toss or stir the carrots (you can see the nice brown underside!) for 1 more minute.

5. Pour the carrots onto a pan or plate so they'll stop cooking while you make the sauce.

6. Turn off the heat and add the whiskey to the same skillet. Stir and scrape the pan for about 30 seconds . . .

7. Then add the remaining 7 tablespoons butter and turn the heat to medium.

8. Add the brown sugar, salt, and maple syrup . . .

9. And stir, letting the brown sugar dissolve. Cook the glaze, stirring constantly, until it has reduced and thickened by about one-third, 5 to 7 minutes.

10. Slide the carrots back in . . .

11. Then stir and let the carrots cook in the glaze until they are tender but still have a nice bite to them, about 5 more minutes. Taste a coated carrot (be careful, the glaze is very hot!) and sprinkle in more salt if it's a little too sweet.

12. Spoon the carrots onto a deep platter or into a serving bowl and spoon the remaining pan glaze over the top. (Note: If the glaze is a little thin, just let it cook for 5 to 7 more minutes after you remove the carrots.)

13. Top with the chives before serving.

Serve with

- *Meatloaf, Mastered (page 163)*
- *Chicken-Fried Steak (page 167)*
- *Prime Rib au Jus (page 197)*
- *Ravishing Roast Chicken (page 216) or Slow-Roasted Chicken (page 219)*
- *Crunchy Buttermilk Fried Chicken (page 232)*
- *Fried Pork Chops (page 251)*
- *Fabulous Fish Almondine (page 273)*

Saucy, boozy,
and delightful!

STEAMED BROCCOLI WITH CHEESE SAUCE

MAKES ABOUT 6 SERVINGS

When I think about the essential recipes I have used to feed my family through the years, I just couldn't discount the significance of steamed broccoli with some kind of cheese sauce. It is responsible for first encouraging the Drummond kids to eat their veggies, and even though they've since broadened their repertoire, they still go back to this as a bright green (and orange!) comfort food. The broccoli part of this is hardly a recipe at all, but I wanted to include it in this cookbook to reassure you that simple steamed broccoli is still very much a thing. You can use any ol' velvety cheese sauce you like, but my homemade version (see page 308) is a miracle of modern cheese sauces.

More broccoli and cheese, please!

4 cups broccoli florets

2 teaspoons kosher salt

Very Velvety Cheese Sauce (page 308) or any jarred cheese sauce, warmed

1. Bring a pot of water to a boil over high heat, then set a steamer basket on top and reduce the heat to medium. Put the broccoli into the basket and cover the pot.

2. Steam the broccoli for no longer than 2½ minutes, to ensure that it's tender but still has a little bit of a bite. (Steamed veggies lose their loveliness once the bite is gone!) Sprinkle the steamed broccoli with the salt . . .

3. Then transfer it to a serving bowl.

4. Serve it with a generous topping of warm cheese sauce!

Variation

- *Instead of steaming, cook the broccoli using the Charred Broccolini method on page 320. This adds some nice flavor (though it isn't quite as kid-friendly).*

Serve with

- *Crispy Chicken Cutlets (page 222)*
- *Ravishing Roast Chicken (page 216) or Slow-Roasted Chicken (page 219)*
- *Chicken Nuggets (page 235)*
- *Crunchy Buttermilk Fried Chicken (page 232)*
- *Fried Pork Chops (page 251)*
- *Tender, Flaky Baked Salmon (minus the cheese sauce) (page 266)*
- *Fabulous Fish Almondine (minus the cheese sauce) (page 273)*

Very Velvety
Cheese Sauce
(page 308)

VERY VELVETY CHEESE SAUCE

MAKES ABOUT 3 CUPS

This sauce is so wildly fun to make, it's surely going to become a staple for you! The end result is a cross between a jar of Cheez Wiz and the stuff they ladle over tortilla chips at sports stadiums, and while it would probably be frowned upon by those with more sophisticated palates, it really does the trick anytime you need a silky-smooth middle America–inspired cheese sauce. From chips to broccoli to chili dogs, you'll want to pour it over everything!

1 cup evaporated milk

1 cup grated cheddar cheese

½ teaspoon seasoned salt

½ teaspoon kosher salt, plus more as needed

½ teaspoon dry mustard

1 teaspoon Worcestershire sauce

¼ teaspoon paprika

6 slices American cheese (I used Kraft slices that aren't individually wrapped)

1. Pour the evaporated milk into a medium saucepan over medium heat and heat it until it starts to steam.

2. Meanwhile, in a blender, combine the cheddar, seasoned salt, kosher salt, dry mustard, Worcestershire, and paprika.

3. When the evaporated milk is hot, add the American cheese . . .

4. And whisk until the cheese is melted.

5. Pour the hot mixture into the blender . . .

6. Then secure the lid and blend on low for about 20 seconds.

7. Scrape the sides of the blender with a rubber spatula and keep blending . . .

8. For another 20 to 30 seconds, until the cheese sauce is totally smooth and velvety! Taste and blend in another pinch or two of salt if needed. The sauce can be served immediately, right out of the blender . . .

9. Or poured into a jar for the fridge. The cheese sauce will keep in the fridge for up to 1 week. To warm it, spoon the amount you need into a bowl or ramekin and microwave for 10 seconds at a time, stirring in between, until hot and smooth. Or, you can heat up the entire amount in a small saucepan over low heat, stirring frequently.

Ways this cheese will change your life

- *Spooned over any cooked vegetable*
- *Poured over the meat on a Marlboro Man Sandwich (page 170) or French Dip (page 201)*
- *Spooned on a Big, Thick Burger (page 191) or a Super-Thin Double Burger (page 195)*
- *Used as a dipping sauce for French Fries (Thick or Thin) (page 287) and/or Chicken Nuggets (page 235)*
- *Poured over tortilla chips with jarred jalapeño rings!*

These cook for nine hours!

BURGUNDY MUSHROOMS

MAKES 8 TO 10 SERVINGS

So many of my food memories involve my late mother-in-law, Nan, and I would say 90 percent of my favorite Nan recipes were sides. There's her legendary corn (see page 318), her Thanksgiving dressing, and her decadent mashed potatoes (see page 284), which I still make today. But in a whole other category are her nothing-short-of-splendiferous Burgundy mushrooms, which she made every single Christmas Eve. They are insanely delicious, and pretty much insane all around: They cook for no fewer than nine hours on the stove, which makes zero sense until you taste one. My gosh, these are otherworldly—almost like some kind of heavenly meat. And to add to their appeal, the mushrooms are actually better heated up the next day, so feel free to make them a day ahead and store them in the fridge. These shrooms are impossible to forget, so I'm just gonna say it: If you haven't made these yet, please, please remedy that as soon as possible.

4 pounds white button mushrooms, cleaned

1 teaspoon dill seeds

5 garlic cloves, peeled but whole

4 chicken bouillon cubes

4 beef bouillon cubes

One 750ml bottle Burgundy or Cabernet Sauvignon (about 4¼ cups)

1½ teaspoons Worcestershire sauce

1 cup (2 sticks) salted butter

1 teaspoon ground black pepper

2 teaspoons kosher salt

1 tablespoon fresh thyme leaves, for garnish

1. Throw the mushrooms into a large Dutch oven and add the dill seeds . . .

2. As well as the garlic cloves and bouillon cubes.

3. Pour in the wine . . .

4. 2 cups of very hot water . . .

5. The Worcestershire . . .

6. And the butter and pepper.

Bryce and Todd at Paige and David's rehearsal dinner. Brother toasts are always interesting!

7. Turn the heat to medium-high, put the lid on the pot, and bring the mixture to a boil. Reduce the heat to low and simmer, covered, for 6 (that's 6!) hours.

8. After that stage, remove the lid and continue cooking on low for 3 hours. Add a cup of hot water if the liquid looks like it's getting a little low.

9. Stir in the salt at the end of the cooking. Your house will smell like mushroom heaven, and that's nothing compared to how amazing they taste!

10. Serve with a sprinkle of thyme leaves on top.

Serve with

- *Prime Rib au Jus (page 197)*
- *The Most Perfect Pot Roast (page 157)*
- *The Creamiest Mac and Cheese (page 119)*
- *Ravishing Roast Chicken (page 216) or Slow-Roasted Chicken (page 219)*
- *Or serve leftovers on "I'm a Fun-gi" Mushroom Pizza (page 111)!*

SAUTÉED GREEN BEANS

MAKES 6 TO 8 SERVINGS

On one hand, it's hard to mess up green beans too badly. They are what they are, and as long as they're bright green and fresh, they're pretty nice. On the other hand, it can sometimes be hard to make green beans utterly delicious. Either they're underseasoned, or they're too firm (or too limp), or they're just overall lacking in flavor or interest. So after decades and decades (okay, maybe two decades) of trial and error, I finally landed on a green bean side dish that will be my forever favorite. Just a couple of simple touches make all the difference: First, I steam the green beans for a few minutes before sautéing them. This locks in the bright green color and keeps the beans from losing it as easily during the cooking process. Second, in addition to the butter and garlic they're sautéed with, I add just a bit of soy sauce, which really is *the* secret sauce in this dish. It adds an absolutely essential umami touch that turns these green beans from "nice" to "yummmmmmm!" You're gonna go crazy for these.

2 pounds green beans, stem ends removed

5 tablespoons salted butter

4 garlic cloves, minced

1 tablespoon soy sauce

Kosher salt and ground black pepper

1. Bring a pot of water to a boil over high heat. Add a steamer basket and fill it with the green beans.

2. Turn the heat to medium and put the lid on the pot. Steam the green beans until bright green and starting to turn tender, about 5 minutes. (They should still have a nice firmness to them.)

3. In a large skillet, heat 4 tablespoons of the butter over medium heat. When the butter is just starting to turn golden brown, dump in the green beans.

4. Add the garlic . . .

5. And the soy sauce.

6. Increase the heat to medium-high and carefully toss or stir the green beans until they've become nicely tender, 4 to 5 minutes. Take care not to overcook them; if they seem like they're plenty tender, you can shorten this step to 2 or 3 minutes.

7. Sprinkle in salt and pepper to taste, then turn off the heat.

8. Add the remaining 1 tablespoon butter to the bottom of the pan and toss or stir to coat the beans as it melts.

9. Transfer the beans to a serving platter and dive in immediately!

Serve with

- *Meatloaf, Mastered (page 163)*
- *Prime Rib au Jus (page 197)*
- *Crispy Chicken Cutlets (page 222)*
- *Ravishing Roast Chicken (page 216) or Slow-Roasted Chicken (page 219)*
- *Crunchy Buttermilk Fried Chicken (page 232)*
- *Fried Pork Chops (page 251)*
- *Tender, Flaky Baked Salmon (page 266)*
- *Fabulous Fish Almondine (page 273)*

Paige's big day.

Fried Pork Chops
(page 251)
Mysterious and
magical flavor!

ROASTED ASPARAGUS

MAKES 4 TO 6 SERVINGS

One of the very best things about roasted vegetables is that the roasting process brings out so much amazing natural flavor that you can keep the rest of the ingredient list pretty short. It's always so gratifying to see the gorgeous veggies come out of the oven and go onto a platter and realize I had almost nothing to do with how delicious they're going to be. Asparagus will always be a favorite veggie for me to roast—but as a confession, in this recipe it isn't actually roasted in the strictest sense. I actually use the broiler to get as much black on the asparagus as I can before it gets overcooked and limp. Try this method—I think you'll be sold!

1 large bunch asparagus, tough ends removed

2 tablespoons olive oil

1 teaspoon kosher salt

½ teaspoon ground black pepper

Grated zest of 1 lemon

2 tablespoons finely chopped parsley (optional)

1. Preheat the oven to the highest broil temperature and place the oven rack at the highest level.

2. Arrange the asparagus on a sheet pan, separating the spears as much as possible. Drizzle on the olive oil . . .

3. Sprinkle on the salt and pepper . . .

4. And shake the pan or roll the asparagus around to coat it in the oil. Broil the asparagus for 5 to 6 minutes . . .

5. Until blackened in areas. Remove the pan from the oven before the asparagus loses its bright green color.

6. Zest the lemon over the top and sprinkle with parsley, if using, before serving. I could eat this whole platter like candy!

Serve with

- *Scalloped Potatoes with Ham (page 121)*
- *Meatloaf, Mastered (page 163)*
- *Prime Rib au Jus (page 197)*
- *Ravishing Roast Chicken (page 216) or Slow-Roasted Chicken (page 219)*
- *Barbecue Pork Tenderloin (page 252) or Cajun Pork Tenderloin (page 255)*
- *Spicy Shrimp Scampi (page 270)*
- *Tender, Flaky Baked Salmon (page 266)*

CREAMY CORN

MAKES 4 TO 6 SERVINGS

This is a quick, easy stovetop version of my mother-in-law, Nan's, famous (and enormous) corn casserole, which is still legendary in our family. Nan used every single bit of corn she could extract from each cob, and the only other ingredients in the casserole were butter, cream, salt, and pepper. It was a side dish casserole at all the important moments in our family, and none of the rest of the family has ever been able to make it quite like she did! I like to make this smaller-batch version for a weeknight dinner. It always reminds me of Nan. We miss her!

4 ears of corn, shucked

5 tablespoons salted butter

2 green onions, thinly sliced, plus more for garnish

3 garlic cloves, sliced

1 cup heavy cream

½ teaspoon kosher salt, plus more as needed

½ teaspoon ground black pepper

1. With a sharp knife, shave the kernels from the cobs.

2. One by one, place the cobs in a bowl and use the dull side of the knife to scrape the corn milk and corn remnants into the bowl. You want to strip the cobs clean!

3. In a medium saucepan, melt 4 tablespoons of the butter over medium heat. Add the green onions and garlic.

4. Stir and cook for 2 minutes, so they start to soften . . .

5. Then add the corn and the corny contents of the bowl.

6. Stir and cook for about 5 minutes . . .

7. Then add the heavy cream, salt, and pepper.

8. Stir and bring the mixture to a simmer, letting it cook for 3 more minutes, until the corn is tender. Turn off the heat and stir in the remaining 1 tablespoon butter. Taste and add more salt as needed.

So rich and buttery!

CHARRED BROCCOLINI

MAKES 4 SERVINGS

Broccolini, when it's good, is so very, very good. I've had some broccolini fails in my life, usually as a result of undercooking it (it's much tougher than broccoli and takes longer to get tender). But for Paige's wedding, we had charred broccolini on the menu, and I decided that is the way broccolini was meant to shine. The blackened flavor is such a beautiful complement to the mild sweetness of the vegetable, and it's become one of my top choices whenever I need a green side dish. It's a good one!

1 to 2 bunches broccolini (about 10 ounces)

2 tablespoons olive oil

2 tablespoons salted butter

½ teaspoon kosher salt, plus more as needed

½ teaspoon ground black pepper, plus more as needed

½ lemon

1. Trim off the ends, then cut each stem of broccolini in half, making sure to slice evenly down the middle of the stalks.

2. In a large skillet, heat the olive oil and butter over medium-high heat.

3. Place the broccolini in the pan, cut side down, alternating their direction to make sure they all fit. Sprinkle on the salt and pepper.

4. Place the lid on the skillet, then turn the heat to medium and cook the broccolini undisturbed until the bottoms are blackened and blistered and the broccolini is tender, about 8 minutes.

5. Remove the broccolini to a serving platter and squeeze the juice of half a lemon all over before serving.

Serve with

- *Crispy Chicken Cutlets (page 222)*
- *Ravishing Roast Chicken (page 216) or Slow-Roasted Chicken (page 219)*
- *Crunchy Buttermilk Fried Chicken (page 232)*
- *Fried Pork Chops (page 251)*
- *Tender, Flaky Baked Salmon (page 266)*
- *Fabulous Fish Almondine (page 273)*

The secret's in the char!

Desserts & Drinks

Desserts are the living embodiment of the phrase "saved the best for last." But before you dive into the sweets you're about to see, I wanted to let you know what you will *not* find in this chapter: impressive layer cakes, perfect pastries, and artisanal tarts. What you will find are homey, simple, and utterly delicious treats that are as *un*fancy as they are *in*credible. Enjoy every single (or double, or triple) bite!

CHOCOLATE SHEET CAKE

MAKES ONE 18 × 13-INCH CAKE

This recipe needeth not a lengthy introduction. It is the best chocolate cake you'll ever make, and probably the easiest, too (short of tearing open a box of cake mix). It's a version of the recipe my mother-in-law shared with me when I was weeks away from marrying her son, and because of some departures from her recipe based on my misreading her quantities (I wound up using twice the cocoa and butter), it's way richer and butterier than it was supposed to be. It's a mistake Ladd and I still chuckle about, and one I'll never be sorry for! Enjoy this cake, friends. (And eat it warm!)

CAKE

2 cups all-purpose flour

2 cups granulated sugar

¼ teaspoon kosher salt

½ cup buttermilk, homemade (see page 5) or store-bought (I always use homemade here)

2 large eggs

1 teaspoon baking soda

1 teaspoon vanilla extract

1 cup (2 sticks) salted butter

4 heaping tablespoons unsweetened cocoa powder

1 cup boiling water

ICING

14 tablespoons (1¾ sticks) salted butter

4 heaping tablespoons unsweetened cocoa powder

6 tablespoons whole milk

1 pound minus ½ cup powdered sugar, sifted

1 teaspoon vanilla extract

½ cup finely chopped pecans

1. Preheat the oven to 350°F.

2. Make the cake: In a large bowl, combine the flour, granulated sugar, and salt.

3. In a medium pitcher or bowl, combine the buttermilk, eggs, baking soda, and vanilla . . .

4. And whisk with a fork.

5. In a medium saucepan, melt the butter over medium heat.

6. Add the cocoa . . .

7. And stir to combine.

Best chocolate cake
in history!

8. Add the boiling water . . .

9. Turn the heat to medium-high and give the mixture a few seconds to start to boil. Turn it off quickly so it doesn't overflow!

10. Pour the chocolate mixture into the dry ingredients . . .

11. And stir with a spatula to incorporate it, stopping when it's about halfway mixed. (This will give the chocolate a chance to cool down a bit.)

12. Pour in the buttermilk mixture, stirring as you add it.

13. Fold the mixture until you can no longer see streaks of flour or buttermilk . . .

14. Then pour this batter into an 18 × 13-inch sheet pan . . .

15. And spread it evenly across the whole pan. Bake the cake until the center is just barely set, 18 to 20 minutes.

16. While the cake is baking, make the icing so it will be ready to pour on the hot cake. In a medium saucepan, melt the butter over medium heat and add the cocoa.

17. Stir until smooth . . .

18. Then add the milk and stir to combine.

19. Turn off the heat and add the powdered sugar. Stir vigorously until it's all incorporated. (The icing will be dark in color and runny, and that's exactly what you want!)

20. Add the vanilla and pecans . . .

21. And stir until it looks impossibly irresistible.

22. Remove the cake with the center just barely set . . .

23. And pour the icing all over the top.

24. My goal is always to get the icing to cover every square millimeter of cake without my having to spread it at all. (It's a fun challenge!) Slice the cake into squares and serve it warm or at room temperature.

The best birthday cake!

This cake has seen generations of Drummonds through countless birthdays, including my own kids. It's easy to customize, and I've never made a fancy cake that has ever gone over as well as this basic ol' sheet cake. Here are some ways I've made it more festive through the years:

- *Omit the pecans for a perfectly plain chocolate sheet cake, and let the kids decorate the top after icing with M&M's, colorful sprinkles, chopped candy bars, and other fun decorations.*
- *Let the cake cool to room temperature and decorate the top with miniature action figures. I've done a cowboy/ranch scene, a football scene, and a butterfly scene!*
- *Before icing, let the cake cool and cut it in half crosswise. Make the icing a little thicker by increasing the powdered sugar by 2 cups, then make a two-layer cake with icing in the center.*
- *Use the batter to make cupcakes instead of cakes! Bake the cupcakes in papers for 15 minutes and spoon the icing over each one. (The amount of batter makes shorter cupcakes, so there's room for the icing inside the paper.)*
- *Let the iced cake cool, then use M&M's to make a gigantic number (for their new age!).*

VANILLA SHEET CAKE WITH 7-MINUTE FROSTING

MAKES ONE 18 × 13-INCH CAKE

As a contrast to the deep, chocolatey sheet cake we usually enjoy, I love this tender vanilla cake with 7-minute frosting, which is light and billowy and so beautifully old-fashioned. I remember Grandma Helen making the frosting on the stove; I thought it looked like a cloud in Heaven probably looked, and I still think it tastes like icing in Heaven probably tastes. The frosting takes seven minutes to beat to perfect fluffiness (and a few minutes to prep before that), but it always astounds me how really simple it is to make. So perfect with the simply perfect white cake!

CAKE

Baking spray

6 large egg whites, at room temperature

1 cup whole milk, at room temperature

1 tablespoon vanilla bean paste

3 cups cake flour

1½ cups sugar

1 tablespoon baking powder

½ teaspoon table salt

¾ cup (1½ sticks) salted butter, softened

¼ cup vegetable oil

7-MINUTE FROSTING

1½ cups sugar

2 large egg whites

2 teaspoons light corn syrup

¼ teaspoon cream of tartar

Pinch of table salt

⅓ cup cold water

1. Preheat the oven to 350°F. Spray an 18 × 13-inch metal sheet pan with baking spray.

2. Make the cake: In a small bowl, combine the egg whites and ½ cup of the milk.

3. Add the vanilla bean paste . . .

4. And whisk it with a fork until well mixed.

5. In a stand mixer fitted with the paddle attachment, combine the flour, sugar, baking powder, and salt.

6. Add the butter and oil . . .

7. Then turn the mixer on low and slowly pour in the remaining ½ cup milk.

The fluffiest frosting!

8. When the milk is mixed in, slowly add half of the egg white mixture and let it mix in . . .

9. Then turn off the mixer and scrape down the sides of the bowl.

10. Turn the mixer back on low and slowly pour in the rest of the egg white mixture.

11. Turn the mixer to medium-high and mix for about 1 minute more, until the batter is smooth. (Scrape the bowl one more time if it needs it, mixing for 15 to 20 seconds after scraping.)

12. Pour the batter into the sheet pan . . .

13. And spread it into an even layer.

14. Bake until the cake is set in the middle but hardly browned at all, 13 to 14 minutes. (The browner the top, the drier the cake! You want it to stay moist and soft.) Set the cake aside and let it cool completely.

15. When the cake is cooled, make the 7-minute frosting: In a double boiler (or heatproof glass bowl set over simmering water), combine the sugar and egg whites.

16. Add the corn syrup, cream of tartar, a pinch of salt, and the cold water . . .

17. Then stir and let the mixture heat up for 4 to 5 minutes, making sure the sugar is fully dissolved.

18. Using a hand mixer on low speed, beat the mixture, moving it slowly around the bowl so it mixes everything evenly.

19. Beat the frosting for 7 minutes (hence the name!), until the frosting is light, fluffy, and glossy and stiff peaks form.

20. Immediately remove the frosting from the heat and plop it on top of the cake in piles.

21. Spread it over the center of the cake . . .

22. Then out to the edges, covering every visible part of the cake.

23. The frosting starts to set on the surface and will lose its gloss before long, so it's best to make this for an occasion when you have plenty of cake eaters!

GRAINY FROSTING?

A common mishap with 7-minute frosting is a discernibly grainy texture once the frosting is whipped. To avoid this, make sure the sugar is fully dissolved in step 17! Once dissolved, the grains are gone for good.

PERFECTLY PUCKERY LEMON BARS

MAKES 24 BARS

I'm a little weird about lemon bars since I'm sensitive to tart things, and I tend not to love them if they're mostly made of lemon filling, with just a paper-thin layer of crust on the bottom. I need other things to break up the puckery lemony tartness, and that's how these lemon bars were born! They're perfectly tart (my father-in-law had a high tolerance for lemon and loved these!), but with a sweet, sugar cookie–like crust and an unapologetically thick layer of powdered sugar on top; enough to get all over your nose and blow across the room if you happen to sneeze! If you already have a favorite lemon square recipe, I dare ya to give these a try. You will fall in love!

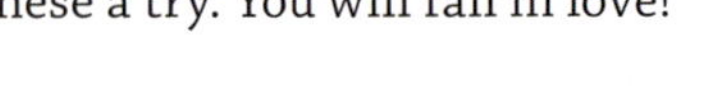

CRUST

1 cup (2 sticks) salted butter, cut into small cubes, plus softened salted butter for the pan

2 cups all-purpose flour

½ cup granulated sugar

¼ teaspoon kosher salt

LEMON FILLING

1½ cups granulated sugar

¼ cup all-purpose flour

Pinch of kosher salt

4 large eggs

Grated zest and juice of 4 medium lemons (about ¾ cup)

Powdered sugar, for topping

1. Preheat the oven to 350°F. Butter a 9 × 13-inch baking dish (or use an 8 × 10-inch pan if you'd like the layers to be a little thicker).

2. Make the crust: In a large bowl, whisk together the flour, granulated sugar, and salt.

3. Add the cubes of butter and use a pastry blender or two knives to work it into the dry ingredients . . .

4. Until the mixture is moist and crumbly.

5. Dump the crumb mixture into the baking dish . . .

6. And press it into an even crust. Bake until golden around the edges, about 20 minutes.

7. When the crust has about 5 minutes left to bake, make the lemon filling: In a large bowl, combine the granulated sugar, flour, salt, eggs, lemon zest, and lemon juice . . .

So tart and tasty!

8. And whisk until everything is well mixed and there are no more visible streaks of egg.

9. Remove the crust from the oven . . .

10. Pour on the lemon mixture . . .

11. Return to the oven and bake until the filling is set, about 20 minutes. (Don't worry if there are bubbles on top! That's normal.) Chill for 2 hours . . .

12. Then, once chilled, completely cover the surface with a generous layer of sifted powdered sugar.

13. Cut them into whatever size squares you'd like! Keep leftovers in the fridge for up to 1 week.

A cowgirl's work is never done.

THE BEST BLACKBERRY COBBLER

MAKES ONE 9 × 13-INCH COBBLER

It's impossible to live among cowboys and not have a super-delicious blackberry cobbler recipe up your sleeve. It's an absolute classic in our neck of the woods. That said, there sure are a lot of different approaches to what amounts to baked fruit with crust! There's a clafouti-type cobbler, where the berries are baked in a thin cake batter. There's a deconstructed pie-type cobbler, where the berries are topped with a big piece of pie crust. Both of those are yummy, and I've made them a million times. But after years of testing and tasting, I've decided my favorite cobbler is this one—berries baked with a cobblestone-like sweet biscuit topping. Good fruit cobbler is good beyond measure . . . and this one is even better than that.

2 tablespoons softened salted butter, for the pan

BLACKBERRIES

6 cups fresh blackberries (or you can use frozen!)

⅓ cup granulated sugar

Grated zest and juice of 1 lemon

1 tablespoon vanilla bean paste or vanilla extract

COBBLER TOPPING

2 cups all-purpose flour

¾ cup granulated sugar

¼ teaspoon kosher salt

1 tablespoon baking powder

8 tablespoons (1 stick) cold salted butter, cut into cubes

½ cup whole milk

½ cup heavy cream

1 large egg

1 tablespoon vanilla bean paste or vanilla extract

2 tablespoons turbinado sugar

Whipped cream or vanilla ice cream, for serving

1. Preheat the oven to 425°F. Grease a 9 × 13-inch baking dish with the softened butter.

2. Prep the blackberries: In a large bowl, combine the blackberries, granulated sugar, lemon zest, lemon juice, and vanilla bean paste.

3. Stir to combine, then let the mixture sit while you make the topping.

4. Make the cobbler topping; In a separate large bowl, whisk together the flour, granulated sugar, salt, and baking powder.

5. Add the butter . . .

6. And use a pastry blender or two knives to work the butter into the dry ingredients until the mixture is mostly crumbs with some small bits of butter.

7. In a medium pitcher, combine the milk, heavy cream, and egg . . .

8. Along with the vanilla bean paste. Whisk with a fork to mix . . .

9. Then slowly pour the mixture into the dry ingredients, stirring gently as you go.

Pre-wedding brother hugs.

10. Stop stirring as soon as the topping comes together.

11. Spread the blackberries out in the buttered dish . . .

12. Then pinch off clumps of the dough and place them all over the blackberries, creating the effect of cobblestones.

13. Sprinkle the turbinado sugar all over the dough.

14. Bake the cobbler until the biscuit topping is golden brown and the berries are juicy and bubbling, 25 to 28 minutes. Serve warm by itself or with whipped cream or vanilla ice cream!

Cobbler the way it should be!

Pecan perfection!

MY PECAN PIE

MAKES ONE 9-INCH PIE

There is nothing better than this pie. I used to call it "the pie that'll make you cry," as in cry tears of bliss, because it's just the perfect package of a pecan pie. The flaky crust, the gooey filling, the crispy pecan topping—it's almost too much. I've always chopped my pecans into small bits rather than keep them in halves, because I think you get more toasty pecan flavor that way, and you don't have big pecan pieces to drag through the filling and make things awkward. You'll never feel awkward eating this pie . . . unless, of course, you accidentally keep cutting yourself sliver after sliver because it's just too good to resist. I may or may not have done that the night before Thanksgiving one year, but we'll just keep that between us.

½ recipe (1 disc) Perfect Pie Crust (page 341) or All-Butter Pie Crust (page 344)

1 heaping cup pecans, finely chopped

1 cup granulated sugar

3 tablespoons packed brown sugar

½ teaspoon kosher salt

1 cup light corn syrup

⅓ cup (⅔ stick) salted butter, melted

3 large eggs, whisked

¾ teaspoon vanilla extract

Whipped cream (optional), for serving

1. Preheat the oven to 350°F with a rack in the bottom third of the oven. Line a sheet pan with parchment paper.

2. Roll out the crust, lay it in a 9-inch pie pan, and tuck under the overhang. Crimp the crust however you wish . . .

3. Then sprinkle the pecans into the crust.

4. In a large pitcher, combine the granulated sugar, brown sugar, and salt.

5. Pour in the corn syrup . . .

6. The melted butter . . .

7. The eggs . . .

8. And the vanilla.

9. Stir the mixture gently with a rubber spatula, scraping the pitcher as you go, until the ingredients are well mixed.

10. Pour the mixture over the pecans . . .

11. Then transfer the pie to the prepared sheet pan. Bake the pie until the crust is light brown, for 55 to 65 minutes. The pecans will rise to the top and slowly brown as the pie bakes; cover the pie loosely with foil when the pecan topping starts to brown, to keep it from burning.

12. The pie should be a little jiggly when you first remove it from the oven, but not overly so. It will firm up as it sits! Set the pie on a wire rack to cool completely.

13. When the pie is at room temperature, you can slice it into wedges and serve it plain or with whipped cream. Store the leftover pie in the fridge.

Mr. and Mrs. Andersen!

PERFECT PIE CRUST

MAKES TWO 9- OR 10-INCH PIE CRUSTS

This is a variation of a pie crust I shared in my very first cookbook, which was released in 2009! It had been shared with me by a reader of my blog, Sylvia Lamon, and I'll always be grateful to her for the almost two decades of perfect, flaky pies. Over the years I've added butter to mine in place of some of the shortening, and tweaked a few ingredient quantities and steps, but the core of the recipe is the same, and it has never, ever let me down. Balls of this dough are great to keep in the freezer; sometimes I stockpile them, particularly when the holidays are approaching.

Note: See page 344 for my All-Butter Pie Crust, plus some considerations to help you make the momentous decision about which to choose for your recipe!

½ cup cold water, plus 1 to 2 tablespoons as needed

2 tablespoons apple cider vinegar

1 large egg

3¾ cups all-purpose flour

1¼ teaspoons kosher salt

¾ cup (1½ sticks) cold salted butter, cut into small cubes

¾ cup cold vegetable shortening (I chill it for 1 hour), cut into small cubes

1. In a small bowl or pitcher, measure ½ cup cold water and add the vinegar . . .

2. Then crack in the egg . . .

3. And whisk to combine. Place the pitcher in the freezer for a few minutes to ensure it's extra cold.

4. While it's chilling, in a large bowl, whisk together the flour and salt.

5. Add the butter and shortening . . .

6. And use a pastry blender or two knives to incorporate them into the dry ingredients. Keep going until the mixture is mostly smaller crumbs but still has a few pea-size bits of butter and shortening.

7. Grab the pitcher from the freezer and slowly drizzle the egg mixture into the bowl, stirring gently to mix.

8. Stir to bring everything together, adding up to 3 more tablespoons of cold water if the dough seems overly crumbly or dry.

9. Pack the dough down a couple of times with the palm of your hand . . .

10. Then dump it out of the bowl.

11. Pack it into a ball, gathering as many loose crumbs as you can, and cut it in half with a bench scraper or knife.

12. Put each half into a gallon storage bag. Pat it into a disc, seal the bag, and freeze for 30 minutes before rolling out, or up to 4 months if you're using the crusts later. When you're ready to use the frozen dough, thaw the discs overnight in the fridge if you have the time, or at room temperature for 1 hour, before rolling out.

Have I mentioned I love Sofia?

ALL-BUTTER PIE CRUST

MAKES TWO 9- OR 10-INCH PIE CRUSTS

It's hard to argue against the delicious merits of an all-butter pie crust, and there are times I want to leave off the shortening and embrace the butter of it all!

Note: See page 341 for my Perfect Pie Crust!

½ cup cold water, plus 1 to 2 tablespoons as needed

3 tablespoons cold apple cider vinegar

3¾ cups all-purpose flour

¾ teaspoon sugar

1¼ teaspoons kosher salt

1½ cups (3 sticks) cold salted butter, cut into small cubes

1. In a small bowl or glass measuring cup, combine the ½ cup cold water and vinegar. Set it aside in the freezer.

2. In a large bowl, whisk together the flour, sugar, and salt.

3. Add the butter . . .

4. And use a pastry blender or two knives to cut it into the flour mixture. Keep going until the mixture is mostly smaller crumbs but still has a few pea-size bits of butter.

5. Grab the pitcher from the freezer and slowly drizzle the vinegar mixture into the bowl, stirring gently to mix.

6. Stir to bring everything together, adding 1 to 2 more tablespoons of cold water if the dough seems overly crumbly or dry.

7. Pack the dough down a couple of times with your hands to bring it together . . .

8. Then turn it out of the bowl and pat it into a ball.

9. Divide the dough in half and place each in a separate gallon storage bag. Pat each into a disc, seal the bags, and freeze for 30 minutes before rolling out, or up to 4 months if you're using the crusts later. When you're ready to use the frozen dough, thaw the discs overnight in the fridge if you have the time, or at room temperature for 1 hour, before rolling out. Use flour on the board and on top of the dough as you're rolling it out.

WHICH PIE CRUST TO CHOOSE?

The differences between my Perfect Pie Crust (page 341) and All-Butter Pie Crust (opposite) aren't wildly noticeable: "Perfect" results in a more crumbly crust and is a little easier to work with because the shortening doesn't get as soft and melt as quickly, while "All-Butter" has an unmistakably buttery flavor and a flakier texture. My Perfect Pie Crust is a best-of-both-worlds situation when it comes to dessert pies, but the all-butter version is a favorite for Chicken Pot Pie (page 212) and other savory uses (or, yes, dessert pies, too!). No egg is used in the all-butter crust, so it's also a good option if you're egg-free in your house. Also, because of the salted butter in the all-butter version, I add a small bit of sugar to balance things a bit. Try them both and you'll get a sense of which one you prefer for which pies! You really can't go wrong with either.

I LOVE THIS APPLE PIE

MAKES ONE 9-INCH APPLE PIE

Apple pies are so personal! Whether to do cinnamon and other spices in the apples or leave them plain, whether to do a streusel topping or a top crust, and whether to add the apples raw or precook them are just a small sampling of the agonizing apple pie decisions most home cooks face at some point in their baking life. And I'm no different; I have searched and searched for the most foolproof collection of factors that result in the perfect apple pie, and it's been an odyssey! I finally landed on this beauty, which is the culmination of a ton of trial and error through the years. The crust is flaky and crunchy-sweet, the apples are thick and caramelly, and the apples are so perfect. It takes time and few key steps, but oh man, is the result worth it!

½ cup apple cider

½ cup (1 stick) salted butter

1¾ cups packed brown sugar

2 tablespoons fresh lemon juice

1 pound Granny Smith apples (about 3 medium apples), peeled, cored, and sliced ¼ inch thick

1¼ pounds Honeycrisp apples (about 3 medium apples), peeled, cored, and sliced ¼ inch thick

1¼ pounds Pink Lady apples (about 3 medium apples), peeled, cored, and sliced ¼ inch thick

2¼ teaspoons ground cinnamon

1½ teaspoons ground ginger

¼ teaspoon ground cardamom

1½ teaspoons kosher salt

½ teaspoon ground nutmeg (I used freshly grated)

½ cup plus ¾ teaspoon granulated sugar

¼ cup plus ¾ teaspoon all-purpose flour

¼ cup cornstarch

1 tablespoon vanilla extract

Perfect Pie Crust (page 341) or All-Butter Pie Crust (page 344), rolled into two ¼-inch-thick crusts

1 large egg, for an egg wash

1 generous tablespoon turbinado sugar

Vanilla ice cream or whipped cream, for serving

1. Pour the apple cider into a large pot or Dutch oven and bring it to a boil over medium-high heat.

2. Cook until it's reduced by about half, about 3 minutes, then reduce the heat to medium and add the butter.

3. When the butter has melted, add the brown sugar and lemon juice . . .

4. And cook, stirring constantly, until the sugar has melted and the mixture is mostly smooth, about 2 minutes.

5. Add the apples and stir to coat them in the sugar mixture. Cook, stirring occasionally, until the apples begin to cook down and release their liquid, about 5 minutes.

6. Add the cinnamon, ginger, cardamom, and salt . . .

Pre-cooking the apples makes a big difference!

7. Then grate in the nutmeg, if you're using fresh! (If not, just add the ground nutmeg with the rest of the spices.)

8. Cook, stirring, for about 2 minutes, to incorporate the spices and cook the apples down a bit more.

9. In a small bowl, whisk together ½ cup of the granulated sugar, ¼ cup of the flour, and the cornstarch.

10. Sprinkle the mixture evenly over the apples . . .

11. Then cook, stirring, until bubbling and very thick, 3 to 4 minutes. (The cornstarch needs to bubble in order to thicken, so be sure to get it to that stage!) Remove from the heat and stir in the vanilla.

12. To stop the cooking process, pour the apples onto a sheet pan . . .

13. And spread them out to cool to room temperature, about 30 minutes.

14. Place one of the rolled-out crusts into a 9-inch pie pan, draping the excess over the edge. Sprinkle the remaining ¾ teaspoon granulated sugar and ¾ teaspoon flour over the bottom of the crust. This will help soak up the excess juices in the pie and keep the crust from getting soggy!

15. Scrape the apples into the crust . . .

16. Even them out, leaving them a little higher in the center.

17. Roll the second crust on a rolling pin to easily transfer it to the top of the pie, then unroll it over the apples.

18. Trim off the excess of both crusts so that there's only about ¼ inch of overhang. Working around the pie, tuck the edge of the top crust under the edge of the bottom crust.

19. Once the edge is tucked and neat, crimp the edge however you like, using the tines of a fork or (as shown) pinching with one hand while pressing with a knuckle on your other hand. At this point, if you have time, you can refrigerate the pie for 1 hour before baking, to help it bake more evenly.

20. When you're ready to bake the pie, preheat the oven to 400°F with a rack set at the lowest level. Cut four slits in the pie's top crust.

21. Brush the top with egg wash . . .

22. And sprinkle the whole surface with the turbinado sugar.

23. Set the pie on a sheet pan and bake until the crust begins to turn golden, about 30 minutes. Reduce the temperature to 350°F and rotate the pie. Bake until the pie is deep golden and the filling is bubbling through the vents, about 1 hour 10 minutes. If the pie seems to be getting brown too quickly, cover it loosely with foil for the rest of the baking process.

24. Let the pie cool to almost room temperature before slicing (the apples will hold together better that way!) Serve it with vanilla ice cream on the side, or a big dollop of whipped cream on top!

Leftover pie can be stored in the fridge. Heat up individual slices in the microwave for about 25 seconds. (The apples will be hot!)

LADD'S VERY BASIC CHOCOLATE PIE

MAKES ONE 9-INCH PIE

My longtime love, who conveniently happens to be my husband, loves chocolate pie more than most things in life. After a few years of making him everything from French Silk pies to deep chocolate custard pies, I finally figured out that what the dude likes best is the kind of chocolate pie served in diners and cafeterias in the old days—basically a pie crust (whether standard or graham cracker) filled with thick chocolate pudding. This is one of the many "if you can't beat 'em, join 'em" culinary situations I've come to terms with involving Ladd, but I don't mind it one bit. It may be pudding in a crust, but it's seriously delicious!

Ladd eats this pie totally plain, which I don't understand at all. I heap on enough whipped cream for both of us! Factor in the chilling time of a few hours when you make this. I often make it the night before to mark it off my "day-of" list!

CRUST

12 whole graham cracker sheets

½ cup sugar

¼ teaspoon kosher salt

½ cup (1 stick) salted butter, melted

1 teaspoon vanilla bean paste (optional)

FILLING

6½ ounces bittersweet chocolate, chopped (or semisweet chocolate, if you like a slightly sweeter pie)

1½ cups sugar

¼ cup cornstarch, sifted

¼ teaspoon kosher salt

3 cups whole milk

4 egg yolks, whisked

2 teaspoons vanilla extract

2 tablespoons salted butter, softened

Freshly whipped cream, for serving (optional)

1. Preheat the oven to 350°F.

2. Make the crust: Pulse the graham crackers into fine crumbs in a food processor and pour them into a bowl.

3. Add the sugar and salt and stir to combine . . .

4. Then add the melted butter while stirring constantly.

5. Drizzle in the vanilla bean paste, if using, and stir to distribute. (The paste is a little easier to distribute than liquid vanilla extract.)

6. Pour the crumbs into a 9-inch pie dish and firmly pat them into the pan, pressing up the sides of the pan and making a nice well for the filling.

7. Bake the crust for 7 minutes, then let it cool.

Just the way Ladd likes it!

8. Make the filling: Chop the chocolate into small chunks and set aside.

9. In a medium saucepan, combine the sugar, cornstarch, and salt.

10. Pour in the milk, whisking as you add it.

11. Add the egg yolks and whisk them in, then turn the heat to medium and cook, whisking gently . . .

12. Until the mixture comes to a gentle boil, 5 to 7 minutes. Let it gently boil for 30 seconds, until very thick but still pourable.

13. Turn off the heat and add the chocolate and vanilla . . .

14. Then stir as the chocolate melts.

15. Add the butter and again stir until melted . . .

16. Then pour the pudding filling into the crust, letting it reach the top edge. (If there's extra filling, you can pour it into small bowls or ramekins and chill them. Pudding cups!)

17. Chill the pie for at least 4 hours until firm. Note: Before you put it in the fridge, you can cover the pie with plastic wrap, lightly pressing it onto the surface of the filling. (This will prevent a skin from forming on the pie while it's cooling.) After chilling, it should peel off the surface without disturbing the topping too much. Before serving, if the surface has any imperfections that bother you, you can cover the whole pie with whipped cream (or top individual slices!).

Variation

- *Add 1 tablespoon instant espresso granules with the chocolate for a lovely, deep flavor.*

CHUCK'S HEAVENLY FUDGE

MAKES ONE 9 × 13-INCH PAN

My father-in-law was a generous soul. Yes, he was a tough gravel-voiced rancher, but he would go to great lengths to show love and appreciation to friends and family, usually with the gift of his time. One of my favorite examples of this is his fudge operation every Christmas. For many consecutive days, he'd stand at his stove making batch after batch after batch of this fudge, pouring them into foil pans and delivering them to neighbors and cowboys and family members, including Ladd and me. Chuck's fudge was absolutely delicious and a little legendary; even though it's the same basic back-of-the-marshmallow-creme-package process that so many people make, he had some kind of special touch that made it taste like a fine confection. I've re-created it here with a small change to the chocolate and vanilla (the paste adds so much incredible flavor!), but it'll never be as good as my sweet father-in-law's fudge. I miss it, and I miss him.

¾ cup (1½ sticks) salted butter, plus more softened for the pan

⅔ cup evaporated milk

3 cups sugar

4 ounces semisweet chocolate

4 ounces bittersweet chocolate

1 teaspoon vanilla bean paste or vanilla extract

One 7-ounce jar marshmallow creme

1. Grease a 9 × 13-inch pan with softened butter.

2. In a medium saucepan, combine the butter and evaporated milk over medium-low heat.

3. Add the sugar . . .

4. And stir, allowing everything to heat up and the butter to melt.

5. Heat the mixture slowly, stirring constantly, until the sugar has dissolved. (Press a little between your fingers to make sure you don't feel any sugar grains.)

6. Raise the heat to medium-high and boil it for 5 minutes, stirring constantly.

7. Remove the mixture from the heat and add both chocolates and the vanilla bean paste . . .

8. Then stir to melt the chocolate.

9. Add the marshmallow creme . . .

10. And fold gently . . .

11. Until just combined.

12. Immediately pour the fudge batter into the prepared pan . . .

13. And work fast to smooth the top into an even layer before it starts to set.

14. Let the fudge cool to room temperature before slicing into squares. Small squares or large squares are both fine! Uneaten fudge can be stored at room temperature, but it's also lovely chilled in the fridge.

We miss you, Chuck!

CRAZY-GOOD CHOCOLATE CHIP COOKIES

MAKES 12 BIG COOKIES

I have something to share with you. I am in a stage of my life where I really, really need to be wowed by cookies in order to eat them. I suppose once someone has lived on this beautiful Earth for more than five decades, they have tried every cookie there is to try. When a cookie is just okay, it can be pretty mediocre, but when a cookie is really good, it can be an otherworldly experience—which is exactly what you're in store for once you make these cookies later today! (Promise me you will, okay?)

1 cup (2 sticks) salted butter

1 cup packed brown sugar

½ cup granulated sugar

2 large eggs

1 tablespoon vanilla bean paste or vanilla extract

2 cups plus 2 tablespoons all-purpose flour

1 teaspoon baking soda

1 teaspoon kosher salt

2 heaping teaspoons instant coffee granules

8 ounces good semisweet chocolate

Flaky sea salt, for garnish

1. Start by browning the butter. In a medium skillet, melt the butter over medium heat and once completely melted . . .

2. Remove the spatula or spoon and let the butter continue to heat. A light-colored foam will form all over the surface.

3. Swirl the pan occasionally . . .

4. And before too long, you'll see the foam start to turn golden.

5. Keep a close watch, swirling constantly, and when the butter under the foam is deep golden, remove it from the heat . . .

6. And pour it into a heatproof bowl.

7. Let the browned butter cool completely to room temperature (or set it in the fridge to hasten this process). The butter solids will collect on the bottom—and the flavor of the cookies is going to be amazing.

8. Scrape the cooled browned butter (both the browned solids and the butterfat) into the bowl of a stand mixer fitted with the paddle attachment.

9. Add the brown sugar and granulated sugar . . .

10. And mix on medium speed until well combined.

11. Add the eggs one at a time, allowing each one to mix for about 45 seconds. (I crack them into a ramekin before adding them to avoid getting any shell in the bowl!)

12. Add the vanilla bean paste and mix it in, then turn off the mixer.

13. In a medium bowl, mix the flour, baking soda, kosher salt, and instant coffee.

14. Whisk until combined . . .

15. Then add the flour mixture to the mixer in five separate additions, mixing on low speed after each one. Scrape the bowl after the last addition, then mix for a few more seconds.

16. Chop 6 ounces of the chocolate into small chunks. Cut or break the remaining chocolate into small uniform pieces.

17. Add the chopped chocolate to the mixer . . .

18. And mix on low until the chocolate is evenly distributed.

19. Use a ⅓-cup scoop or measure to scoop 12 large mounds of dough onto a quarter sheet pan lined with parchment.

20. Press a chunk of chocolate onto each mound. Refrigerate the dough for 15 to 20 minutes to firm it up a bit. Preheat the oven to 375°F.

21. Divide the dough mounds between two parchment-lined sheet pans.

22. Bake until golden but still soft and chewy, 9 to 10 minutes, switching racks halfway through. As soon as the cookies come out of the oven, sprinkle the tops with a little flaky sea salt.

23. Let the cookies sit on the pan for 5 minutes, then transfer them to a wire rack. Enjoy them warm!

So happy for Paige and David!

PEANUT BUTTER COOKIES

MAKES 12 BIG COOKIES

Peanut butter desserts have never been my absolute favorite, so I have had to work hard to create a peanut butter cookie that's so good, I actually crave it. This is that cookie, and I encourage you to try this recipe as soon as possible! The significance of the crunchy turbinado sugar coating is not to be underestimated. These are fantasterrific!

2 cups all-purpose flour

¾ teaspoon baking soda

½ teaspoon baking powder

¾ teaspoon kosher salt

½ cup (1 stick) salted butter, at room temperature

1 cup packed brown sugar

¼ cup granulated sugar

1 large egg

1 large egg yolk

1 tablespoon vanilla bean paste

¼ cup vegetable oil

1 cup smooth peanut butter (not all-natural)

½ cup turbinado sugar

1. In a medium bowl, whisk together the flour, baking soda, baking powder, and salt.

2. In a stand mixer fitted with the paddle attachment, combine the butter, brown sugar, and granulated sugar. Cream on medium-high speed for 2 minutes, scraping the bowl once halfway through.

3. Reduce the speed to medium-low and add the whole egg and egg yolk one at a time, letting each one mix for 30 seconds.

4. Add the vanilla bean paste . . .

5. And the vegetable oil and mix for 1 minute . . .

6. Then add the peanut butter and mix for 30 seconds.

The crispy sugar topping is divine!

7. Add the dry ingredients in three additions, letting the dough mix for 30 seconds after each one.

8. Scrape the bowl really well and mix for 30 more seconds, until uniformly mixed.

9. Using a large cookie scoop, portion the dough into 12 large (2-ounce) cookies and set them on a parchment-lined sheet pan. Chill for 30 minutes. When you're ready to bake the cookies, preheat the oven to 350°F.

10. Pour the turbinado sugar into a small bowl and drop the balls of dough one by one into the sugar. Roll and sprinkle the sugar all over the surface, pressing to get it to stick.

11. Place the coated balls of dough onto a parchment-lined sheet pan, leaving plenty of room for the cookies to spread.

12. Flatten the discs of dough until they're about half the thickness . . .

13. Then use a dinner fork to press a crosshatch pattern onto the surface of each cookie.

14. Bake the cookies until the edges are golden but the tops are still soft and light in color, 14 to 16 minutes. Let the cookies cool on the sheet pan for 5 minutes, then remove them to a wire rack. Repeat to bake the rest of the cookies. These are delicious!

After chilling the balls of dough, you can freeze them in plastic bags and bake them according to how many you need. Thaw them for 15 minutes, then crosshatch them with a fork and bake as usual. I love making four at a time: 3½ for me, ½ for Ladd! (Just kidding. Sort of.)

MY FAVORITE SUGAR COOKIES

MAKES 12 BIG COOKIES

When I think about the kind of sugar cookie I have loved most throughout my life, I always go back to a big, chewy-cakey cookie that has the perfect balance of butter, vanilla, and sweetness. Decorated sugar cookies are fine, but they're more about the festive colors and icing techniques. Thin, crisp sugar cookies are nice, but they're more for a little nibble with coffee or tea. These totally delightful sugar cookies are my favorite, and while you *can* top them with icing and sprinkles, they can absolutely stand on their own. These may not necessarily look different from any other ol' sugar cookie, but make no mistake about it, these are positively dreamy!

1 cup (2 sticks) salted butter, at room temperature

1⅓ cups plus ¼ cup sugar

2 large eggs, at room temperature

2 teaspoons vanilla extract

2½ cups all-purpose flour

2 teaspoons baking powder

½ teaspoon kosher salt

1. Preheat the oven to 350°F.

2. In a stand mixer fitted with the paddle attachment, combine the butter and 1⅓ cups of the sugar. Cream on medium-high speed until light and fluffy, about 2 minutes, scraping the bowl halfway through.

3. Turn the speed to medium-low and add the eggs one at a time, allowing each one to mix for 30 seconds.

4. Add the vanilla, mix for 30 more seconds, then turn off the mixer.

5. In a large bowl, combine the flour, baking powder, and salt and stir to mix.

6. With the mixer on low, add the flour mixture to the dough in three additions, letting each mix in for 20 seconds before adding the next one.

7. Scrape the bowl well and give the dough a final 20-second mix.

A combination of fluffy, chewy, and cakey!

8. Line a plate with parchment paper and place the remaining ¼ cup sugar in a small dish. Use a ⅓-cup scoop to grab a ball of dough . . .

9. And form the dough into a thick disc.

10. Drop the disc in the sugar and turn it to totally coat all sides in a layer of sugar.

11. Place the disc on the parchment-covered plate and repeat with the rest of the dough. Chill the cookies for 15 minutes.

12. Divide the dough discs between two sheet pans, leaving plenty of space for each cookie to spread.

13. Bake the cookies until the bottom edges are just starting to turn golden, about 14 to 15 minutes, switching racks halfway through. It's very important not to let them brown on top! That's part of the magic. Let the cookies cool on the pans for 5 minutes, then remove them to a wire rack.

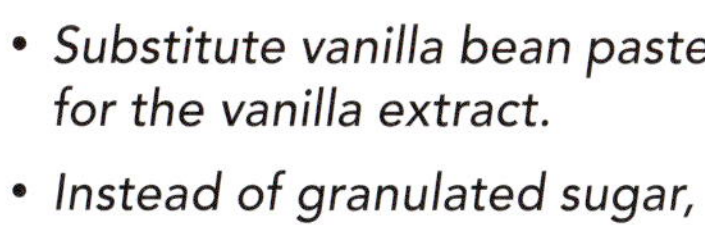

How to have fun with these sugar cookies

- *Substitute vanilla bean paste for the vanilla extract.*
- *Instead of granulated sugar, roll the dough in sanding sugar, whether white or brightly colored.*
- *Ice them in any color of buttercream frosting to suit the holiday or occasion you're in.*
- *Sandwich a scoop of coffee ice cream between two cookies, then freeze.*

ICE, ICE, BABY!

While these cookies are delicious on their own, I sometimes spread icing on them to make them ultra luscious and/or to decorate them for different holidays. Here is the best basic buttercream to use.

½ cup (1 stick) salted butter, softened

1½ cups powdered sugar, sifted

3 tablespoons heavy cream

½ teaspoon vanilla, almond, or lemon extract

Food coloring of your choice (I use gel)

Sprinkles or other decorations (optional)

Beat the butter until fluffy using a stand mixer or hand mixer. Gradually beat in the sugar, then add the cream 1 tablespoon at a time. Add the extract and food coloring of your choice and mix until everything is a uniform color! Spread the icing on cooled cookies, then sprinkle on decorations if you wish. Icing can be stored in the fridge but needs to be brought to room temperature in order to be spreadable.

Perfect for all holidays! Or any old day.

CLASSIC LEMONADE

MAKES 6 TO 8 SERVINGS

Everyone knows how to make lemonade! But I can't imagine including all my favorite family recipes in this cookbook and not sharing my basic, time-tested recipe for the happiest beverage in the world. Who has ever held a glass of lemonade in their hand and not felt a little sunnier?

1 cup cold lemon juice (from about 5 lemons), plus more to taste

1 cup cold Simple Syrup (see sidebar), plus more to taste

Lots of ice cubes

Lemon wedges, for serving

1. Measure the lemon juice and pour it into a pitcher.

2. Measure out 1 cup of the Simple Syrup . . .

3. And add it to the lemon juice. Then add enough ice to the pitcher to come close to the rim. Top with 3 to 4 cups water, to fill.

4. Stir with a long spoon and give it a taste. Add more lemon juice or Simple Syrup in order to get it to just the right sweetness and tartness!

5. Serve it in glasses over ice, garnished with a lemon wedge.

To make the lemonade ahead of time, just put the pitcher with the lemon and Simple Syrup mixture in the fridge. Right before serving, fill the pitcher with ice and add the water. Stir and serve it cold!

Simple Syrup

MAKES ABOUT 1½ CUPS

Great for lemonade and cocktails! See page 372 for a minty version.

1 cup sugar

In a small saucepan, combine the sugar and 1 cup water. Heat over medium heat until the sugar dissolves. Transfer to a jar with an airtight lid. Cool completely, then secure the lid and store in the refrigerator.

CHERRY LIMEADE

MAKES ONE 16-OUNCE DRINK

I don't know for certain whether cherry limeades were invented in Oklahoma, but they sure feel like they were. There are many different versions, but the drink basically comes down to maraschino cherries, a whole bunch of lime, and some kind of sparkling pop. I like my cherry limeades a little less sweet, so I opt for super-crispy sparkling water instead of the classic lemon-lime pop. (And psst. Even though this is a Prohibition-era nonalcoholic drink, it's fun to turn it into an adult beverage from time to time!)

8 maraschino cherries

Ice cubes

2 tablespoons fresh lime juice, plus 3 lime slices, for garnish

1 tablespoon cold Simple Syrup (page 366), plus more to taste

6 to 8 ounces cold sparkling water (I use Topo Chico; it's the crispiest!)

1 tablespoon maraschino cherry juice from the jar (optional)

1. Place the cherries in a 16-ounce mason jar . . .

2. And use a muddler or the end of a wooden spoon to smash them. You just want to break them apart a bit to release the intense maraschino cherry flavor!

3. Fill the jar to the brim with ice . . .

4. Then add the lime juice and the Simple Syrup.

5. Arrange the lime slices in a circle around the inside of the jar . . .

6. Then pour the sparkling water all the way to the top.

7. Finish it off with a tablespoon of juice from the jar of cherries if you'd like a little more bright-red, sugary sweetness!

Adulting

- *Make a Grown-Up Cherry Limeade by adding 2 tablespoons vodka, tequila, or rum to the jar with the lime juice and Simple Syrup (page 366)*
- *Switch to a cherry lemonade by substituting lemon juice for the lime juice.*

An Oklahoma classic!

DRY GIN MARTINI

MAKES 1 COCKTAIL

A good martini is *soooooo* easy to drink, which is why this recipe is for one and only one. For years I made the mistake of ordering my martinis flavored, with things like lychee or elderflower liqueur (or even cranberry juice!). But lately I have absolutely fallen in love with the sophisticated smoothness of the gin-vermouth combo. I guess I'm growing up! (But not enough to not also love a super-dirty version of the original. Both options are wonderful!)

Ice cubes

2½ ounces gin

½ ounce dry vermouth, plus more to taste

1 or 2 pimento-stuffed Spanish Queen olives

OPTIONAL
(FOR A DIRTY MARTINI)

½ ounce olive brine

2 blue cheese–stuffed olives

3 pimento-stuffed Spanish Queen olives

1. Fill a cocktail shaker halfway with ice.

2. Measure the gin and add it in . . .

3. Then do the same with the vermouth.

4. Shake vigorously for about 20 seconds . . .

5. Then pour the drink through the strainer into a martini or coupe glass.

6. Add an olive or two on a pick!

7. Optional: For a dirty martini (my favorite!), pour the cold olive brine (from the jar) into the glass.

8. Drop in the blue cheese–stuffed olives . . .

9. Then add a pick with the pimento-stuffed olives to the top.

Variation

- *Substitute vodka for gin if you like a more neutral flavor.*

MARVELOUSLY MINTY MOJITO

MAKES 1 COCKTAIL

This marvelous mint masterpiece is . . . a miracle. I'm never not amazed by how irresistible it is, and how strong that fresh mint flavor comes through. How could it not? Not only are there a bunch of fresh mint leaves in the glass, the simple syrup is spiked with massive amounts of mint as well. There's nothing better on a hot summer evening than a mojito, especially if you've got mint growing in a planter on your porch!

MINT SIMPLE SYRUP

1 cup sugar

1 cup packed mint leaves

MOJITO

5 or 6 fresh mint sprigs

2 ounces silver rum

1 ounce lime juice

1 ounce mint simple syrup

Ice cubes

Sparkling water, to top (I use Topo Chico!)

1. First, make the mint simple syrup: In a small saucepan, combine the sugar and 1 cup water. Heat over medium heat, stirring to dissolve the sugar. When it is just barely about to simmer, remove it from the heat.

2. Immediately plunge a generous cup of mint leaves into the syrup . . .

3. And use a spatula to push the mint leaves into the syrup so they're mostly submerged. Let the mint steep for 10 minutes . . .

4. Then strain the syrup through a fine-mesh strainer set over a jar.

5. Let the syrup cool to room temperature, then cover the jar and chill it for at least 2 hours, or until very cold.

6. To build the mojito: Add a few mint sprigs and leaves to a tall glass.

7. Use a muddler or the back of a wooden spoon to smash the mint a few times . . .

8. Then measure in the rum . . .

9. The lime juice . . .

10. And the mint simple syrup.

11. Add some ice, some more mint on top of it, and a little more ice.

12. Top off the drink with sparkling water . . .

13. Stir it with a long spoon . . .

14. And drop in one more sprig of mint!

PITCHER OF MARGARITAS

MAKES ABOUT 8 SERVINGS

A good on-the-rocks margarita is something I was unfamiliar with in my young adult life, when I thought "margarita" meant a syrupy lime slushie spiked with tequila. Through the years I've come to appreciate the details and balance of ingredients a little more, and today a pretty pitcher of margs is one of my favorite ways to chill out with friends on a Friday night. To sum up where my margaritas are these days: bright and lime-forward, light on the sweetness, super-heavy on the ice. See my variations opposite for ways to customize yours!

2 cups chilled tequila blanco

½ cup chilled orange liqueur

⅓ cup chilled agave nectar or Simple Syrup (page 366)

1¼ cups cold freshly squeezed lime juice, plus 1 lime, sliced

Lots of ice

1. Important: Measure your tequila to avoid a too-boozy pitcher (and too-boozy flavor).

2. Add it to a 2 quart pitcher.

3. Measure the orange liqueur and add it to the pitcher as well . . .

4. Along with the agave or Simple Syrup.

5. Pour in the lime juice and give the mixture a stir.

6. Right before serving, add enough ice to come close to the top of the pitcher. Ice-cold margs are the best margs!

7. Drop several lime slices into the pitcher . . .

8. And push them into the pitcher with a wooden spoon.

9. Add a little ice to each glass before pouring in the margaritas.

10. Drop a slice of lime into each drink.

Customize your margs!

- *My favorite: Stick a generous mint sprig into each glass, slapping it on your hand first to release the oils. Such a nice addition!*
- *Dip the rim of the glass in a little agave, then onto a small plate of margarita salt, turbinado sugar, or Tajín (chili-lime seasoning!)*
- *Add a little fruit puree, sold in many supermarkets. Blackberry is my favorite!*
- *Add fresh raspberries or blueberries to the pitcher*

Dr Pepper
Diet

Acknowledgments

To Trey Wilson, my culinary main man, who tirelessly tests, preps, manages, troubleshoots, organizes, and perfects. We make so much food together, and you make work wonderful. Thank you, Trey!

To Savanna Givens, who brings light and love to our cookbook shoots and who doesn't ever slow down. You are the best, Sav!!

To our whole cookbook team: Jess Palace, Abigail Derethik, Matt Taylor, Ed Anderson, Bethany Gregory, Kat Call, and Tiffany Taylor. From power outages to ice storms, tornado warnings to oven meltdowns, by the time we finished that last recipe, we all had lived nineteen lives together. You're all pros in your field, and I can't thank you enough for the time you choose to spend with me!

To Cassie Jones Morgan, my editor. Thank you for believing in me and giving me such a high standard to strive for. I look up to you (have I ever told you that?) and feel so lucky we found each other nine hundred years ago!!

To my awesome agent, Susanna Einstein, and the fantastic team at William Morrow: Nicole Braun, Rachel Meyers, Lucy Albanese, Mumtaz Mustafa, Anna Brower, Anwesha Basu, and Melissa Esner. It's been a long and exciting decade-plus together!

To Kris Tobiassen, my book designer, who makes beautiful sense out of hundreds of photos and dozens of recipes—I couldn't do it without you!

To Haley Carter, the superhero I could never live without. You are my favorite!

To my family and friends. I love you all more'n my luggage.

To my children. You are everything.

To Ladd. My rock!! No other way to say it.

To all of you, for being here for me through the ages and stages and adventures. I feel the love, and I hope you know I love you too!!

The awesome cookbook team! Left to right: Ed, Trey, Savanna, me, Bethany, Jess, Abigail, and Matt.

Universal Conversion Chart

OVEN TEMPERATURE EQUIVALENTS
250°F = 120°C
275°F = 135°C
300°F = 150°C
325°F = 160°C
350°F = 180°C
375°F = 190°C
400°F = 200°C
425°F = 220°C
450°F = 230°C
475°F = 240°C
500°F = 260°C

MEASUREMENT EQUIVALENTS

Measurements should always be level unless directed otherwise.

⅛ teaspoon = 0.5 mL

¼ teaspoon = 1 mL

½ teaspoon = 2 mL

1 teaspoon = 5 mL

1 tablespoon = 3 teaspoons = ½ fluid ounce = 15 mL

2 tablespoons = ⅛ cup = 1 fluid ounce = 30 mL

4 tablespoons = ¼ cup = 2 fluid ounces = 60 mL

5⅓ tablespoons = ⅓ cup = 3 fluid ounces = 80 mL

8 tablespoons = ½ cup = 4 fluid ounces = 120 mL

10⅔ tablespoons = ⅔ cup = 5 fluid ounces = 160 mL

12 tablespoons = ¾ cup = 6 fluid ounces = 180 mL

16 tablespoons = 1 cup = 8 fluid ounces = 240 mL

Index

DODGE

D

E

F

R

S

T

V

W

The End